ArtScroll Tanach Series®

A traditional commentary on the Books of the Bible

Rabbis Nosson Scherman/Meir Zlotowitz
General Editors

THE BOOK OF Ruth

THE BOOK OF Ruth

MEGILLAS RUTH / A NEW TRANSLATION
WITH A COMMENTARY ANTHOLOGIZED FROM
TALMUDIC, MIDRASHIC AND RABBINIC SOURCES.

Published by

Mesorah Publications, ltd

Translated and compiled by
Rabbi Meir Zlotowitz

'An Overview/Ruth and the Seeds of Mashiach'
by:
Rabbi Nosson Scherman

FIRST EDITION
First Impression . . . April, 1976

SECOND EDITION
Revised and Corrected
Seventeen Impressions: December 1976, March 1977, January 1978,
June 1979, May 1981, May 1983, June 1985, March 1986, May 1987, May 1988, May 1989,
October 1990, January 1993, December 1994, February 1996, August 1998, July 1999

Published and Distributed by
MESORAH PUBLICATIONS, Ltd.
4401 Second Avenue
Brooklyn, New York 11232

Distributed in Europe by
J. LEHMANN HEBREW BOOKSELLERS
20 Cambridge Terrace
Gateshead, Tyne and Wear
England NE8 1RP

Distributed in Israel by
SIFRIATI / A. GITLER – BOOKS
10 Hashomer Street
Bnei Brak 51361

Distributed in Australia & New Zealand by
GOLDS BOOK & GIFT CO.
36 William Street
Balaclava 3183, Vic., Australia

Distributed in South Africa by
KOLLEL BOOKSHOP
Shop 8A Norwood Hypermarket
Norwood 2196, Johannesburg, South Africa

THE ARTSCROLL TANACH SERIES ·
THE BOOK OF RUTH / MEGILLAS RUTH
© *Copyright 1976, 1977, 1978, 1979, 1989*
by MESORAH PUBLICATIONS, Ltd.
4401 Second Avenue / Brooklyn, N.Y. 11232 / (718) 921-9000

	ISBN	THE FIVE MEGILLOS
THE BOOK OF RUTH / MEGILLAS RUTH		(set of five volumes)
	0-89906-002-1 (hard cover)	0-89906-010-2 (hard cover)
	0-89906-003-X (paperback)	0-89906-011-0 (paperback)

Typography by CompuScribe at ArtScroll Studios, Ltd.
4401 Second Avenue / Brooklyn, N.Y. 11232 / (718) 921-9000

Printed in the United States of America by Moriah Offset
Bound by Sefercraft, Quality Bookbinders, Ltd. Brooklyn, N.Y.

Table of Contents

הסכמת הגאון האמיתי שר התורה ועמוד ההוראה
מורנו ורבנו מרן ר' משה פיינשטיין שליט"א

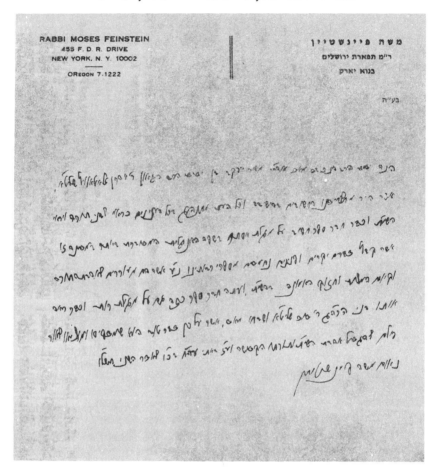

RABBI MOSES FEINSTEIN
455 F. D. R. DRIVE
NEW YORK, N. Y. 10002

OREGON 7-1222

משה פיינשטיין
ר"מ תפארת ירושלים
בנוא יארק

הנה ידידי הרב הנכבד מאד מוה"ר מאיר יעקב בן ידידי הרב הגאון ר'
אהרן זלאטאוויץ שליט"א, אשר היה מתלמידנו החשובים בהישיבה וכל
העת מתנהג בכל העניינים כראוי לבני תורה ויראי השי"ת וכבר חבר ספר
חשוב על מגלת אסתר בשפה האנגלית המדוברת ביותר במדינה זו, אשר
קבץ דברים יקרים ופנינים נחמדים מספרי רבותינו נ"ע אשר הם מעוררים
לאהבת התורה וקיום המצות וחזוק האמונה בהשי"ת. ועתה חבר ספר
כזה גם על מגילת רות וכבר ראה אותו בני הרה"ג ר' דוד שליט"א ושבחו
מאד, אשר על כן דבר טוב הוא שמדפיסו ומוצאו לאור עולם להגדיל
אהבת השי"ת ותורתו הקדושה, וע"ז באתי עה"ח בכ"ו לאדר השני
תשל"ו

נאום משה פיינשטיין

מכתב ברכה מאאמו"ר
הרב הגאון ר' אהרן זלאטאוויץ שליט"א

בעזהשי"ת

הרב אהרן זלאטאוויץ

Rabbi Aron Zlotowitz

CONGREGATION ETZ CHAIM ANSHEI LUBIN
EXECUTIVE DIRECTOR: BOARD OF ORTHODOX RABBIS OF BROOKLYN

RESIDENCE:
1134 EAST 9 STREET
BROOKLYN, N.Y. 11230
(212) 252-9188

[Handwritten Hebrew letter of approbation]

Preface

הַמַּתְחִיל בְּמִצְוָה אוֹמְרִים לוֹ גְמֹר

T his volume marks the second in a planned series to be presented to the
Jewish public.

The overwhelming response with which the previous offering — Megillas Esther, published two months ago — has been received, has clearly in-
dicated that the Torah audience is anxious for unadulterated traditional
commentaries, lucidly, dignifiedly, and literately presented, and
aesthetically and attractively packaged.

With this in mind, I approached my good friend REB NOSSON
SCHERMAN and asked him again to take part in such a noble project: to
make accessible to the Torah public a Chazal's-eye view of another of the
twenty-four sacred Books of the Bible, a book that is deceiving in its seem-
ing simplicity, but which holds the inscrutable secrets of Mashiach and the
Kingship of the Davidic Dynasty.

I approached Reb Nosson with some trepidation, knowing how deeply
involved he is in chinuch and service to k'lal and how precious little personal time he has.

But his erudition and flowing style, as well as his insights and
philosophical presentation of the sublime thoughts of our Sages were in-
dispensable to the success of this venture. He consented to put the public's
needs before his own and gave freely of himself.

The resulting work is prima-facie evidence of his erudition: his associa-
tion has raised its level beyond description.

SCOPE OF THE COMMENTARY

T he commentary was meant to appeal to the needs of a large cross-
section of people — from the early-teenage day school student to the
Hebrew teacher; from the college student with a limited Hebrew
background to the young Kollel scholar who has neither access to all the
sources in their original nor the time to investigate them individually —
therefore, a serious attempt has been made to bridge the very wide gap and
fill the unique individual needs of each reader.

The Book of Ruth was more difficult than Esther in this area. The commentary on every nuance of every word is more copious and abundant; the
Book of Ruth is more laden with Halachic implications; the Book is more

"compact" in its narrative — the first few verses alone condensing ten years of events into a few words — the commentators are, on the whole, more esoteric and require more elaboration and interpretation. There were many concepts such as the sin of Elimelech and his sons, the conversion of Ruth, Moabite marriage, the period of the Judges, Davidic monarchy, etc., which needed a fuller treatment in order for the reader to comprehend the Book of Ruth — not as a 'love story,' God forbid; but as a Book of the Holy Scriptures aglow with inner meaning and understandable only in the light of our Sages who expounded every word בִּקְדֻשָׁה וּבְטָהֳרָה — with sanctity and purity.

To this end a new, free-flowing translation of the main text — not literal, but true to the interpretation of our Sages — was prepared. This new translation, designed to be as readable as possible, eliminated many of the 'surface difficulties' dealt with by the Midrash, Rashi and Ibn Ezra because their interpretations were incorporated directly into the translation.

Continuing with the method used in Esther, the Gemara, Midrashim, and Zohar Chadash were then consulted and virtually every Chazal directly concerned with פְּשַׁט, — the literal and intended meaning of the text, which could be meaningfully incorporated into the framework of an English-language commentary, was included.

The classic commentaries, Rashi, Ibn Ezra, Alshich and Vilna Gaon — were then painstakingly culled for essential comments not suggested in the translation, or quoted in the Talmudic source.

Next, the major commentaries were consulted: primarily the monumental Iggeres Shmuel by Rav Shmuel de Uzeda; Meishiv Nefesh by the Bach; Akeidas Yitzchak by Rav Yitzchak Arama; Simchas haRegel and Nachal Eshkol by the Chidah; Kol Yaakov by the Dubno Maggid; and the Malbim.

What was sorely missed is the encyclopedic and erudite commentary of Me'am Loez on Ruth which is not at this time available.

[In response to many readers of Esther, an extensive bibliography — with enlarged biographical description of the authorities quoted — has been added to the back of this volume as well.]

The major problem here was limiting and condensing the vast amount of commentary on every word, into a book of meaningful and intelligible proportions that would satisfy both the scholar and the casual reader. Often, concepts briefly noted in the commentary are treated fully in the Introduction/Overview. I hope the resulting volume does justice both to these readers and to the Gaonim whose sublime writings are quoted.

HASHEM's Name

It was decided that wherever the Hebrew Four Letter Name of God appears, it would be translated in large and small caps: "HASHEM," i.e. 'The' Name — the Holy name of God. Where the Hebrew has Elokim, the more general and less 'personal' Name of the Diety — it was translated 'God.' Although the name of the Creator is generally written 'G-d' and not spelled out in its entirety, since this Book is a portion of the Holy

Scriptures and the full Four Letter Name of HASHEM appears in the Hebrew, it would have been ludicrous to abbreviate the spelling of the English word God. אֶרֶץ יִשְׂרָאֵל was translated Eretz Yisrael (Land of Israel). Where the word Israel is found, it refers to the Jewish people.

A cross between the Sephardi and Ashkenazi transliteration of Hebrew words was used: Ashkenezi consonants, so to speak, with Sephardi vowels. Thus: Yisrael, not Yisroel; Iggeres Shmuel not Iggeret Shmuel, etc. Proper names that have become generally accepted have been retained; thus: Ruth, Bethlehem, Jesse were retained and not changed to conform to our method of transliteration. Although there are several inconsistencies, the style has generally been held throughout the work.

ACKNOWLEDGEMENT'S

This work is not entirely my own. That it is in any way worthy of the reader's attention is because I have the honor of benefiting from the friendship and counsel of some of the most scholarly and intellectually gifted personalities on the contemporary Torah scene. They have graciously given of their free time and genius to read the manuscript in its evolutionary stages, saving me, in many cases, from my own ignorance. I am indebted to:

My father HARAV HAGAON ARON ZLOTOWITZ who has reviewed the work and allowed me to benefit from his hashkafa and erudition. May he and my dear mother תחי', be rewarded בְּכָל מִילֵי דְמֵיטַב.

A very great note of thanks is due רַבִּי אַלוּפִי וּמְיוּדָעִי, RAV DAVID FEINSTEIN, who, seeing the importance of such a series, again made an exception to his general policy, to assist in the preparation of this work. He graciously allowed me to remain in constant communication with him, and he patiently clarified many difficult Chazals, reading the entire manuscript and offering most sensitive suggestions. He allowed me the freedom to decide what to include and what to omit — and hence is absolved from any responsibility for the final redaction — but his scholarship and בְּקִיאוּת is something I could not have done without.

RAV JOSEPH ELIAS, who kindly consented to read through the whole manuscript and who spent hours offering many concepts from the storehouse of his vast scholarship and in many ways raising up the level of the work.

My very good friend RAV DAVID COHEN, who graciously took time from his hectic schedule to read and comment upon the entire manuscript, guiding me to thoughts and interpretations, elucidating upon many of the underlying concepts and tenderly removing many stumbling blocks. He performed "constant righteousness" — עוֹשֵׂה צְדָקָה בְּכָל עֵת, by lending me many of the volumes I needed for researching this anthology. He freely gave of his time allowing me to "air out" important insights before commiting them to writing. I am grateful for his loving concern.

My long-time friend, RABBI ELI MUNK, was good enough to meticulously read the entire manuscript. He diligently checked the comments against the original sources and pointed out several discrepancies which were corrected before publication. These tangible fruits of his long friendship are appreciated.

MR. DAVID H. SCHWARTZ, as always, was near at hand with his warmth and friendship. He made many practical suggestions which are gratefully acknowledged.

RABBI RONALD GREENWALD, a dear and devoted friend, has been kind enough to make invaluable and encouraging suggestions, many of which were incorporated into the final work. His wife, MIRIAM תחי׳, was kind enough to read the manuscript, and offered several suggestions.

My dear friend and colleague, REB AVI SHULMAN, who, along with his wife, תחי׳, made many very important stylistic and conceptual observations on portions of the commentary. Avi shouldered the burden at ArtScroll during my involvement with this work and, seeing the need for such a commentary, almost single-handedly ensured its dissemination on a broad scale.

RABBI NISSON WOLPIN has again offered much in the way of stylistic approach to the commentary. He reviewed sections of the manuscript and offered invaluable suggestions.

The proprietors of J. BIEGELEISEN CO., Booksellers, are to be thanked for providing me with many of the difficult to obtain volumes on Ruth from which the anthology was culled. They have always warmly responded to my needs and have gone out of their way to help.

The efforts of my friend REB ZUNDEL BERMAN, seforim dealer and publisher, are deeply acknowledged. He envisioned the harbatzas-Torah-value of this series and he undertook to distribute it to the broad spectrum of b'nai Yeshivah with whom he enjoys a fine reputation, and with whom he is so intimately involved. He has gone out of his way to cooperate in every way possible.

A note of thanks is due to my friends at ARTSCROLL STUDIOS, LTD., whose high degree of professionalism and self-sacrificing devotion and loyalty ensured a beautiful production:

MRS. JUDY GROSSMAN and MISS RIVA ALPER gave of their personal time to proofread the manuscript through the various stages of editing. They ensured a nearly error-free publication. They gave the gift of time, which is greatly appreciated.

MISS MAZAL LANIADO, MISS MIRIAM FLAM, MISS PEARL EINHORN, and MISS NANCY LEFF have followed through the technical end with great devotion and dedication. My great thanks to them.

To be adequately appreciated, spirituality must be esthetically clothed, and my חָבֵר נֶאֱמָן REB SHEA BRANDER is the 'master-tailor.' The finished volume could not possibly have attained this degree of graphic excellence were it not for his efforts. He labored strenuously to assure a perfect product בִּפְנִים וּבַחוּץ, inside and out. He has my eternal gratitude for his every kindness, patience, and courtesy — both in the compilation of the anthology — which he (and his wife Henny תחי׳) were kind enough to read with a most critical eye; and the final layout and design. He let nothing stand in the way of ensuring a beautiful production. Words do not adequately express my appreciation.

My devoted wife, RACHEL, is the recipient of my most profound blessings. Her patience continues to mystify me. She creates a home for me and our children which is conducive to Torah study, and which, to her delight, has become בֵּית וַעַד לַחֲכָמִים, a gathering place for scholars. She inspires my efforts for Harbatzas Torah — in that merit may she be abundantly rewarded. תְּהִי מַשְׂכֻּרְתָּהּ שְׁלֵמָה מֵעִם ה׳.

I again end with a prayer that the work be received by the Torah world as a tool toward understanding and appreciating yet another one of the Sacred Books of the Bible as our Sages wanted us to understand and appreciate it; without recourse to so-called 'scientific' or other untraditional sources, so that the hidden depths of the Torah will become the possession also of non-Hebrew reading Jews — too many of whom have been condemned to varying degrees of spiritual pauperdom — so that 'their souls will be drawn to HASHEM and His Torah.'

Meir Zlotowitz

Brooklyn, N.Y. Rosh Chodesh Nissan, 5736

An Overview —
Ruth and the Seeds of Mashiach

Ruth and the Seeds of Mashiach

בשביל שני פרידות טובות [רות המואביה ונעמה העמונית]
חס הקב״ה על שתי אומות גדולות ולא החריבן   (ב״ק לח:)

Because of two good 'doves' [pure and righteous
Ruth the Moabite and Na'amah the Ammonite], the
Holy One, blessed be He, had mercy on two great
nations [Ammon and Moab] and did not destroy
them.   (Talmud)

שתי נשים היו שמהם נבנה זרע יהודה ויצא מהם דוד המלך
שלמה המלך ומלך המשיח ... תמר ורות ... ושתיהם עשו
בכשרות כדי לעשות טובה עם המתים   (זהר)

There were two women from whom were built the
seed of Judah and from whom descended King
David, King Solomon, and the King Mashiach ...
Tamar and Ruth ... Both acted properly in order to
do good with the dead.   (Zohar)

שבטים היו עסוקים במכירתו של יוסף, יוסף היה עסוק
בשקו ותעניתו, ראובן היה עסוק בשקו ותעניתו, יעקב היה
עסוק בשקו ותעניתו, ויהודה היה עסוק ליקח לו אשה,
והקב״ה היה עוסק בורא אורו של מלך המשיח   (בראשית רבה)

The tribes were occupied with the sale of Joseph,
Joseph was occupied with his sackcloth and fast,
Reuben was occupied with his sackcloth and fast,
Jacob was occupied with his sackcloth and fast, and
Judah was occupied with taking a wife. And the
Holy One, blessed be He, was occupied in creating
the light of the King Mashiach.   (Midrash)

I. The Period—A Moral Perspective

The Book of Ruth begins with a phrase that, at
first glance, appears designed to place the story in a
historic time frame: בִּימֵי שְׁפֹט הַשֹּׁפְטִים — *And it was*
in the days when the Judges judged. Upon closer ex-

amination, however, we see that Samuel, author of *Megillas Ruth* has, in fact, told us very little. The period of Judges began with the death of Joshua and extended until King Saul introduced monarchy to *Eretz Yisrael* — a period of roughly 350 years. By telling us that the story of Ruth occurred during the period of the judges, the prophet is hardly telling us when the events took place.

By telling us that the story of Ruth occurred during the period of the Judges, the prophet is hardly telling us when the events took place.

True, the Talmud says אִבְצָן זֶה בֹעַז — the Judge Ivtzan was Boaz *(Bava Basra 91a)* in which case the marriage of Ruth and Boaz took place in the year 2792 (968 BCE), 304 years after Joshua led *B'nai Yisroel* into the Land and 259 years after the period of Judges began *(Toldos Am Olam)*. Nevertheless, *Scripture* does not declare explicitly that Boaz and Ivtzan were one and the same, a statement that would be of utmost necessity if the opening phrase of *Megillas Ruth* were indeed intended to establish the chronology of the succeeding events.

Thus it is that our Sages interpret the phrase "When the Judges judged" not as a historical, but as a moral statement (see *Commentary* 1:1). Ruth emerged during a chaotic period in Jewish history. It was a time when people did not respond to their leaders and too many of the leaders did not earn the allegiance of the people. During such a period, famine struck the land — not only physical but spiritual; when there are no leaders and no followers, the soul of Judaism hungers with pangs no less severe or lethal than those of an emaciated body *(Ohr Yohel)*.

When there are no leaders and no followers, the soul of Judaism hungers with pangs no less severe or lethal than those of an emaciated body.

When there was no King

Although *Megillas Ruth* is a separate book of the Twenty Four, it is strikingly similar in many ways to two of the sorriest tales in Scripture, both at the conclusion of the Book of *Judges* — פִּלֶגֶשׁ בְּגִבְעָה, The Concubine in Giv'ah [*Judges 19*] the story of an atrocity that led to a civil war resulting in over 80,000 dead and the virtual decimation of the tribe of Benjamin; and פֶּסֶל מִיכָה, The Idol of Michah that led astray a sizeable portion of the tribe of Dan [*Judges*

18]. Those episodes, too, are placed in an indefinite time frame and the commentators disagree concerning when they occurred. But the author of the Book of Judges describes the respective periods very pithily:

בַּיָּמִים הָהֵם אֵין מֶלֶךְ בְּיִשְׂרָאֵל אִישׁ הַיָּשָׁר בְּעֵינָיו יַעֲשֶׂה

In those days there was no King in Israel, every man did what was right in his own eyes (Judges 17:6, 18:1, 19:1, 21:25).

How striking! The precise year of the event is unimportant. Even the name of the contemporary Judge matters not at all ... The Scriptures are not a history book.

How striking! The precise year of the event is unimportant. Even the name of the contemporary Judge matters not at all. Were we to know these historical curiosities, they would not add to our understanding of the episodes or instruct us for the future. And, in the final analysis, the Scriptures are not a history book. The narratives are often incomplete and the chronology indefinite. Any number of inspirational and miraculous tales are told only in the *Talmud* and *Midrash*. Why aren't they in Scripture? They aren't because they needn't be; the Torah is neither a history book nor a story book. God in His infinite wisdom gave us the סֵפֶר תּוֹלְדוֹת אָדָם, *the 'Book of the Generations of Man' (Genesis 5:1)* and included in it what was necessary for us to know. The Jewish people produced over a million prophets until the period of prophecy came to an end with the Babylonian Exile, but only fifty five are mentioned in the Twenty-four Books of the Torah. Only those stories and prophecies needed by posterity were recorded. The others, too, were manifestations of the mind, hand, and word of God — but, needed only in the period when they were revealed, they were not immortalized in the eternity of Torah *(Maharal).*

The Jewish people produced over a million prophets ... but only fifty-five are mentioned in the Twenty-four Books of the Torah ... Only those stories and prophecies needed by posterity were recorded.

But the closing tragedies of the Book of Judges: the concubine in Giv'ah and the Idol of Michah, were. They were indelibly inscribed in Jewish thought because they are more than tales. They are expressions of what can occur when *'there is no king in Israel, every man does what is right in his own* eyes.' As such, they are timeless and eternal. The Jew in every age must know what his fate can become if he refuses to accept authority and leadership. Ruth is of a piece with those other illustrations of what can happen when there is no vested authority in Israel. *Megillas Ruth*, too, begins with a cryptic phrase '*in the days when the Judges judged.*' The prophet, in three Hebrew words captures the attitude of an era. As the Talmud interprets, it indicates that the people judged, criticized, flouted their judges. Under such conditions authority breaks down. When that happens, there is famine — physical and spiritual. When that happens, even so great a man as Elimelech — learned, honored, wealthy — can cast off his responsibility to his people and flee to the fields of Moab (see *Commentary*).

The Story of Ruth

Ruth, princess of Moab, might never even have seen a Jew, much less married one, had it not been for the lapse of Elimelech and the Jewish people.

... She became the matriarch of the family that produced David, bearer of God's glory on earth.

Seen in this light, the story of Ruth as the background of מַלְכוּת בֵּית דָּוִד, the kingship of the House of David takes on a new perspective. Ruth, princess of Moab, might never even have seen a Jew, much less married one, had it not been for the lapse of Elimelech and the Jewish people. Because there was relative anarchy, a family from Bethlehem went to Moab and set in motion a chain of events that resulted in a princess from Moab becoming אִמָּא שֶׁל מַלְכוּת, the mother of Jewish royalty, matriarch of the family that produced David, bearer of God's glory on earth, and will ultimately produce *Mashiach* who will lead Israel and all mankind to the spiritual splendor intended by God when He said יְהִי אוֹר, '*let there be light!*'

It is axiomatic in Jewish belief that God's hand is everywhere and that the seeds of salvation can often be planted in a greenhouse of tragedy. Joseph was sold into slavery and his righteous father grieved for twenty-two years, but meanwhile God was preparing for Joseph to become the gracious and merciful viceroy who would ease the way into an Egyptian exile that had to be. A Jewish baby was placed in a basket to die in the sea, but he became Moses, the

ward of Pharaoh's daughter and the faithful
shepherd of the Jewish people. Elimelech fled his
destiny and we can only imagine how mortified the
tribe of Judah must have been that its most
illustrious son deserted it in its time of desperate
need, but God was preparing the genesis of the
Davidic house which would bring to Judah at long
last the glory that Jacob pledged it in his final
blessing.

Elimelech fled his destiny ... but God was preparing the genesis of the Davidic house.

II. The Sins of the Ancients

A Frame of Reference

Before proceeding further, it is important to
understand that the sins of the ancients cannot
even be mentioned in the same breath as ours. The
Torah creates no cult of hero worship; it freely and
frankly discloses the transgressions and
shortcomings of the Jewish people as a whole and of
the most exalted figures in its history. When such
greats as Moses and David fall short of the exacting
standards expected of them, they are criticized in a
way that can make modern-day readers smug and
complacent in their own fantasies of self-
righteousness. Superficial readings of Torah have
resulted in the images of violence, cruelty, and lust
profitably merchandized by by writers and
producers who dare to cheapen history's greatest
souls to turn on easy profit. Yet one of our great
scholars and righteous men of recent generations expressed the Torah view succinctly and well when he
said, "If only our *mitzvos* could be as holy as their
aveiros (transgressions)." It is ingrained in our
system of belief that earlier generations — because
they were closer to the wellsprings of revelation and
to Sinai — were infinitely more holy than ours. So
much so that, even in *Halacha*, the outstanding
decisors of any era can only interpret and compare,
but never dispute, the findings of their predecessors

When such greats as Moses and David fall short of the exacting standards expected of them, they are criticized in a way that can make modern-day readers smug and complacent in their own fantasies of self-righteousness.

It is ingrained in our system of belief that earlier generations — because they were closer to the wellsprings of revelation and to Sinai — were infinitely more holy than ours.

of a previous period. The demarcations of periods were decreed by the leading scholars of a generation when they, themselves, realized that they did not approach the stature of the preceding greats. Thus it was that the sages of the Talmud decided that the illustrious period of the Mishnaic *Tannaim* had come to an end. In the same way, the personal conduct of the ancients — and especially the greatest among them — was measured by a standard infinitely higher and more exacting than ours.

The personal conduct of the ancients — and especially the greatest among them — was measured by a standard infinitely higher and more exacting than ours.

Such a concept should not be entirely foreign to us. We expect higher standards of conduct from people holding positions of responsibility. One might feel extreme annoyance at the sight of a drunken bicycle rider — after all he could collide with someone or something, endangering himself and others. But we would be appalled at the thought of a drunken airline pilot with hundreds of passengers, and of untold innocents below at the mercy of his inebriated mind and uncontrollable hands. Similarly, succeeding generations have learned to shrug at the corruption of leaders and magnates, but *Baruch Hashem*, we could not even conceive of such behavior on the part of our Torah giants.

Conversely, because more is expected of greater people, their lapses must be judged by a higher standard as well. The standard the Torah imposes on the holy figures of ancient times is harsh and unforgiving — and it is proof of their greatness: one does not expect big things of small people, nor should one be indulgent of "human" weakness in mighty figures.

One does not expect big things of small people, nor should one be indulgent of "human" weakness in mighty figures.

Condemnation — But no Sin

וַיֵּלֶךְ רְאוּבֵן וַיִּשְׁכַּב אֶת־בִּלְהָה פִּילֶגֶשׁ אָבִיו

And Reuben went and slept with Bilhah, his father's concubine (Breishis 35:22).

A horrible sin! The children of Jacob had only recently exterminated the city of Shechem for a lesser abomination, and yet Reuben remained a son in good standing, a respected father of the Jewish nation. The

The Talmud
explains that Reuben
did not commit the
sin of adultery:
'whoever says
Reuben sinned is
mistaken'.

Talmud explains that Reuben did *not* commit the sin of adultery; מי שאמר ראובן חטא אינו אלא טועה, 'whoever says Reuben sinned is mistaken' (*Shabbos 55b*). After the death of Rachel who had had the status of Jacob's principal wife, Leah and her children felt that the honor of family primacy was due her. When, instead, Jacob's personal belongings were moved to the tent of Bilhah, Reuben felt that his mother had been slighted. To right the wrong, he removed Jacob's things to the tent of Leah. An understandable, even commendable, deed by most standards.

For a person of
Reuben's stature to
tamper with his
father's privacy, to
interfere in the
personal life of the
Patriarch Jacob, was
a gross, coarse act.

But for a person of Reuben's stature to tamper with his father's privacy, to interfere in the personal life of the patriarch Jacob, was a gross, coarse act. By the standard of behavior expected of a Reuben, such an indiscretion is tantamount to adultery and the Torah so labels it.

וַיְהִי לְעֵת זִקְנַת שְׁלֹמֹה נָשָׁיו הִטּוּ אֶת־לְבָבוֹ אַחֲרֵי
אֱלֹהִים אֲחֵרִים ... וְלֹא שָׁמַר אֵת אֲשֶׁר צִוָּה ה'

And it happened when Solomon was old that his wives turned his heart away to other gods ... he kept not that which HASHEM commanded. (I Kings 11:4-10).

Scripture apparently makes it clear that the aging Solomon became an idol worshipper. Again, the

Solomon's wives
attempted to draw
him after the idols,
but he did not heed
them. Just the same,
he is condemned as
an idolator, the
harshest approbrium
the Torah can
confer.

Talmud says no (*Shabbos 56b*). His wives attempted to draw him after the idols, but he did not heed them. Just the same, Solomon is condemned as an idolator, the harshest approbrium the Torah can confer because, by his indulgent attitude toward the sins of his foreign wives, he allowed them to think that they could sway his heart from the service of God. This might be excusable in lesser men, but never in Solomon.

An Exalted Nation

Similarly, higher standards are expected of the Jewish people, especially during the period of Scriptures when they were witness to miracles, audience to prophecy. The classic, indisputable case in point is the incident in *Joshua 7*, which tells of the

Higher standards are expected of the Jewish people, especially during the period of Scriptures when they were witness to miracles, audience to prophecy.

shocking, demoralizing defeat suffered by Israel in their attack upon the small town of Ai. After the miracle of Jericho and the Divine promises that they would conquer the land without a casualty, this setback cast a pall upon the entire people. Joshua and the elders tore their clothes, put ashes on their heads, and fell before the Holy Ark pleading with God to tell them why the tragedy happened.

God responded with a shocking and frightening litany of the transgressions of His once holy and righteous people:

חָטָא יִשְׂרָאֵל וְגַם עָבְרוּ אֶת־בְּרִיתִי ... וְגַם לָקְחוּ
מִן הַחֵרֶם וְגַם גָּנְבוּ וְגַם כִּחֲשׁוּ וְגַם שָׂמוּ בִכְלֵיהֶם

Israel has sinned and they have also transgressed my covenant ... and they have taken of the devoted property, and have also stolen, and falsified, and they have put it among their own goods.

How bold and all-encompassing a condemnation! A nation of traitors and thieves had Israel become!

Joshua investigated and it was discovered that Achan — only one man from an entire nation — had violated Joshua's prohibition against looting the spoils of Jericho. Because of one man's lapse, the nation was castigated in the sharpest terms and doomed to defeat in the wars commanded by God. Because of only one man's frailty, the Divine pledge to the patriarchs and their children was jeopardized.

Because of only one man's frailty, the Divine pledge to the patriarchs and their children was jeopardized.

Did Scripture not tell the story explicitly, we could not imagine that Achan's deed could even be considered a serious sin, much less imperil a nation. That it was considered so grievous an act points up to an inspiring and unimaginable degree how great was the nation that, because of its malfeasance in winking at his act, could be so stringently judged for the failure of one of its insignificant members. (For a fuller treatment of the above concept and further examples of it, see *Michtav Me'Eliyahu* I p. 162.)

How great was the nation that could be so stringently judged for the failure of one of its insignificant members, because of its malfeasance in winking at his act.

Ruth in Perspective

It is a valid indication of the depth of ignorance and the shallowness of scholarship with which most of T'nach is studied — or, better said, read.

Megillas Ruth has been referred to ignorantly and sacrilegiously by people far from Torah as history's first love story. That such a statement makes any Torah Jew shudder with disgust and bristle with anger goes without saying. Just the same, it is a valid indication of the depth of ignorance and the shallowness of scholarship with which most of *T'nach* is studied — or, better said, read. True, a literal reading of much of *T'nach* presents a blood-and-guts, lust-and-transgression picture of the Jewish people in what should have been the most spiritual and fulfilling period of its history. To be sure, Israel fell short of the goals set for it — but let us never forget that it fell short of *its* goals, not of ours. Even during its period of deepest decline; Israel was far, far above the moral, ethical, scholarly, and religious standards of the twentieth century which so enjoys basking in the self-anointed status of occupant of civilization's highest rung.

Even during its period of deepest decline, Israel was far, far above the moral, ethical, scholarly, and religious standards of the twentieth century.

Our Sages make it clear that Ruth's visit to Boaz in the dark of night was, in truth, the dawn of the blazing sun of the Davidic dynasty. Far from lusting after a Moabite woman, Boaz dedicated the last day of his life and the last strength of his aging body to the holy task of preparing the source of *Mashiach* with the righteous and pure 'dove' for whose sake God spared incestuous, selfish, iniquitous Moab for over seven hundred years. Even the sins of a generation judging its judges, the shortcomings of judges unequal to their responsibilities (see *Commentary* 1:1), and the lapse of the great Elimelech and his family (*Commentary* 1:1-5) cannot be understood in terms of the corruption, cowardice and rebellion with which we have become inured in recent years.

The Book of Judges is called סֵפֶר הַיָּשָׁר, The Book of the Just, because during the three-and-a-half centuries of the judges, the Jewish people, as a rule, did what was 'upright in the eyes of God' (*Avodah Zarah* 25a). This in no way contradicts the many tales of sinfulness found in the pages of *Judges*. The years of sin were relatively few, they did not enmesh

Their sins, however real, were defined by a standard as elevated from ours as is heaven from earth.

the entire nation, and the sins, however real, were defined by a standard as elevated from ours as is heaven from earth.

III. Monarchy in Israel

A Command-ment Deferred

There is a basic difference between a king and a judge and, in order to understand the period, we must understand the difference.

As is made clear in the opening of *Megillas Ruth* and the references to the lack of a king in the chapters of the concubine in Giv'ah and the Idol of Michah, the rule of Judges was not the ideal condition of Israel, and the absence of a king was, from time to time, sorely felt. Clearly there is a basic difference between a king and a judge and, in order to understand the period, we must understand the difference. Further, if monarchy is the ideal condition of Jewish government, why was it not established as soon as Israel entered *Eretz Yisrael*? And why, when the Jews finally asked Samuel to give them a king, did he criticize them so bitterly for doing so? The Torah ordains as one of the Six Hundred Thirteen Commandments that Israel request a king (*Deuteronomy* 17:14-15) according to the halachically accepted view of Rabbi Yehudah (*Sanhedrin* 20b, *Rambam Hilchos Melachim*) that:

שלוש מצות נצטוו ישראל בכניסתם לארץ:
להעמיד להם מלך, ולהכרית זרעו של עמלק,
ולבנות להם בית הבחירה

'The Jews were charged with three commandments upon entering the Land: to appoint a king, to cut off the seed of Amalek, and to build the Bais Hamikdosh...

If so, why did God scathingly describe the request for a king as

לֹא אוֹתְךָ מָאָסוּ כִּי אוֹתִי מָאֲסוּ מִמְּלֹךְ עֲלֵיהֶם,
Not you [Samuel] have they rejected, but Me have they rejected that I should not reign over them (I Samuel 8:7)?

Govern-ment in Israel

The Jewish concept of government is unique and always has been. Josephus Flavius put it this way:

> *Some nations place the sovereignty of their land in the hands of a single ruler (monarchy), some in the hands of a small number of rulers (oligarchy), and some in the hands of the people (democracy). Moses our Teacher taught us to place our faith in none of these forms of government. He taught us to obey the rule of God, for to God alone did he accord kingship and power. He commanded the people always to raise their eyes to God, for He is the source of all good for mankind in general and for each person in particular and in Him will people find help when they pray to Him in their time of suffering, for no act is hidden from His understanding and no hidden thought of man's heart is hidden from Him (Contra Appion).*

Josephus's description of Jewish government is often mistakenly described as theocracy, but it is not that at all. Jewish government was never the province of priests, an exchange of ermine for cassock. The Chashmonaim established a royal dynasty after their overthrow of the Syrian-Greeks, it is true, but the attempted perpetuation of that priestly monarchy was in violation of Jewish law in that it usurped the prerogative of the House of David and perverted the purpose of the priesthood. For their persistance in occupying the seat of power, the Chashmonaim were punished with extermination in a slave rebellion (*Ramban, Genesis* 49:10).

Jewish government was never the province of priests, an exchange of ermine for cassock.

The government described by Josephus is not one of priests, but of God. It mattered not whether the throne was occupied by a king or, as in earlier days, the accepted authority was a Judge — the true King of Israel is God; whatever human hands hold the reins of government are but His tools.

The true King of Israel is God; whatever human hands hold the reins of government are but His tools.

King Too Soon

Why, then, the commandment to install a king?

כִּי תָבֹא אֶל הָאָרֶץ אֲשֶׁר ה׳ אֱלֹקֶיךָ נֹתֵן לָךְ
וִירִשְׁתָּהּ וְיָשַׁבְתָּה בָּהּ וְאָמַרְתָּ אָשִׂימָה עָלַי מֶלֶךְ
כְּכָל הַגּוֹיִם אֲשֶׁר סְבִיבֹתָי

When you come into the land which HASHEM your God gives you and you take possession of it and dwell in it — and you say: I would set a king over me like all the nations around me (*Deut.* 17:14).

The commandment makes it clear that it is *not* the purpose of a king to serve as a charismatic conqueror uniting the nation behind him, meting out judgment to the enemy, and conquering and securing the land for his people (*Kiddushin* 37b). For it was only *after* having conquered and inhabited the land that a king was to be sought. Israel needed no mighty warlord to win its land — for had not God Himself promised them speedy conquest and total victory? ה׳ אִישׁ מִלְחָמָה ה׳ שְׁמוֹ, *God is a Man of war, with His Name HASHEM* — what need had they of a mortal conqueror? Security, prosperity, fruitfulness, happiness, and health were to be theirs as a natural consequence of observing the commandments, not for allegiance to a becrowned head or awe of a bemedaled breast (*Deut.* 28:1-14).

For Israel upon its entry into *Eretz Yisrael* to have a king with all his royal trappings would have cheapened itself and its king. Had Israel been a conquering army with a king at its head, the presence and assistance of God would have been obscured by the glitter of a crown and the plush of royal robes. The fiction would indeed have been created that Israel had won its land by force of arms rather than *by grace of God; that the foe had been slain by a* flesh and blood king rather than by the King of Kings, blessed be He.

During the days of Samuel, significant stretches of *Eretz Yisrael* had not yet been conquered. Indeed, it was to the enduring shame and centuries-long discredit of Israel that it allowed such a condition to persist. Rather than take advantage of Divine assistance and heed the Divine command that it purge the Holy Land of its profane inhabitants and turn it in its entirety into the land of Abraham, Isaac, and Jacob,' Israel was content to settle what had been won, retire to its vineyards and fig trees, and allow the less fortunate tribes — those whose inheritance was still in alien hands — to bemoan their fate in isolation. For not uniting as a nation and carrying out its destiny, it was condemned to endure the presence and invasions of its enemies in a centuries-long cycle of fall, punishment, repentence, and deliverance (*Judges* 2).

Rather than take advantage of Divine assistance ... Israel was content to settle what had been won and allow the less fortunate tribes to bemoan their fate in isolation.

It was a weary people fearing invasion by Ammon and seeking a defender and military leader that confronted aging Samuel and demanded a king. But it was not for defense and conquest that God ordained royalty upon Israel — for those purposes, Israel had to worry less about the weaknesses of its fortresses than about the stubbornness of its spirit; less about crumbling the defenses of its enemies than about shattering its own nature-conditioned heart.

It was not for defense and conquest that God ordained royalty upon Israel.

So it was an angry and disappointed Samuel who recited the catalog of miraculous Divine interventions in behalf of Israel, interventions that should have been more than sufficient to clarify the road of deliverance from their enemies. Samuel said:

וַתֹּאמְרוּ לִי, לֹא כִּי מֶלֶךְ יִמְלֹךְ עָלֵינוּ וַה׳ אֱלֹקֵיכֶם מַלְכְּכֶם,

'And you said to me, No; but a king shall reign over us — but HASHEM, your God is your King! (Samuel 12:12).

Yes, the Torah indeed commands Israel to request a king, but, in Samuel's day, the request was premature.

Yes, the Torah indeed commands Israel to request a king, but, in Samuel's day, the request was premature. They got their king, Saul — a great and righteous man, head and shoulders above the rest of the nation — but his monarchy ended in tragedy because the people were wrong in demanding it then.

The Role of a King

The ideal Jewish king ascends his throne in a time of tranquility. The nation is secure and prosperous because its ultimate King, God, has made it so, and its way of life is charted by the Torah. The king plays a unique role. He, as first citizen of the nation, is the living embodiment of Torah and how its statutes and holiness ennoble man. Holder of immense and almost unbridled power, he submits to the laws in the *Sefer Torah* which he carries with him at all times; required by his duty to the nation to hold wealth and exhibit pomp, he acquires what he must, but shuns excess; enabled by his station to indulge his passions, he sets an example of sobriety and self-control; inhibited by no mortal restraint, he turns his energies to the selfless service of his people; able to establish the absolute dominion of his own will, he does not rest until his people know the rigors of Torah study and a discipline of honesty and morality in their personal and business lives that would earn sainthood in any other nation.

The king is the living embodiment of Torah and how its statutes and holiness ennoble man.

The King does not rest until his people know the rigors of Torah study and a discipline of honesty and morality in their personal and business lives that would earn sainthood in any other nation.

When the nation sought its king, it had not yet attained the stature it needed to be worthy of that type of monarch. Nevertheless, it did possess a man suited to the role — David, an unknown shepherd who was unappreciated even by his own family. Had Israel been worthy, David would have become the final *Mashiach* and the eternal *Bais Hamikdosh* would have been built by him. As it was, he became the father of the dynasty whose ultimate heir will one day proclaim the kingdom of heaven upon earth. (Although there are many sources for the above treatment of Jewish monarchy, it is based primarily upon *Rav S.R. Hirsch, Deut.* 17:14).

Had Israel been worthy, David would have become the final Mashiach and the eternal Bais Hamikdosh would have been built by him.

Powers of the King

It is the function of the king to safeguard the Torah and see to it that the people study it and obey its commandments. Nor is he to be considered above the Halacha — on the contrary, it is his duty to be a model of scrupulous adherence to the laws of the Torah. His office, however, carries with it a unique legal status which may be divided into two categories:

a) As the sovereign embodiment of the nation, the king is entitled to respect and reverence exceeding anyone elses. All must step aside to make way for him and even property may be destroyed for his convenience. Nor may the king voluntarily forfeit any of his prerogatives; to do so is to demean the nation he leads. He is as obligated to exercise his claim upon the awe of the nation as is each of its members to grant it.

b) The king has extra-legal powers to confiscate, punish, and condemn to execution. A Jewish court of law may not execute a murderer save under a set of extraordinarily strict rules of evidence and testimony; a king may have the murderer killed, so long as he is satisfied that sufficient proof of guilt exists, even if the evidence is circumstancial. Whoever is disrespectful or defiant of the king is liable to the death penalty upon his command and at his pleasure.

All this is to insure that he has the power to inspire the fear of, and destroy the capacity of evil-doers (*Rambam, Hilchos Melachim* 3).

In the exercise of his extra-legal powers, the king is guided by one consideration — '*to correct any situation, as required by the times*' (*ibid*).

Thus it becomes clear why Samuel, author of Judges, explains the worst aberrations of the people with the unadorned statement, *In those days there was no king in Israel, every man did what was right in his own eyes.* A king would not have permitted the barbaric city of Giv'ah to go unpunished after its *act of wantonness against a helpless concubine* innocently seeking nothing more than a place to rest her head before going on with her craven Levite husband. Nor would a king have allowed the Levite, in his grief and anger, to incite the other tribes against Benjamin. Nor would he have allowed a jurisdictional dispute between the Sanhedrin of Benjamin

A king would not have permitted the barbaric city of Giv'ah to go unpunished.

and the rest of the nation to result in such tragic bloodshed. The existing legal system at the time could not cope with the travail engendered by the atrocity of Giv'ah, but a king transcends and overrides the legal system.

Nor would a king have allowed the marauders of Dan to make off with Michah's idol and carve out a little kingdom of their own up north. His duty to maintain the spiritual standard of the nation would have forced him to act; no lack of power or jurisdiction could have stood in his way.

The defection of Elimelech, too, at the beginning of *Megillas Ruth* was a result of the 'judging of the judges' — a lack of constituted, accepted, powerful leadership. Elimelech, great and wealthy, felt a *responsibility but feared its burden. He would be expected* to establish some sort of order to cope with the ravages of famine and his treasury would have to be thrown open to the poor and hungry. Elimelech felt unequal to the task — and fled. Trying to conserve his fortune and peace of mind, he lost both — and his Jewish identity. Save for the sacrifice and idealism of Ruth, he would have lost his posterity, as well. Had there been a king — who knows? The responsibility upon Elimelech might not have been so overwhelming and the majesty of the throne might have been employed to prevent the flight of the erstwhile patron of Bethlehem.

Elimelech, great and wealthy, felt a responsibility but feared its burden ... felt unequal to the task — and fled.

Had there been a king — who knows?

The Power of a Judge

Extra-legal powers are not the province of a king alone. The Sanhedrin, too, has the power to ordain coercive measures in defense of the nation and its mission. There were such courts in the days before the monarchy. The Torah commands that judges and officers of the court be established in all cities (*Deut.* 16:18). They were, and they performed valiantly throughout the period, even under foreign occupation and terror; these were the judges whom Deborah praised several times in her song (*Judges* 5).

But the courts were loath to exercise their extra-legal powers as is shown from the formula, *In those days there was no king*, to explain how such tragedies could have happened.

For there is a basic difference between the residual power of the monarchy and the Sanhedrin:

כל אלו הרצחנים שאינם חייבים מיתת ב"ד אם
ירצה מלך ישראל להורגם בדין מלכות ותקנת
עולם הרשות בידו. וכן אם רצה ב"ד להורגם
בהוראת שעה, אם היתה השעה צריכה לכך יש
רשות להם כפי מה שיראו

All these murderers who are not liable to execution — if a Jewish king wishes to kill them using his regal powers and for the benefit of society, he may do so. So, too, if a court wishes to execute them by an extraordinary decree, if the times require it, the court has the right as it sees fit (Rambam, Hilchos Rotzeach 2:4)

Rav Tzvi Hirsh Chayes (in *Toras Nvi'im* 7) deduces from the subtle differences in Rambam's descriptions of the respective authority of king and court, that the king's powers, while identical to those of the court in the case under discussion, may be more freely exercised. Rambam (*Hilchos Sanhedrin* 18:6) differentiates between הוֹרָאַת שָׁעָה, extraordinary decree, and דִין מַלְכוּת, the law of the king. This further indicates a presumption of authority that is automatically attributed to the king purely by virtue of his office — an authority that the court cannot exercise unless it is absolutely convinced by the particular circumstances that the national interest and severity of the situation require it to act extra-legally.

Plainly, any Sanhedrin, local or national, would be most ginger in annexing such powers to itself. Only in the most serious of cases would it tamper with the laws of the Torah; it is no small matter for a court of Torah law to go beyond the strictures of Torah law.

The king is bound by no such restrictions. His very position and resultant responsibility to the nation demand and require that he exercise the powers of his position. A weak king does the nation no good — he becomes an invitation to religious lassitude and the paralysis of leadership that results in spiritual famine, atrocity, and idolatry. Indeed, the constant obligation to respect the king's personal majesty — the neglect of which can result in the death penalty — is in order to strengthen his position as national leader so that he can better serve the nation.

The judges of old were national leaders, but their leadership was based on law and public acceptance. They did not have the power inherent in the office of the king. They could lead if the people followed and they could exercise the extra-legal powers of a Sanhedrin under such conditions as allowed a court to exercise those powers. But the ability to lead varies with many factors, and Jewish judges did not exercise extra-legal powers with impunity.

There was another circumstance conferring power on a judge. The people could accept him upon themselves with all the rights and powers of a monarch — including the right to execute the disrespectful and disobedient. Joshua was given such acceptance (*Joshua* 1:16-18) and the people were anxious to establish a Gideonic dynasty (*Judges* 8:22).

Generally, however, the period of the judges was one of striving imperfectly toward goals that were never achieved — the goal of national unity under God, sovereignty over all of *Eretz Yisrael*, the attainment of the Divine blessings of peace, prosperity, and security. Had that goal been achieved, the people could have gone on to the fulfillment of the Torah's commandment that they ask God to select a king to lead them to even greater spiritual heights. It was not achieved. The result was the turbulence of the period of judges and flawed monarchy aiming at a spiritual summit that has, for millennia, awaited the coming of *Mashiach*.

The judges of old were national leaders, but their leadership was based on law and public acceptance. They did not have the power inherent in the office of the king.

The period of the judges was one of striving imperfectly toward goals that were never achieved.

The result was the turbulence of the period of judges and flawed monarchy aiming at a spiritual summit that has, for millennia, awaited the coming of Mashiach.

IV. The Murky Roots of Monarchy

The Kingship of Judah

Jewish monarchy is no mere political system; when it is ordered according to the Divine Will, it is an end unto itself.

Jewish monarchy is no mere political system; when it is ordered according to the Divine Will, it is an end unto itself. It is this end which is particularly represented by the kingdom of Judah. The final one of the Ten *Sefiros*, the stages through which God's will is carried out in creation, is מַלְכוּת, *malchus* (kingship.) *Malchus* represents the final revelation, the coming to fruition of His will. To the extent to which His will is obscured by the human fiction of *'my strength and the power of my hand has created for me all this accomplishment,'* His rule on earth fails to find expression in our lives.

When Leah's fourth child was born, she named him Judah saying הַפַּעַם אוֹדֶה אֶת ה', *now I will praise HASHEM*. Rashi explains that she gave special praise then, rather than previously with the birth of her first three sons, שנטלתי יותר על חלקי, *for I have taken more than my share*. The matriarchs knew that Jacob would have twelve sons; that should have meant three sons for each of Jacob's four wives. When Leah gave birth to her fourth son, she gave special thanks because God had given her more than her share. That is why Jews are called *Yehudim* (implying that they are descended from Judah) no matter what tribe they belong to. Even Mordechai, a Benjaminite, is referred to in *Megillas Esther* as *Mordechai haYehudi*. We are Yehudim because we always thank God for giving us more than our share, more than we deserve. The Jew is ever conscious of the graciousness and mercy of God. To him, health, prosperity — life itself — are never his by right; he thanks God for everything, for it is all an undeserved gift (*Chidushei HaRim* in *Sefer haZechus*).

The matriarchs knew that Jacob would have twelve sons; that should have meant three sons for each of Jacob's four wives. When Leah gave birth to her fourth son, she gave special thanks because God had given her more than her share.

To the Jew, health, prosperity — life itself — are never his by right.

The strength of Judah lay in his readiness to be a willing receptacle of God's talent, blessing, and responsibility while ascribing nothing to himself. His very name indicates this quality. The Hebrew spelling of Judah's name, יְהוּדָה, contains the sacred four-letter name of God — plus one more letter, a ד *dalet.* The word דָּל, *dal* in Hebrew means a pauper. Judah has within himself the majesty of his Creator; his kingship is no less than the kingship, in a mortal guise, of God Himself, — in his own eyes, Judah remains דָּל, a pauper. No matter how exalted his position, whatever he has is an undeserved gift of God.

David, first of the Judean kings and model for all his successors, embodies the same concept in his name. It begins with *dalet* and ends with *dalet.* For all his grandeur and achievement, for all the love his Maker bore for him and the holiness that made even the blood of his war victims seem like holy offerings before the altar of God, David, from beginning to end, considered himself a pauper, an impoverished mortal who carried only the gifts of God, but nothing of his own. The future *Mashiach* is described by Zechariah as עָנִי וְרוֹכֵב עַל חֲמוֹר, *a poor man riding a donkey.* He will finally fulfill the purpose of creation by bringing the kingdom of heaven to earth and by crowning God as King of all mankind — but he is a pauper riding the humblest of domestic beasts of burden.

Such kings represent the final stage of revelation. They are themselves but an embodiment of God's will on earth (*Sfas Emes, Vayigash*).

Tainted Origins

It is no less than astounding that the conception of the Davidic dynasty was shrouded in mists of impropriety.

Lot and his daughters were miraculously saved from the destruction of Sodom. His daughters thinking they were the only people left on earth, intoxicated him, lived with him, and gave birth to Ammon and Moab. Centuries later, Ruth the Moabite became the great-grandmother of David. Even later, Naamah the Ammonite became the wife of King Solomon and mother of his successor, Rechavam. True, the righteousness of Ruth and Naamah was of such magnitude that their nations were spared by God for all the centuries spanning traditions of selfishness and cruelty, but why was it neccessary for God to defile His servant David by planting his origin in a guise of incest? And what luster could it add to the Holy Name for His מַלְכוּת, kingship, to trace its source to so ignoble a beginning?

Why was it necessary for God to defile His servant David by planting his origin in a guise of incest?

After the sale of Joseph into slavery, Judah left his brothers to found his own family. First his oldest and then his second son married Tamar. Each of the young men died because of his own sin (see *Genesis* 38). Judah, fearing that Tamar had some blame in the unusual pair of tragedies, delayed the יבום, levirate marriage of Tamar to his youngest son, Shelah. She realized that Judah would not allow her to marry Shelah but she wanted to share in building God's Kingdom, so, posing as a harlot, she lured Judah into spending a single night with her. She conceived and gave birth to twins, Peretz and Zerach. Her ambition was fulfilled — Peretz was the ancestor of David.

Tamar's ambition was fulfilled — Peretz was the ancestor of David.

> *Rabbi Yochanan said, Judah sought to pass by Tamar. The Holy One, blessed be He, dispatched the angel of lust to waylay him. The angel said to Judah, 'Where are you going? From where will kings arise, from where will great men arise?' 'Then he [Judah] turned to her by the way' — he was coerced, against his good sense (Breishis Rabbah 85:8).*

Not only did Judah father the twins in an apparently illicit manner, the shame of his action became public knowledge by his own admission in an act of moral courage that remains a shining example of honesty even under the most distasteful circumstances. But Judah's tryst with Tamar left him no less righteous and chaste than before. It was more than Divinely inspired — it was forced by the Hand of God. But why? Why did God's design require so convoluted an execution; why did His plan require such unbecoming conduct?

Judah's tryst with Tamar left him no less righteous and chaste than before. It was more than Divinely inspired — it was forced by the Hand of God.

The next episode in the strange Divine scheme was the marriage of Ruth and Boaz. (See Commentary 3)

Why a Moabite? Why a blot in the family— ... לֹא יָבֹא
מוֹאָבִי בִּקְהַל ה׳, 'a Moabite may not come into the Assembly of HASHEM' — that took years to erase? Why
a stealthy night-time visit by the Moabite woman to
the field where the righteous, aged Judge slept
guarding his harvest? Why so profane a method to
carry out so sacred a mission?

A Bribe for the Satan

That evil exists and that it has the ability to becloud the senses of even the wisest of men is in order to create the battleground for man's free-will struggle to choose correctly.

The eternal struggle between good and evil
revolves essentially around man. It is not God who
struggles with evil; the Satan exists only as long as he
suits God's purpose. That evil exists and that it has
the ability to becloud the senses of even the wisest of
men is in order to create the battleground for man's
free-will struggle to choose correctly. People are
rewarded only for having prevailed in the struggle to
choose right over wrong; if the emptiness of evil and
the virtues of good are so obvious that the choice
becomes automatic, then there is no justification for
rewarding the righteous. One does not reward a child
for not reaching into a blazing fire; the consequences
of doing so are so plain that no sane person would
try it. On the other hand, the child who is all alone
with a tempting cookie jar and conquers his greed is
amply deserving of recognition. Had there been no
prophets of Ba'al with their 'miracles' and appearance of rectitude, no one would have been fool
enough to reject Elijah. The forces of evil must have
the power to confuse, confound, convince —
otherwise man's mission would be an exercise in the
obvious (Derech Hashem).

The forces of evil must have the power to confuse, confound, convince — otherwise man's mission would be an exercise in the obvious.

A direct frontal attack on the יצר הרע, the evil inclination, is too often doomed to failure. The powers
of the Satan are usually too great for mortal man.
Indeed, his own flesh-and-blood drives and desires
are too strong to be vanquished and sublimated
without a long, complex, and devious struggle.

But there are ways. The evil inclination is far from
invincible — in fact, it is eminently deceivable. The
Sages have an interesting expression: שוחד לשטן, a
bribe for the Satan. All of us know the popular methods

for developing self-control. 'I won't allow myself a piece of cake until I finish forty-five minutes of study.' 'I will take a vacation if I am successful.' To a serious thinker these ploys are ridiculous — except that they work! People have an awesome capacity for self-deception — the sincere and intelligent person uses this capacity for the good; the self-indulgent and shallow person uses this same capacity to cause his own downfall. The old witticism 'it's the easiest thing in the world to stop smoking — I've done it thousands of times,' is all too true!

The strategems in the battle against evil are like one step backward and two steps forward.

The strategems in the battle against evil are like one step backward and two steps forward. They are a means of utilizing the frailities of human nature to combat, weaken, and eventually conquer the evil inclination that is part of the very humanness of man.

Man is fully capable of knowing and understanding himself well enough to cope with his urges, and to utilize rather than be defeated by them. Even base desires — like greed and vanity — can be sublimated by using money for charity or accepting honor only for worthwhile accomplishments (see *Ramban, Lev. 16:8* and *Michtav meEliyahu I p. 262*):

But it remains true that our world is a balance of good and evil with every person facing the challenge of choosing one over the other.

But it remains true that our world is a balance of good and evil with every person facing the challenge of choosing one over the other. And man seldom succeeds by directly attacking the forces of evil; in order to maintain the balance, they were given too much power to be easily defeated. They will bounce back with a counter-attack that will leave the presumed victor bloodied and disarrayed.

No greater good exists than the kingdom of God on earth and its champions, the tribe of Judah with its most distinguished son, David. Its development began with Judah's apparently inexplicable weakness in straying from the path — literally and figuratively — after Tamar in harlot's disguise. The

The Satan will not — cannot — permit spiritual heights to be scaled without a fierce struggle.

episode illustrates that the Satan will not — cannot — permit spiritual heights to be scaled without a fierce struggle. To take the direct path would be to court failure by inviting the Satan ferociously to thwart the attainment of good. The Satan must be appeased. Judah's act had the appearance of a lamentable fall as the great leader of Jacob's sons was powerless to control his lust for a stranger. Satan laughed, the Canaanites snickered, Judah was ashamed — but God was doing His work by striking the spark that would ultimately become the brilliant light of *Mashiach* (*Chafetz Chaim on Torah*).

Drawing out the Sparks

מִי יִתֵּן טָהוֹר מִטָּמֵא?

'Who can withdraw purity from impurity?' (Job 14:3)

Abraham came from Terach, Hezekiah from Achaz, Yoshiah from Omon, Mordechai from Shim'i, Israel from the nations, the world to come from this world. Who could do this? Who could command this? Who could decree this? No one but [God] the only One on earth! (Bamidbar Rabbah 19:1).

In a deeper sense, there is more to the strange and distasteful circumstances surrounding Lot, Judah, and Ruth than a bribe to the Satan. There is a constant refrain in Kabbalist and esoteric literature that this world is a mixture of good and evil symbolized by עֵץ הַדַּעַת טוֹב וָרָע, the Tree of Knowledge of Good and Evil. In all evil there is some good — otherwise it could not exist. Man's highest purpose is to extract the sparks of good from the evil. Obviously this is no simple task. It demands a high degree of self-perfection before it can even be attempted, but the mission of mankind on earth is to withdraw the spiritual good from its captivity.

It is known to all who have been given understanding that the soul of David was clothed in the shell of Moab and that it was freed from Moab through Ruth. Concerning this, too, Scripture says: Who could withdraw purity from impurity [see Midrash above]. These were the intentions of the inscrutable wisdom of the Creator in guiding His world to bring every act to its proper path. Every act of God travels through byways, often in complex, crooked ones . . . For such has occured to all great souls as they go among the 'shells' of impurity to capture and extract the good (Rabbi Moshe Chaim Luzatto in Megillas Sesarim).

The sparks of goodness are scattered throughout creation. One was in Lot and remained glimmering even in the moral filth of Sodom. To salvage that spark, God sent the angel Rafael, who, after healing Abraham, went to Sodom to save Lot, bearer of the spark that would become the soul of David. It went down the generations until the time came for it to leave the impurity of Moab and enter the Jewish nation through Ruth.

There was a spark in Canaan and it was lodged in Tamar. Judah had to unite with her, but of his own free will he would never have done it.

There was a spark in Canaan and it was lodged in Tamar. Judah had to unite with her, but of his own free will he would never have done it. An angel forced Judah into the path of a harlot when God was ready to begin the creation of the Davidic dynasty.

Lot's spark travelled through his Moabite descendents for seven centuries until it reached its ultimate destination. When the proper time came, Ruth went from the field of Moab to the field of Boaz. While popular wisdom held that no Moabite could ever enter the community of God, the scion of Judah, leader of his people, unearthed the long-neglected law that a Moabitess was not forbidden to marry a Jew. One fateful night, the last one of Boaz's life, the spark of Lot and the brilliance of Judah were united as Ruth and Boaz were married. That night, Oved, the grandfather of David, was conceived.

V. The Marriage—Levirate and Moabite

The Torah's first mention of the obligation of יִבּוּם, levirate marriage, appears when Er, first-born son of Judah, died and Judah instructed his second son, Onan to marry the widow and וְהָקֵם זֶרַע לְאָחִיךָ, *raise up seed for your brother (Gen. 38:8).*

The *Holy Zohar (Vayeishev 177)* explains that the death of a person does not remove him from his eternal roots on earth because his children carry on his role in life. When someone dies without children, his mission on earth would go uncontinued and unfulfilled. To prevent this tragedy and maintain the departed's link in the chain of life, the Divine Wisdom ordained that his widow and his brother marry and produce children . . . The newborn child becomes the receptacle for the soul of the departed so that his mission in life can be completed through the children of his widow and closest relative.

Shaar Bas Rabim (Vayeishev) explains further that man and wife are considered like one body, one unit. It is her duty to perpetuate his life through levirate marriage because, with the death of her husband, it is as if part of her own body had died. The closest relative is a brother because he and the deceased are products of the same parents. Therefore, the commandment of levirate marriage applies to the brother.

Man and wife are considered like one body, one unit.

In early generations, לִפְנֵי מַתַּן תּוֹרָה, *before the Torah was given*, the secret of levirate marriage was known to wise men of the caliber of Judah. They knew that in the absence of a brother to marry the widow, the closest blood relatives, too, could function to make "whole" the disrupted family unit. Therefore, Judah's unwitting marriage to Tamar was legal, even commendable. Only its mode — the apparent wanton act with a "harlot" and the resulting humiliation of Judah — was degrading. When the Torah was given with the statutes that most forms of family marriages were incestuous, a relationship such as Judah's and Tamar's became forbidden. Still,

In early generations, לפני מתן תורה before the Torah was given, the wise men knew that in the absence of a brother to marry the widow, the closest blood relatives, too, could function to make "whole" the disrupted family unit.

levirate marriage was so holy that God continued to permit, even command, it in its highest form — that of a brother marrying his widowed, childless sister-in-law (*Ramban*).

Boaz was a "redeemer" and a potential participant in a levirate marriage with Ruth by virtue of the fact that he was a close relative — but not so close that a marriage would be forbidden as incestuous. He was second in line; the closest relative was Tov, a brother of Elimelech and an uncle of Machlon. The next relative was Boaz, a cousin of Machlon. True, the Torah does not ordain levirate marriage except for a brother of the deceased, but, as is apparent from *Megillas Ruth*, in those days, Jews acknowledged a moral obligation to provide a resting place for the soul of the departed by providing an offspring from his wife (see Commentary 3:1; 3:10).

It is apparent from Megillas Ruth that, in those days, Jews acknowledged a moral obligation to provide a resting place for the soul of the departed by providing an offspring from his wife.

Moabite But Not Moabitess

In prohibiting converts from Ammon and Moab from ever marrying into the 'congregation of God,' the Torah explains the reason why:

עַל דְּבַר אֲשֶׁר לֹא קִדְּמוּ אֶתְכֶם בַּלֶּחֶם וּבַמַּיִם
בַּדֶּרֶךְ בְּצֵאתְכֶם מִמִּצְרָיִם

Because they met you not with bread and water on the way when you came forth from Egypt (Deut. 23:5)

The Sages interpret the verse to indicate that עַמּוֹנִי וְלֹא עַמּוֹנִית, מוֹאָבִי וְלֹא מוֹאָבִית, only male Ammonite and Moabite converts may not marry into the nation (*Yevamos 76b*). This interpretation is implicit in the verse itself. The Torah gives us a reason for the prohibition: that the accused nations failed to show simple human decency in not greeting the travel-weary Jews with food and drink. It is customary for men to travel into the desert to meet travelers, point out our Sages, but it is not proper for women to do so. Therefore, women were absolved from the national guilt and hence welcome to convert and marry into the Jewish nation.

The Torah gives us a reason for the prohibition that accused nations failed to show simple human decency in not greeting the travel-weary Jews with food and drink.

Like all interpretations that modify Scriptural prohibitions, this one was transmitted to Moses by

The Sages did not
legislate; they
merely pointed out
the Scriptural basis
for an apparently
incongruous law.

God. The Sages did not legislate; they merely pointed out the Scriptural basis for an apparently incongruous law — nowhere do we find a law of this type that applies to one sex, but not to the other. Egyptian converts, male and female alike, are forbidden to enter the congregation of God until their third generation as Jews. *Mamzeirim* (people born of incestuous or adulterous unions which can never be legitimized by marriage) are forbidden to marry other Jews no matter what their sex. Why, then, should the Ammonite and Moabite nations be different? The answer — our Sages *explain*, but do not originate — is found in Scripture itself as cited above.

This law was known to Moses and his disciples. During the three centuries between Israel's entry into the Land and the time of Ruth and Boaz, the law gradually became forgotten, probably because it fell into disuse. Those were the times when the Oral Law was still oral — the interpretations of Scripture were not committed to writing; they passed from teacher to student down through the generations. If no Ammonites or Moabites sought to convert — a natural consequence of the long-standing hostility between them and Israel — the legal question of their marital status would never have required decision by a court. And the average Jew, even most scholars, would have assumed that the prohibition upon them was as sexless as those upon Egyptians and *mamzeirim*. Of course, had the question come before the Great Sanhedrin or any of the other distinguished courts of the Land, it is virtually certain that a decision would have been rendered in favor of Ammonite and Moabite women. Indeed, it *did* arise in the court of Boaz at that pivotal time in Jewish history and it *was* so decided. Many legal concepts become hazy with disuse, however, and this was one of them. So it was that it was almost universally thought, even by a minority of the greatest sages, that Ruth's marriage to a Jew was prohibited.

Those were the times
when the Oral Law
was still oral — the
interpretations of
Scripture were not
committed to
writing; they passed
from teacher to
student down
through the
generations.

Many legal concepts
become hazy with
disuse, however, and
this was one of them.

An analogy can be found in the prohibition against eating certain species of birds. The Torah

When Ruth's baby was born, the birth was celebrated by few because, for many, it was not a blessed event at all, this product of a 'forbidden' marriage (*Ruth* 4:14-17; see Commentary).

This popular misconception died hard; it hung like a black cloud over the family until the time of David — and very nearly changed and embittered the course of Jewish history.

Marriage in Moab

The flight of Elimelech and his family to Moab in itself is enough to strain the credulity of even the casual reader. The simple text makes abundantly clear that Elimelech's was a most distinguished family. The Sages go even further in extolling Elimelech and in pointing out the enormity of his sin in deserting his people — imagine the blow to them when the great man to whom they look for encouragement, guidance, and material support during the famine defected to an antagonistic neighbor. But the marriage of Machlon and Kilion to Ruth and Orpah hurt even more. How could they intermarry with Moabites? Whatever their lack of loyalty to their people, surely there was no justification for the marriages that kept them anchored in Moab until their deaths!

Whatever their lack of loyalty to their people, surely there was no justification for the marriages that kept them anchored in Moab until their deaths!

The commonly known view is that of Rabbi Meir as expounded in the *Midrash*:

לא גיירום ולא הטבילו אותם

'They neither converted nor ritually immersed them'.

(Ruth Rabba 1:4)

In that view, the marriage is but one more unpleasant indication of how far lapsed people can sink once they cut loose from their moorings. Support is lent to this view by the Talmud (*Yevamos* 47b) which derives the laws of proselytes from the exchange between Naomi and Ruth (See *Commentary* 1:16). It would also explain why Naomi tried so hard to encourage Ruth and Orpah to return home rather than go to *Eretz Yisrael* with her. If her daughters-in-law had converted prior to their marriages, Naomi would

It would also explain why Naomi tried so hard to encourage Ruth and Orpah to return home rather than go to Eretz Yisrael with her.

specifies that only twenty kinds of fowl may not be eaten. All others — the overwhelming majority of all birds on earth — are permitted. With the passing of time, successive exiles, and the increasing disuse of the Scriptural Hebrew names of the forbidden birds, the exact identities of the forbidden fowl were forgotten. Not knowing with any degree of certainty which birds are forbidden, the Jewish people have refrained from eating any fowl save for those which were in constant use down through the centuries. Those are permitted only because uninterrupted traditions guarantee that they are not among the forbidden twenty. Turkey, for example, was once of doubtful status until it was learned that in some areas such a tradition existed; that being established, the permitted status of turkey was accepted by the overwhelming majority of Jews.

Not knowing with any degree of certainty which birds are forbidden, the Jewish people have refrained from eating any fowl save for those which were in constant use down through the centuries.

Boaz's proclamation that any Jew might marry Ruth must be understood in this way. Boaz permitted nothing new; he merely popularized a law that had been forgotten by the majority of the population. That many found it difficult to accept this repudiation of the popular misconception is obvious from the reaction of Tov, the *Ploni Almoni* of *Megillas Ruth* who refused to marry Ruth on the grounds that he would be tainting his posterity by marrying a forbidden Moabitess (*Ruth* 4:6).

Boaz permitted nothing new; he merely popularized a law that had been forgotten by the majority of the population.

An ensuing tragedy lent credance to those who disputed Boaz and his court. Righteous Boaz married Ruth and lived with her for only one night — the next day he was dead. The wags of the generation were convinced they knew why: Boaz had publicly defied the Torah's prohibition by marrying a forbidden daughter of Moab — for that he was struck dead. The truth, of course, was just the opposite. God kept an aging Boaz alive and in good health so that the centuries-old design could come to fruition. The holiness lodged in the seed of Lot, the holiness lodged in the seed of Tamar and the holiness lodged in the seed of Judah joined that night to produce the grandfather of David. But the truth is not always visible.

The holiness lodged in the seed of Lot, the holiness lodged in the seed of Tamar and the holiness lodged in the seed of Judah joined that night to produce the grandfather of David.

have had no right to send them back to idolatry.

On the other hand, if, indeed, the Moabite brides were unconverted during their marriage, several other difficulties arise. Scripture repeatedly refers to Naomi as the mother-in-law of Ruth — had Ruth been a Moabite during her marriage to Machlon, the marriage would not have been legally binding under Jewish law, thus rendering incongruous the references to 'mother-in-law.' But the problems are more than semantic. If Ruth was never legally married to Machlon, then much of the succeeding story of Ruth is incomprehensible. Boaz was a redeemer of Ruth's property — what property? Under Jewish law she had no right to any property of Machlon. Boaz accepted a moral responsibility to enter into a levirate marriage with Ruth — but only the widow of a Jewish marriage falls within the purview of the levirate relationship. A non-Jewish Ruth would no more obligate Boaz than any other widowed Moabite.

If Ruth was never legally married to Machlon, then much of the succeeding story of Ruth is incomprehensible.

Indeed, there is a second view, that of *Zohar Chadash* that Ruth and Orpah *did*, in fact, convert to Judaism prior to their marriages:

> *Rabbi P'dos asked the son of Rav Yosi, a man from Socho: Since Ruth was a proselyte, why did they not call her by another [Jewish] name? He answered him: So have I heard — she did have another name and when she married Machlon, they renamed her Ruth and from then on she used that name. For her conversion came when she married Machlon, and not afterwards.*
>
> *He said to him: But it is written later, 'where you sleep, I will sleep and your God is my God,' etc. (Ruth 1:16). Naomi gave her many warnings [against the rigorous life of a Jew] as we have learned, and Ruth accepted them all. If she had already converted previously, why was all this necessary at that time?*

*He replied to him: God forbid that
Machlon married her while she was still a
gentile. Rather, when she married she converted and she remained under the
presumption of* אִימַת בַּעֲלָה, *fear of her
husband, she and Orpah, in this matter.
When their husbands died, Orpah
returned to her abominable ways, and
Ruth remained in her goodness, as it is
written, 'behold your sister-in-law has
returned to her nation and her god, but
Ruth clung to her' (Ruth 1:14) as she had
earlier. When her husband died [Ruth]
cleaved to her of her own free will (Zohar
Chadash Ruth 180-182).*

According to this view, how could Naomi have allowed, much less urged, the widows to return to
Moabite idolatry?

It may be that the key words in solving this serious
difficulty are אימת בעליהם, *'the fear of their husbands'*. Machlon and Kilion came to Moab as very
wealthy, highly eligible young אֶפְרָתִים, *'Ephrathites'* — distinguished citizens of Judah's leading
city [see *Commentary* 1:2]. So esteemed was the
family of Elimelech that the royal family of Moab
wanted two of its daughters to marry the newly arrived Jewish brothers. In those days, the prospective
bride had little say in such an arrangement, especially
when it was a marriage of state made for considerations transcending personal preferences. If Machlon
and Kilion had insisted that their brides convert to
Judaism as a condition of marriage, the young
women would surely have felt compelled to accede.

This could well have constituted a coerced conversion. In the case of such a conversion, the mere fact
that the marriage took place and that the converted
woman lived as a Jewess would not in and of itself
prove that the conversion was valid. Should she have
become widowed and then — newly freed — declared
her refusal to continue her fiction of Jewishness, her

conversion would have been proven invalid from the start.

When Machlon and Kilion died, Naomi put Ruth and Orpah to the test. Was their original conversion sincere? Had they become committed Jews in the course of their marriages? Or were they accompanying her back to *Eretz Yisrael* merely out of pity? Orpah turned her back with a parting kiss thereby proving that her conversion had never been sincere. Ruth withstood the test — she demonstrated her commitment thus proving that her membership in the Jewish nation was entirely unfeigned.

The problem of conversion was not limited to Machlon and Kilion. A similar, though not identical, question was raised concerning far greater *tzaddikim* than they, Solomon and Samson, who also married non-Jewish wives. Rambam raises the question in *Hilchos Issurei Biah* 13:14-16. He states categorically that it is inconceivable that those two great men married unconverted women. Their wives were converted. Rambam explains that a convert must demonstrate that his conversion is sincerely motivated — that it is not done for money, prestige, or fear, and that it is not done for love of man or woman. If there are no ulterior motives, the rabbinical court teaches the would-be convert the responsibilities of Torah and its commandments. When the court is convinced of his sincerity, he is accepted. As an example of the sincere convert, Rambam cites Ruth.

During the reigns of David and Solomon, *Rambam* continues, converts were not accepted because the lures of conversion were too great to insure that sincerity was present. Despite this ban, many non-Jews did join Israel thanks to conversions performed by uninformed, unsophisticated, makeshift courts. Those converts were ignored by the legitimate courts — not ostracized, and not embraced — until time and experience showed whether or not they were truly sincere.

The wives of Samson and Solomon, *Rambam* concludes, converted for the sake of marriage, without any true motivation for Jewishness. For this reason *Scripture* refers to them as non-Jews; in terms of the standards expected of sincere converts, they were. Their outcomes told the story — they remained idolators proving that their conversions were but a sham.

It may be that it was this knowledge that motivated Naomi's attempts to dissuade her daughters-in-law. Were they truly her daughters-in-law or were they merely the Moabite common-law widows of her sons? She performed her task well. Orpah was never truly a Jew; Ruth was one of the finest daughters — and mothers — Israel ever had.

(It should be unmistakably clear that the above discussion is not meant and must not be taken as the basis for any halachic decision. The laws of conversion, like most areas of Halacha are based on a two thousand year accumulation of Mishnaitic, Talmudic, and post-Talmudic literature. Especially in so sensitive an area as conversion, only highly qualified rabbis are competent to render decisions.)

VI. The Emergence of David*

O ved, son of Ruth and Boaz, and Jesse, son of Oved, were outstandingly righteous men, among the greatest of their age. Inevitably, people began to feel that such people could not have been the progeny of a sinful marriage — surely God would not invest holiness so promiscuously. So Jesse's family was the most respected in Bethlehem.

Surely God would not invest holiness so promiscuously.

God revealed to Samuel that the successor to King Saul would be a son of Jesse the Bethlehemite. The

---

* *A superlative treatment of this topic can be found in Sefer haToda'ah by Eliyahu Ki Tov. Much of his essay is beyond the scope of this paper, but is highly recommended reading.*

prophet was commanded to go to Bethlehem where God would show him the future king (*I Samuel* 16). Samuel asked Jesse to come with his sons to a feast. As we can well imagine, the great prophet's invitation was a rare privilege. Jesse came with seven of his sons; David was left behind. David — red of complexion, short of stature, tender of sheep, desert hermit — could not possibly become God's anointed. There wasn't a soul in Bethlehem, not even his father or brothers, who thought that. No one knew that he was not alone in the fields, that he was attuning his soul to his Maker; that his very being was a harp in the hands of holiness, reverberating with the sweet songs that would become part of one of Israel's most precious legacies — *The Book of Tehillim*. No one knew that the love he would later lavish on his people was being nurtured in his care of helpless sheep. No one knew that the fearless warrior of the future was single-handedly slaying lions and bears, learning that only God is to be feared.

No one knew that the love David would later lavish on his people was being nurtured in his care of helpless sheep.

The moment of anointment came and Samuel asked that Jesse's sons come before him one by one. They were outstanding products of an outstanding family. The great prophet was impressed with Eliav, Jesse's first-born; he was sure that he was in the presence of God's chosen anointed — only to be told by God:

> *Look not on his countenance nor on the height of his stature, because I have refused him: for it is not as a man sees, for a man looks on the outward appearance, but G-d looks on the heart.*

So it was. One by one, each was rejected. Finally, Samuel asked Jesse if he had any more sons and Jesse answered strangely, "*There remains yet the youngest and he is tending the sheep.*" Samuel ordered that he be brought. He was — and he was anointed David, King of Israel.

"There remains yet the youngest and he is tending the sheep."

As soon as he arrived, Samuel knew that they were in the presence of God's chosen. Samuel knew that this was to be no temporary, transitory king like

As soon as he arrived, Samuel knew that they were in the presence of God's chosen.

Saul. When Samuel picked up the horn of the holy oil, it began to bubble as though it could not wait to drop on the forehead of David. When Samuel anointed him, the oil hardened and glistened like pearls and precious stones, and the horn remained full (*Yalkut haMakiri Tehillim* 118).

But the taint on David's origin was a stubborn one:

וְכִרְאוֹת שָׁאוּל אֶת דָּוִד יוֹצֵא לִקְרַאת הַפְּלִשְׁתִּי
אָמַר אֶל אַבְנֵר שַׂר הַצָּבָא בֶּן מִי זֶה הַנַּעַר אַבְנֵר

— *And when Saul saw David go out against the Philistine [Goliath] he said to Avner the captain of the host, Avner, whose son is this youth?* (I Samuel 17:55).

Didn't Saul know who David was? The Talmud asks (*Yevamos* 76b), Scripture says (*I Samuel* 16:21) that Saul loved David very much and appointed him his personal armor-bearer — obviously Saul knew him well!

Saul became apprehensive and began to fear that David was more than a talented singer and devoted shepherd.

Saul became apprehensive and began to fear that David was more than a talented singer and devoted shepherd. When David volunteered to defend the honor of Israel by facing Goliath in combat, Saul offered the young man his own armor. David put it on and it fit — but Saul was head and shoulders above even the tallest of Israel and David was shorter than average! That the royal armor fit could well be a Divine indication that David was to be Saul's successor as king. He asked Avner which branch of Judah David was from. If he was from Zerach, then he would be illustrious, but no threat to Saul. But if he was from Peretz, then he was royalty, for it was from Peretz that the kings of Judah would descend.

Then, Doeg the Edomi stepped forward. Doeg was one of the greatest scholars of the age, head of the Sanhedrin, and a close friend and adviser to the king. Doeg said,

> *"Instead of asking whether or not he is worthy of kingship, ask whether or not he is fit to enter the congregation of God! He is descended from Ruth the Moabitess."*

Avner defended David's legitimacy with the dictum expounded by the court of Boaz and reaffirmed by the court of Samuel.

Avner defended David's legitimacy with the dictum expounded by the court of Boaz and reaffirmed by the court of Samuel: A Moabite, but not a Moabitess, is forbidden to enter the congregation of God. Doeg fought back and, halachic great that he was, no one was able to refute his arguments against the fitness of David. Then Amassa, son of Yisra, arose and declared,

> *"Whoever refuses to acknowledge this law will be stabbed with my sword. This I have learned from the court of Samuel of Ramah — a Moabite, but not a Moabitess!"*

These were the passions awakened by David. The greatest men of his generation questioned and agonized over his status. Finally it was only through a violent insistence upon the unshakable Jewish belief in its tradition as transmitted by the Torah greats that the royal house of David — embodiment of God's kingdom on earth — could come into being.

Finally it was only through a violent insistence upon the unshakable Jewish belief in its tradition as transmitted by the Torah greats that the royal house of David — embodiment of God's kingdom on earth — could come into being.

Doeg did not rest. Throughout the reign of Saul he was David's nemesis, inflaming Saul against the young Judean shepherd whose love for, and loyalty to the king were unmatched. He urged Saul to kill David as a rebel (see above Powers of the King) and he succeeded in having eighty-five priests of the city of Nob executed for having harbored David (*I Samuel* 22)

David endured patiently all the barbs slung at him throughout his lifetime. Yet even this patient, long-suffering model of righteousness lashed out at Doeg in a passionate, poignant appeal to conscience and decency:

> *'You, a powerful and wealthy man, head of the Sanhedrin — stoop to such a low level of evil and slander! Is it a show of strength to see someone teetering at the edge of an abyss and push him over? Or to see someone at the edge of a roof and throw him down? The true hero is the one who sees his fellow at the brink and pulls him back to safety! You saw how Saul*

The true hero is the one who sees his fellow at the brink and pulls him back to safety!

became angry with me and you attacked me further — is this how one serves his God? Do you think that if Achimelech [High Priest of Nob] had not yet welcomed me and given me a crust of bread that no one in all Israel would have given me food? A man who is occupied with God's goodness, the study of Torah, has no right to act this way. Why did you do this?' (Midrash Shocher Tov).

The Talmudic sages [*Sanhedrin 106b*] hold Doeg up to rebuke as a person who made a mockery of his learning. 'His learning was from the lips outward' — it had no inner meaning. God asked him, "Wicked one, why do you study My statutes — what will you say when you come to the sections of the Torah that forbid murder and slander?"

Brilliant man though he was, Doeg was condemned to prove by his own downfall that his tirades against David were baseless. He forgot his learning before his death and lost the respect of even his own students. Scintillating Doeg, who held sway over the great minds in Israel, died in disgrace as a ridiculed caricature of a Torah scholar. Of him the Talmud says: אַנְשֵׁי דָמִים וּמִרְמָה לֹא יֶחֱצוּ יְמֵיהֶם, *bloody and deceitful men shall not live out their days (Psalms 55:24)* —Doeg died when he was only thirty-three.

Not until then could David hold up his head without fear that the canard 'Moabite' would be slung at him.

But his days of adversity were not numbered; they lasted throughout his life. War, betrayal, personal tragedy, rebellion, abuse — all of these were his constant lot, but he responded with a life that became אֲנִי תְפִלָּה, *I am prayer*; David became the very embodiment of prayer, his entire being became a song of praise. In the end, David's greatness was acknowledged. He was worthy of his people, but his people were unworthy of him.

David asked God: 'Why can I not build the Holy Temple?'

God answered: *'Because if you build it, it will endure and never be destroyed'* (Yalkut Shimoni, II Samuel 145).

David was so great, so consistent, that any act of his had to endure forever. The Jewish people were not yet worthy of a Temple built by David. It would be too great, too permanent — because it would be his, and his people would not rise to such a level until the coming of *Mashiach (see Michtav me-Eliyahu II,* p. 275).

The Jewish people were not yet worthy of a Temple built by David. It would be too great, too permanent.

When he died, he left us with two treasures:

His *Tehillim,* the songs of praise and prayer that have sustained countless Jewish sparks amid constant storms and holocausts;

And his sacred seed, nurtured through millenia — just as the seed of Moab, Judah, Tamar, Boaz, and Ruth were nurtured — waiting for the time when it would explode into the flame of the seven days of creation; waiting for the day when a poor man will come riding on a donkey; possessing all talents and blessing, but ascribing nothing to himself and everything to God; leading all the world under the protective wings of Divine Presence when HASHEM will be King over the entire universe, on that day when HASHEM will be one and His Name will be one.

Waiting for the day when a poor man will come riding on a donkey; possessing all talents and blessing, but ascribing nothing to himself and everything to God.

Rabbi Nosson Scherman

מגילת רות

א וַיְהִי בִּימֵי שְׁפֹט הַשֹּׁפְטִים וַיְהִי רָעָב
בָּאָרֶץ וַיֵּלֶךְ אִישׁ מִבֵּית לֶחֶם יְהוּדָה לָגוּר
ב בִּשְׂדֵי מוֹאָב הוּא וְאִשְׁתּוֹ וּשְׁנֵי בָנָיו: וְשֵׁם
הָאִישׁ אֱלִימֶלֶךְ וְשֵׁם אִשְׁתּוֹ נָעֳמִי וְשֵׁם
שְׁנֵי־בָנָיו | מַחְלוֹן וְכִלְיוֹן אֶפְרָתִים מִבֵּית

1. וַיְהִי — *And it happened.* 'Where-ever in the Bible we find the term וַיְהִי בִּימֵי, *And it happened in the days*, it indicates the approach of trouble. Thus, *And it came to pass in the days of Ahasuerus* — there was Haman. *And it came to pass when the Judges judged* — there was a famine' *(Megillah 10b).*

שְׁפֹט הַשֹּׁפְטִים — *When the Judges judged.* [Lit. 'in the days of the judgment of the Judges']. . .

The story of Ruth occurred before the reign of King Saul, when the Jews were governed by Judges. The Judge at the time was Ivtzan [*Jud. 12:8*] — whom the Sages identify as Boaz of *Megillas Ruth* [*Bava Basra 91a*] (Rashi).

According to *Seder Hadoros* and *Tzemach David*, the episode happened approximately in the year 2787 (973 B.C.E.)

The *Iggeres Shmuel* quotes *Rav Yosef ibn Yichiah* that Ivtzan was not *specifically* named in our verse in deference to his righteousness, for Scripture did not wish to implicate him in Elimelech's sin.

According to the *Malbim*, these events transpired during the days of the Judges, a period of which it was written [Judges 21:25]: בַּיָּמִים הָהֵם אֵין מֶלֶךְ בְּיִשְׂרָאֵל אִישׁ הַיָּשָׁר בְּעֵינָיו יַעֲשֶׂה, *In those days there was no king in Israel; every man did that which was right in his own eyes.* No *specific* Judge ruled at the time; it was during an interval *between* Judges, when no one individual exercised control over the Jews — that Elimelech came to leave the country — a time when power was seized by lesser men, unable to earn position through their personal merit, and everyone acted independently.

Some understand 'שְׁפֹט הַשֹּׁפְטִים' as the period when 'God judged the Judges' — for they were the cause of the famine *(Ibn Ezra; Vilna Gaon)*..

'It was a generation which judged its Judges. If the judge said to a man: 'Take the splinter from between your teeth,' he would retort: 'Take the beam from between your eyes.' *(Bava Basra 15b).*

'Woe unto the generation whose Judges are judged,' bewails the *Midrash*, 'and woe to the generation whose Judges deserve to be judged.'

All the above interpretations are suggested by the use of the phrase בִּימֵי שְׁפֹט הַשֹּׁפְטִים, [lit. 'the days of the judgment of the Judges], instead of the more direct בִּימֵי הַשֹּׁפְטִים 'days of the Judges' (Torah T'mimah).

A different approach is taken by *Iggeres Shmuel*: The *Midrash* states that a famine comes only upon a strong and righteous people that can withstand the test. Therefore,

[Please note: *The source for every excerpt has been documented. Whenever the author has inserted a comment of his own it is inserted in square brackets.*]

A nd it happened in the days when the Judges judged, that there was a famine in the land, and a man went from Bethlehem in Judah to sojourn in the fields of Moab, he, his wife, and his two sons. ² The man's name was Elimelech, his wife's name was Naomi, and his two sons were named Machlon and

we can say that the generation was not lawless. On the contrary, it was a time when שָׁפט הַשֹּׁפְטִים — *the Judges judged* — and the people listened. It was to *this* generation that God, knowing they would withstand the test and not flee or be contumacious against the Desirable Land [i.e., Eretz Yisrael], brought a famine upon them. And it was so. No one left Eretz Yisrael — except for the single family mentioned by Scripture.

וַיְהִי רָעָב בָּאָרֶץ — *That there was a famine in the land.* ['The' land, *par excellence*; i.e., Eretz Yisrael].

[The judges in those days, say the commentaries, were devoid of Torah knowledge, and it was due to their laxity in rebuking the multitide who strayed from the Torah path that God punished the Jews with a famine.]

The word וַיְהִי is repeated twice in this verse to imply that there were two famines in the days of the Judges: a famine for bread and a famine for Torah. This teaches us that in any generation where there is a lack of Torah, famine must ensue (*Yalkut Shimoni; Mid Zuta*).

'At that moment the Holy One, blessed be He, said: 'My children are rebellious; yet to destroy them is impossible, to take them back to Egypt is impossible, exchange them for another people I cannot; what then shall I do to them? I will

punish them and purify them with famine' (*Midrash*).

וַיֵּלֶךְ אִישׁ — *A man went.* [The appelation אִישׁ, 'man,' throughout the Bible signifies prominence.] The *Targum* here translates 'גַּבְרָא רַבָּא *a great man.*

Elimelech was very wealthy and the פַּרְנָס הַדּוֹר, provider of that generation, who left Eretz Yisrael because he was selfish and was afraid that all the impoverished people would come and knock at his door for help. For this he was punished (*Rashi*).

'He was punished because he struck despair into the hearts of Israel. When the famine came, he arose and fled' (*Midrash*).

Elimelech may have rationalized his departure by claiming that he could not bear to witness the corruption of the judges while powerless to correct the situation, or that he was not required to dispense more than a fifth of his resources to charity — hardly enough to feed all of the hungry (*Kol Yehuda*).

Ima Shel Malchus notes that in those days, the Jews had settled in Eretz Yisrael according to their tribal divisions, their families' and fathers' houses. An added insight into Elimelech's misdeed can be gained if we remember that all the inhabitants of Bethlehem were related to each other in some manner, and that now, in the days of trouble,

Elimelech's family had deserted its relatives and fled.'

[The *Midrash* notes that nothing is said about the wealth he took with him — surely he did not go empty-handed!] . . .

And a certain man went — like a 'dead stump' [to which nothing is attached]! See how the Holy One, blessed be He, favors the'entry *into* Eretz Yisrael over the departure *from* it! When the Jews returned from Babylon it is written: *Their horses ... their mules ... their camels,* etc. [*Ezra 2:66*]. But here the verse simply tells us: *and a certain man went* — like a mere stump. He left the country, and Scripture makes no mention of his property — as though he left empty-handed (*Midrash*).

The word וַיֵּלֶךְ, *went* [lit. *walked*], not וַיִּסַּע, *travelled*, is used. This indicates that he originally planned only a temporary stay (*Kol Yehuda*).

The phrase וַיֵּלֶךְ אִישׁ, *and a certain man went*, appears twice in Scripture: here, and in Exodus 2:1 [referring to Moses' father]. Esoterically speaking, just as there — וַיֵּלֶךְ אִישׁ מִבֵּית לֵוִי '*and a man of the house of Levi went*' resulted in the first Redeemer, Moses — so here, too, did וַיֵּלֶךְ אִישׁ מִבֵּית לֶחֶם יְהוּדָה '*a certain man from Bethlehem in Judah went*' resulted in the final Redeemer — the house of David (*Alshich; Baal haTurim*).

מִבֵּית לֶחֶם יְהוּדָה — *From Bethlehem in Judah.* [The verse could also be translated '*A man from Bethlehem in Judah went...*' i.e., that a man, who was a resident of Bethlehem, went, (the phrase being adjectival)]

[Bethlehem was one of the finest and most fruitful areas of Eretz Yisrael.]

[Perhaps יְהוּדָה, *in Judah*, is mentioned to distinguish it from the other Bethlehem in Zevulun (*Joshua 19:15*)].

Why is the phrase '*from Bethlehem in Judah to dwell in the fields of Moab*' inserted here [between '*a certain man*' and '*he, his wife, and his two sons*']? Grammatically, the verse should read: '*A certain man, along with his wife and two sons, went from Bethlehem in Judah to sojourn in the fields of Moab.*'...

This verse, structured as it is, seems to imply that leaving Eretz Yisrael at that time was his decision alone. וַיֵּלֶךְ אִישׁ, *A certain man went* — the decision to *leave* בֵּית לֶחֶם יְהוּדָה was his alone — and he compelled his wife and two sons to follow. Having unilaterally made the decision to leave, Elimelech asked his family where they wished to go. The ultimate choice — לָגוּר בִּשְׂדֵי מוֹאָב, *to sojourn in the fields of Moab* — was made with the unanimous consent of אִשְׁתּוֹ וּשְׁנֵי בָנָיו, *his wife and two sons* (*Iggeres Shmuel*).

לָגוּר בִּשְׂדֵי מוֹאָב — *To sojourn in the fields of Moab.* 'Fields' are in plural because it was Elimelech's original intention to sojourn and wander about the many fields and cities — not to establish himself permanently in any one place in Moab (*Alshich*).

Elimelech's sin was compounded by his choice of a new homeland. Had he gone elsewhere, his sin would not have been so severe. Our verse specifically elaborates on his shameful act by telling us his destination: the detestable Moab of whom God cautioned us: לֹא יָבֹא '*An Ammonite or Moabite shall not enter into the assembly of HASHEM ... forever*' [*Deut. 23:4*], and also: לֹא תִדְרֹשׁ שְׁלֹמָם וְטֹבָתָם כָּל יָמֶיךָ לְעוֹלָם, '*Thou shalt not seek their* peace nor their prosperity all thy days forever' [Deut. 23:7]. And yet, Elimelech went to live among them, where he would greet them every morning with 'Shalom' or would at the very least respond to them, 'Shalom'! (Iggeres Shmuel).

Elimelech perhaps rationalized that it was better for him to dwell in open fields among Moabites, than to remain in Eretz Yisrael under the circumstances of lawlessness prevalent during the famine (Pri Chaim).

הוּא וְאִשְׁתּוֹ וּשְׁנֵי בָנָיו — He, his wife, and his two sons. 'He was the prime mover, his wife secondary to him, and his two sons secondary to both of them' (Midrash).

Elimelech's additional sin was that he took only his nearest kin — his wife and two sons along with him, not being concerned about anyone else (Iggeres Shmuel).

2. וְשֵׁם הָאִישׁ אֱלִימֶלֶךְ — The man's name was Elimelech. The Midrash explains that his name signified his arrogant attitude; he would boast: אֵלַי תָּבוֹא מַלְכוּת — 'to me shall kingship come. . .'

Being a member of the tribe of Judah and a descendant of Nachshon ben Aminadav, its prince, he reasoned that royalty would descend from him (Torah T'mimah).

Elimelech considered himself to be a prominent individual, always boasting 'to me shall kingship come.' Therefore, he should have considered the consequences of his desertion of the Land — and so, he deserved to be punished (Kol Yehuda).

[The holiness of Eretz Yisrael is such that a sin on its holy earth is more serious and more significant than a sin elsewhere. For this reason

the punishment for sins committed in Eretz Yisrael is quicker in coming and more stringent. (See Lev. 18:25-28; and Ramban there.) In attempting to flee from divine judgment, Elimelech wanted to leave the Holy Land in the belief that if he were in a foreign, non-sacred land, his sins would be of lesser magnitude and less deserving of punishment.]

Elimelech wanted to flee from the Divine Decree — but was unsuccessful in escaping from it. This is implied in the words וַיֵּלֶךְ אִישׁ, a certain man went, i.e., anonymously, incognito. But מִדַּת הַדִּין — God's Attribute of Judgment recognized and identified him, as the verse continues: וְשֵׁם הָאִישׁ אֱלִימֶלֶךְ, the man's name was Elimelech, i.e., the prominent and famous Elimelech, leader of that generation, one who could have protested the injustices of the time but did not. Judgment was then visited upon him and his sons, and they died (Zohar Chadash).

וְשֵׁם אִשְׁתּוֹ נָעֳמִי — his wife's name was Naomi. 'For her actions were pleasant and sweet' [the translation of Naomi being 'pleasant'] (Midrash).

Not only was Elimelech well known, even his wife and two sons were אַנְשֵׁי שֵׁם — famous personages (Malbim).

שְׁנֵי בָנָיו — His two sons. 'Two' is mentioned because they were both equally great (Rashba haLevi).

מַחְלוֹן וְכִלְיוֹן — Machlon and Kilion. The Midrash says that their names indicate שֶׁנִּמְחוּ וְכָלוּ מִן הָעוֹלָם — 'they were blotted out and perished from the world.'

The Talmud enumerates them, along with Elimelech, as the leaders of that generation. They were all punished because they left Eretz Yisrael (Bava Basra 91a).

לֶחֶם יְהוּדָה וַיָּבֹאוּ שְׂדֵי־מוֹאָב וַיִּהְיוּ־שָׁם: **פרק א**

ג וַיָּמָת אֱלִימֶלֶךְ אִישׁ נָעֳמִי וַתִּשָּׁאֵר הִיא **ג-ה**

ד וּשְׁנֵי בָנֶיהָ: וַיִּשְׂאוּ לָהֶם נָשִׁים מֹאֲבִיּוֹת

שֵׁם הָאַחַת עָרְפָּה וְשֵׁם הַשֵּׁנִית רוּת

ה וַיֵּשְׁבוּ שָׁם כְּעֶשֶׂר שָׁנִים: וַיָּמֻתוּ גַם־

According to *Zohar Chadash*, he was called Machlon שֶׁמָּחַל לוֹ הקב״ה לְאַחַר זְמַן, — 'because the Holy One, blessed be He ultimately forgave him [posthumously, by allowing יִבּוּם, a levirate marriage, to take place with his widow Ruth] שֶׁהָיָה מוֹחֶה, because he protested the injustices of his father. Kilion was so named שֶׁנִּכְלָה מִן הָעוֹלָם, for he was utterly blotted out from the world.'

אֶפְרָתִים — *Ephrathites*. [This word, sometimes translated *'Ephraimite'* and sometimes *'Ephrathite,'* is variously interpreted by the Sages]—

The *Midrash* considers the word to be a title of honor, interpreting it to mean 'courtiers,' 'aristocrats.' It may be derived from the word אַפִּרְיוֹן — a 'crown' i.e., one who possesses the 'crown' bequeathed by יַעֲקֹב אָבִינוּ, our Patriarch Jacob, at the time of his departure from the world. . .'

The word usually indicates a descendant of Ephraim, or a native of Ephrath, i.e., Bethlehem [see *Gen. 35:19, 48:7.*] The *Midrash* offers different interpretations because the word אֶפְרָתִים, *Ephrathites*, in our verse could not refer to the tribe of Ephraim since Elimelech and his sons were of the tribe of Judah. Also, the Sages did not define it as *Ephrathite* 'a native of Ephrath' because if Bethlehem is referred to as Ephrath by the author

of *Megillas Ruth*, then he should have used that name in verse 1 as well. Obviously, therefore, *'Ephrathite'* must be taken as a description of the family rather than as a reference to their city (*Torah T'mimah; Gishmei Bracha*).

The *Targum*, translating אֶפְרָתִים, adds the word רַבָּנִין 'masters.'

According to *Rashi*: אֶפְרָתִים means *distinguished persons* ... See how important they were! Eglon, the King of Moab married his daughter [Ruth] to Machlon, as the Master has expounded: Ruth was the daughter of Eglon.'

Bethlehem was originally called 'Ephrath,' and later given the name Bethlehem. Also, there was a very distinguished family in the tribe of Judah called אֶפְרָתִים, *Ephrathites*, because they descended from Ephrath [another name for Miriam, sister of Moses — (*Sotah 11a*)], the wife of Caleb [*I Chronicles 2:19*], a most distinguished lady (*Malbim*).

Pirkei d'Rabbi Eliezer notes that throughout the Bible 'every great man who arose in Israel had the title Ephrathite attached to his name.'

אֶפְרָתִים מִבֵּית לֶחֶם יְהוּדָה — *Ephrathites, from Bethlehem in Judah.* Bethlehem is repeated in this verse as if to say that the sons, as *Ephrathites*, distinguished persons, were also held responsible for the sin of Elimelech's departure from Bethlehem; they should have protested!

Kilion, Ephrathites of Bethlehem in Judah. They came to the field of Moab and there they remained.

³ Elimelech, Naomi's husband, died; and she was left with her two sons. ⁴ They married Moabite women, one named Orpah, and the other Ruth, and they lived there about ten years. ⁵ The two of them,

...They were the most prominent citizens of the most prominent city in Eretz Yisrael (*Pri Chaim; Malbim*).

וַיִּהְיוּ שָׁם — *And there they remained.* [Lit. 'and they were there.']

Although it was their original intention only to *sojourn temporarily* in the fields of Moab, nevertheless, once they arrived they decided to settle permanently (*Malbim*).

They felt themselves drawn to the Moabites whom they resembled. They were mean and ungenerous like the Moabites who *'did not meet Israel with bread and water on the way when they left Egypt'* [compare *Deut. 23:5*] (*Meishiv Nefesh* quoting *Ruth Zuta*).

The word וַיִּהְיוּ, 'they were,' rather than וַיֵּשְׁבוּ, 'they settled,' is used to imply that they achieved a new status [וַהֲוָיָה'] there — they felt no remorse that they had departed from Eretz Yisrael ... and for this reason they died (*Rav Yosef Yavetz*).

The *Targum* translates וַיִּהְיוּ שָׁם as follows: וַהֲווֹ תַּמָּן רוֹפִילִין 'they became officers there' [which, in the context of the traditional enmity between the Jews and Moab must be understood not as praise, but as condemnation, i.e., they stooped so low that they integrated themselves socially and militarily into the culture of Moab].

3. וַיָּמָת אֱלִימֶלֶךְ — *And Elimelech died.* An untimely death (*Midrash*). This punishment was inflicted upon the family 'because they should have begged for mercy for their generation and they did not do so' (*Bava Basra 91b*). Even though one could perhaps rationalize that their departure from the Holy Land was necessary under the conditions of famine and need, they were still not guiltless. It was they who were responsible for the hunger because they did not pray for their generation (*Nachlas Yosef*).

The *Talmud*, giving Elimelech's ancestry, states: 'Elimelech, Salmah, Ploni Almoni, and the father of Naomi were all descendants of Nachshon son of Aminadav [prince of the tribe of Judah]. This teaches us that even זְכוּת־אָבוֹת, the merit of ancestors, is of no avail when one leaves Eretz Yisrael for a foreign country (*Bava Basra 91a*).

אִישׁ נָעֳמִי — *Naomi's husband.* Naomi is mentioned here in conjunction with Elimelech's death, notes the *Talmud*, 'because the death of a man is felt by no one as keenly and as deeply as by his wife' (*Sanhedrin 22b*).

Elimelech, not Naomi, was punished, because, as the verse tells us, he was אִישׁ נָעֳמִי, *Naomi's husband*, and she was subject to his authority. Therefore, the onus of the sin was thrust upon him (*Rashi, Malbim*).

[This great man, this פַּרְנָס הַדּוֹר, (magnate of the generation), is described at his death merely as אִישׁ נָעֳמִי, 'Naomi's husband.' Only she grieved at his loss — to his people he had already died long before.]

וַתִּשָּׁאֵר הִיא וּשְׁנֵי בָנֶיהָ — And she was left with her two sons. 'She became like the שִׁיּוּרֵי מְנָחוֹת, remnants of the meal offerings' [i.e., of little importance, now that her husband was dead] (Midrash).

As translated with the additions of the Targum: 'And she was left' — a widow; 'and her two sons' — orphans.

Had Elimelech's sons sinned only in leaving the Holy Land, the punishment of being orphaned would have been retribution enough. But they sinned further by marrying Moabite women [see next verse] (Pri Chaim).

[Some commentators, however, understand וַתִּשָּׁאֵר in the sense of 'she remained' in a despised foreign land]: When her husband died, she should have seen it as a divine warning to return to Eretz Yisrael. Instead 'she remained there with her two sons' (Malbim), — as a result, her sons stayed on to marry Moabite women, and paid with their own lives (Iggeres Shmuel).

4. וַיִּשְׂאוּ לָהֶם נָשִׁים מֹאֲבִיּוֹת — They married Moabite women, [lit. 'and they married to themselves Moabite women'].

'Shouldn't the sons have learned a lesson from their father's death and returned to Eretz Yisrael? What did they do? They married Moabite women without even having their wives undergo ritual purification and conversion' (Tanchuma, B'har).

עֲבֵירָה גוֹרֶרֶת עֲבֵירָה — 'One transgression leads to another' (Simchas haRegel).

It should be noted that only after their father's death did the sons marry women who were not of their people, an indication that Elimelech, for all his faults, would not have allowed them to stoop so low (Alshich).

The common expression וַיִּשְׂאוּ, 'married' is used rather than the legal term וַיִּקְחוּ, 'took,' — because the women were not ritually converted and were thus not legally married under Torah law (Iggeres Shmuel; Malbim).

The Torah's prohibition of marriage to a Moabite (even after ritual conversion) had within it the implication later expounded by the Sages that the ban extends only to a "Moabite but not to a Moabitess" [see Deut. 23:4]. Thus, their sin could be considered as of lesser magnitude. But Machlon and Kilion did not know that; in their own minds they were transgressing the law against Moabite marriage. Therefore their punishment was greater. (Kol Yehudah).

The word לָהֶם, 'to themselves' implies that they married these women not לְשֵׁם שָׁמַיִם, for the 'sake of heaven', but to satisfy their own selfish, sensual desires . . . and having married non-converted, Moabite women, whatever offspring would have resulted from these unions would have been considered non-Jewish (Iggeres Shmuel).

[There is an opinion (Zohar Chadash and Ibn Ezra), that Machlon and Kilion did subject their prospective brides to conversion and immersion, but the 'fear of their husbands was upon them.' (See Introduction for a detailed explanation of this view, and its ramifications.]

שֵׁם הָאַחַת עָרְפָּה — One named Or-

pah. She was named Orpah because she ultimately turned her back [עֹרֶף — *the nape of her neck*] on her mother-in-law *(Midrash)*.

וְשֵׁם הַשֵּׁנִית רוּת — *And the other Ruth*. [lit. 'and the name of the second, Ruth.] She was named Ruth because she 'saw' [רָאֲתָה — i.e. considered well] the words of her mother-in-law *(Midrash)*.

According to the *Talmud:* 'Rav Yochanan said: Why was she called Ruth? — Because there issued from her David who 'saturated' (רִוָּה) the Holy One, blessed be He with hymns and prayers *(Bava Basra 14b)*.

[The Torah contains 606 Commandments (in addition to the 7 Noachide Laws which are incumbent even upon non-Jews). The commentators note that this number, 606, is equal to the numerical value of the name רוּת, *Ruth*, the convert *par excellence*. This was the number of additional *mitzvos* she accepted upon her conversion.]

Esoterically speaking, the name Ruth [רוּת] is spelled with the letters of 'turtle-dove' [תּוֹר]. 'Just as the turtle-dove is fit for sacrifice on the altar, so was Ruth fit for inclusion in the Assembly of God' *(Zohar Chadash)*.

[The Sages tell us that Machlon and Kilion, wealthy and distinguished, rose to such prominence while living in Moab that Eglon, King of Moab, offered them his daughters' hands in marriage] —

'Ruth and Orpah were the daughters of Eglon, as it is written [Judges 3:19; (when Ehud came to Eglon to deliver God's message)] *". . . and Ehud said: I have a message from God to you. And [Eglon] arose from his throne."* The Holy One, blessed be He, said of him:

"You stood up from your throne in My honor, I will cause to emerge from you a descendent who will sit upon My throne" '*(Midrash)*.

וַיֵּשְׁבוּ שָׁם כְּעֶשֶׂר שָׁנִים — *And they lived there about ten years*. [lit. they 'sat' (dwelt) there about ten years.]

This confirms the view that they had given up all thoughts of returning to Eretz Yisrael *(Malbim)*.

In verse 2 the verb וַיִּהְיוּ, *'and they were there'* is used; here, וַיֵּשְׁבוּ, *'and they lived there'* is used. Elimelech should have known better than to leave Eretz Yisrael. As soon as he 'was' there he was punished. But the sons were helpless in the matter and could not overrule their father. They were not punished until וַיֵּשְׁבוּ שָׁם, *they dwelt there*, and tarried for so long *(Iggeres Shmuel)*.

God waited all these years to give them the opportunity to repent. *(Midrash Zuta)*.

Having married princesses, they couldn't abandon them, nor could they return with them to Eretz Yisrael — they feared the Sages would have forced them to separate themselves from their Moabite wives, who, at the time, were still thought to be forbidden because the Sages had not yet ruled that a Moabitess was permitted. Therefore — divorce and return to Eretz Yisroel being impossible — God punished them with death. *(Simchas haRegel)*.

כְּעֶשֶׂר שָׁנִים — *About ten years*. [lit. like ten years]. The *Bach* explains why 'like' ten years is used. The *Midrash* (on verse 1) states that before the famine, the Jews in Eretz Yisrael had looked upon Elimelech as one who could provide their sustenance for ten years. They placed all their trust in him — rather than in God. When the famine

שְׁנֵיהֶם מַחְלוֹן וְכִלְיוֹן וַתִּשָּׁאֵר הָאִשָּׁה
מִשְּׁנֵי יְלָדֶיהָ וּמֵאִישָׁהּ: וַתָּקׇם הִיא
וְכַלֹּתֶיהָ וַתָּשׇׁב מִשְּׂדֵי מוֹאָב כִּי שָׁמְעָה

broke out, the miserly Elimelech left, and God caused his family to live away for a period *'like the ten years,'* a length of time equal to the ten years which the Jews had misplaced their trust in flesh and blood — until when these ten years were up, and the famine ended *(Meishiv Nefesh).*

5. וַיָּמֻתוּ גַם־שְׁנֵיהֶם *The two of them . . . also died.*

[God first punishes man, via warnings, depriving him of his property, and only after that, if man does not repent, does God smite him in his person.]

'The Merciful One never begins His retribution by taking a human life . . . And so it was with Machlon and Kilion also. First their horses, their asses, and their camels died, then Elimelech, and lastly the two sons' *(Midrash).*

After being stripped of their money and cattle the two of them גַם, *'also'* died *(Rashi).*

The word גַם, *also,* indicates that just as the death of their father was punishment for having remained outside of Eretz Yisrael, so was their death in punishment for that sin. *(Iggeres Shmuel).*

[Just as the death of Elimelech — in verse 3 — follows as punishment for וַיִּהְיוּ שָׁם — *'and they remained there',* so does the death of the sons follow as punishment for וַיֵּשְׁבוּ שָׁם — *'and they lived there']*

'Although [under certain conditions of great distress] one is permitted to emigrate, if one does, the act is not in conformity with the law

of righteousness. Remember Machlon and Kilion! They were the two great men of their generation and they left Eretz Yisrael at a time of great distress; nevertheless they incurred thereby the penalty of extinction' *(Rambam).*

שְׁנֵיהֶם — *Both of them.* Because they were equally guilty *(Pri Chaim).*

מַחְלוֹן וְכִלְיוֹן — *Machlon and Kilion.* Note that they are no longer referred to as *'Ephrathites,'* as above in verse 2 [see Comm. there], nor are they identified as the husbands of Ruth and Orpah. They are stripped of their prestige: they are simply *Machlon and Kilion. (Alschich).*

The verse repeats their names to emphasize that not only did they die physically, but because they were childless, their very names — *Machlon and Kilion* — died with them *(Iggeres Shmuel)..*

וַתִּשָּׁאֵר הָאִשָּׁה מִשְּׁנֵי יְלָדֶיהָ וּמֵאִישָׁהּ — *And the woman was bereft of her two children and of her husband,* i.e., she was left alone without her children or her husband. Her children are mentioned first because when one recounts past events one usually mentions the most recent first; or because of the greater anguish associated with the death of her children who died young, whereas her husband died at an old age *(Ibn Ezra).*

The *Midrash* notes that before punishing their persons, God first struck at their property, completely devastating and impoverishing them. Nevertheless, this verse tells

Machlon and Kilion, also died; and the woman was bereft of her two children and of her husband.

6 She then arose along with her daughters-in-law to return from the fields of Moab, for she had heard

us, Naomi did not anguish over the loss of her property, but over the loss of her children and husband *(Iggeres Shmuel)*.

[After her husband's death Naomi was yet of some importance, but with her sons' death, that remaining prestige, too, left her] . . .

'Rav Chaninah said: She was left as the remnants of the remnants [of the meal offering; i.e., of no value whatsoever. See Comm. to verse 3 s.v. וַתִּשָּׁאֵר *'And she was left'*] *(Midrash)*.

[Unlike verse 3 where they are called בָּנֶיהָ, her 'sons,' here Machlon and Kilion are called יְלָדֶיהָ, her 'children,' i.e., they died like young children without their own offspring].

An excellent insight is offered in *Ima Shel Malchus*:

Naomi had many times asked herself by what merit she had survived. Had she not sinned as much as they? ...Perhaps her sin was a greater one, and therefore her punishment, too was greater ... It was she — of the whole family — who was left, desolate, to bear the burden of sorrow of the entire family. ...

Naomi could not possibly have known, much less have dared to believe at the time, that she had been preserved through the kindness and compassion of HASHEM, who had allowed the spark of life of Elimelech's family to remain glowing in her ... leading to the birth of King David.

6. וַתָּקָם הִיא וְכַלֹּתֶיהָ — *She then arose along with her daughters-in-law*. The next verse tells us, in a seemingly redundant manner, וַתֵּצֵא מִן הַמָּקוֹם, *she left the place*. In this verse, therefore, וַתָּקָם, *she arose*, means: *she 'resolved' to leave (Iggeres Shmuel; Ibn Ezra; Vilna Gaon)*.

The resolve to *leave this ill-fated place* was shared equally by them all, because they surmised that their evil fortune was bound up with their present luckless abode *(Malbim)*.

She was afraid that if they stayed there one more day they would all die *(Alschich)*.

The *Besuras Eliyahu* interprets וַתָּקָם as *'rising up from mourning'* i.e. as soon as the mourning period was over they resolved to leave.

The *Midrash* interprets וַתָּקָם in a spiritual sense: 'Fallen down, she now lifted herself up by returning to Eretz Yisrael' *(Lekach Tov)*.

(According to *Rashi*, however, וַתָּקָם *'she arose'* in this verse implies *actual* departure, [see Comm. next verse]).

וַתָּשָׁב מִשְּׂדֵי מוֹאָב — *To return from the fields of Moab*. The word וַתָּשָׁב [lit. *'and she returned'*] is singular to imply that although the three of them unanimously agreed that they must leave their present luckless abode, at first it was Naomi alone who decided to leave Moab, her daughters-in-law concurring in that decision only later *(Malbim)*.

בְּשְׂדֵה מוֹאָב כִּי־פָקַד יהוה אֶת־עַמּוֹ לָתֵת לָהֶם לָחֶם: וַתֵּצֵא מִן־הַמָּקוֹם אֲשֶׁר הָיְתָה־שָּׁמָּה וּשְׁתֵּי כַלֹּתֶיהָ עִמָּהּ וַתֵּלַכְנָה בַדֶּרֶךְ לָשׁוּב אֶל־אֶרֶץ יְהוּדָה: וַתֹּאמֶר נָעֳמִי לִשְׁתֵּי כַלֹּתֶיהָ לֵכְנָה שֹּׁבְנָה אִשָּׁה

כִּי שָׁמְעָה בִּשְׂדֵי מוֹאָב — *For she had heard in the fields of Moab.* 'She heard from peddlers making their rounds from city to city,' says the *Midrash.* 'And what was it she heard? . . . כִּי־פָקַד ה' אֶת־עַמּוֹ לָתֵת לָהֶם לָחֶם, *That* HASHEM *had remembered His people by giving them food.'* Now that the famine was over, Jewish peddlers resumed their rounds in Moab selling the produce of Eretz Yisrael. It was from these peddlers that she heard the good news. The *Midrash* reasons that she heard it from Jewish peddlers because the Moabites would never have invoked the Name of HASHEM (the proper Name of God) as the Cause of the famine and its removal. Also, as the *Midrash* states, God ended the famine for the sake of עַמּוֹ, *His people;* she was reassured that the cause of the famine [i.e. the lawlessness of the times; see Comm. to verse 1] was remedied, the people having repented, and that the famine had permanently ended (*Malbim*).

Pri Chaim, on the other hand, analyzing the verse, comments that פָקַד ה' אֶת עַמּוֹ *'*HASHEM *has remembered His people'* — is an exact quotation of what the peddlers were going around saying; and since עַמּוֹ *'His people'* is in the third person — implying that the speaker excluded himself — we must say that it was Moabite peddlers who were ac-

knowledging HASHEM's ending of the famine in Eretz Yisrael.

Nachlas Yosef stresses the word עַמּוֹ, *His people* — i.e. the word was out that the Jews once again became God's people, having fully repented from their evil ways.

It should be noted that Naomi did not resolve to return home until she had the assurance that the famine was finally over, and that God had ended it for the sake of עַמּוֹ *His people,* of which she, too, was part. For had He ended it for the sake of Eretz Yisrael, she could not be part of it, having forsaken the land. [The family's affront to the Land would have precluded their sharing in any prosperity granted for its sake. But 'a Jew remains a Jew even after having sinned' — thus Naomi could share in abundance given for the sake of the people] (*Alschich*).

According to the *Targum*: God gave the people food on account of the righteousness of the judge Ivtzan and the prayers of Boaz [who, according to the *Talmud* were the same person].

A homiletical interpretation is offered by *Kol Yehuda*: At first, Naomi was afraid to return home during the famine lest the Jews take revenge against her by not feeding her. She realized, however, that God, Who by warning against being vengeful, פָקַד אֶת עַמּוֹ — *Had* (in effect) *commanded His people* [פָקַד, *'remembered,'* could also mean *in the fields of Moab that HASHEM had remembered His people by giving them food. ⁷ She left the place where she had been, accompanied by her two daughters-in-law, and they set out on the road to return to the land of Judah.*

⁸ Then Naomi said to her two daughters-in-law:

'commanded'], לָתֵת לָהֶם לָחֶם *to give them* [i.e. Naomi and her family] *bread* just as Jews are commanded by the Torah to care for all unfortunates.

7. וַתֵּצֵא מִן־הַמָּקוֹם — *She left the place.* Rashi, who holds that וַתָּקָם, 'she arose', in the previous verse denotes actual departure rather than a resolve to leave, queries: Her return home is already mentioned in the preceding verse; why does this verse speak of her departure?...

[Her departure was particularly noticeable because]: 'The great person of a city is its brilliance, its distinction, its glory, and its praise. When he departs, its brilliance, its distinction, its glory, and its praise depart with him (*Midrash; Rashi*).

וּשְׁתֵּי כַלֹתֶיהָ עִמָּהּ — *Accompanied by her two daughters-in-law.* [Lit. 'her two daughters-in-law with her']. The departure of the daughters-in-law was also particularly significant, as was Naomi's [see preceeding Comm.] (*Meishiv Nefesh*).

וַתֵּלַכְנָה — *And they set out,* [lit. 'they walked'] i.e. they discussed הִלְכוֹת גֵּרִים, the laws of proselytes. [This interpretation is suggested by the seemingly redundant use of the word וַתֵּלַכְנָה, *they walked,* which has the same root as הֲלָכָה, *law.*] (*Midrash*).

בַּדֶּרֶךְ — *On the road.* The *Midrash* offers this explanation for the

seemingly superfluous term בַּדֶּרֶךְ, *on the road:* The way was hard for them because they went barefoot. [i.e nothing cushioned their bare feet from the road — such was the degree of their poverty] (*Torah T'mimah*).

The words בַּדֶּרֶךְ לָשׁוּב 'on the road to return,' are superfluous; the verse could have read: '*And they set out to the land of Judah.'* The verse, as structured, teaches us that when our intentions are good, God rewards us every step of the way (*Kol Yehudah*).

לָשׁוּב — *To return.* This can only refer to Naomi who was 'returning' to Eretz Yisrael. 'Returning,' in this context, could not refer to Ruth or Orpah who had never been in Eretz Yisrael (*Iggerres Shmuel*).

8. וַתֹּאמֶר נָעֳמִי — *Then Naomi said.* Naomi had assumed that her daughters-in-law were merely accompanying her to Judah out of respect and courtesy, with the intention of returning to Moab afterwards. She told them that this was unnecessary. Her maternal suggestion was that they should return to their mother's home, confident that God would reward them for having been good wives and dutiful daughters-in-law (*Malbim*).

לִשְׁתֵּי כַלֹתֶיהָ. The verse mentions 'two' in order to make clear that Naomi showed no bias toward

לְבֵית אִמָּהּ יַעֲשֶׂה יהוה עִמָּכֶם חֶסֶד
כַּאֲשֶׁר עֲשִׂיתֶם עִם־הַמֵּתִים וְעִמָּדִי: יִתֵּן ט
יהוה לָכֶם וּמְצֶאןָ מְנוּחָה אִשָּׁה בֵּית

יַעֲשֶׂ ק'

Ruth. Although she realized that Ruth's determination to convert was much stronger than Orpah's, she addressed them both in the same terms *(Meishiv Nefesh)*.

Quite possibly, Naomi did not yet realize that Ruth's commitment was greater than Orpah's. She addressed them as equals in the hope that each would strengthen the other's resolve *(Rav Yosef Yavetz; Pri Chaim)*.

לֵכְנָה שֹׁבְנָה — *Go return*. She asked them to return home because she did not want to be embarrassed [i.e. by returning to Eretz Yisrael with Moabite daughters-in-law] *(Midrash Zuta)*. . .

[The Sages rule that one must attempt to dissuade a would-be convert three times; this was the first time — the others are in verses 11 and 12]. . .

If Naomi's *only* intention was to fulfill the halachic requirement that a potential proselyte be discouraged, then the word שֹׁבְנָה *return*, would have been sufficient. Since Naomi added לֵכְנָה, *go*, the Rabbis deduced that her intention was sincere, because she reflected that she, Elimelech's widow, was about to return to the Holy Land with non-Jewish daughters-in-law, and, as the *Midrash* tells us, she grew ashamed *(Midrash Zuta)*.

According to *Alshich*, once they reached the *'road to return to the land of Judah,'* Naomi realized that they had not escorted her as a mere courtesy, but that their intention was to remain with her in Judah.

She told them not to follow each other blindly, but, as individuals, to carefully consider the implications of conversion and to act out of a deep personal conviction. She said: "לֵכְנָה, *'go'* along with me, or שֹׁבְנָה, *'return'* to your mother's home, but, whatever course you choose, may God repay your goodness, and may you find husbands".

יַעֲשֶׂה ה' עִמָּכֶם חֶסֶד — *May HASHEM deal kindly with you*. The כְּתִיב — *ksiv*, [the traditional spelling] is יעשה, [the simple future tense],i.e. 'He will *certainly* deal kindly with you'] *(Midrash)*.

[Our translation, of course, follows the קְרִי — *kri*, (the traditional reading) יַעַשׂ — the optative *'may He do'* The juxtaposition of *ksiv* and *kri* indicate that, although Naomi said 'May He do' in the form of a prayer, she was fully confident that God would, indeed, reward their kindness].

'God does not withhold reward from any creature!' [i.e. God repays every good deed accordingly; what special implication did Naomi's blessing have?]. — Naomi's blessing must be understood as saying: Just as you both have gone beyond what is expected of you by doing חֶסֶד, *kindness*, so may HASHEM not only reward you in the usual manner, but may He go beyond the expected and do חֶסֶד, *kindness*, with you *(Nachal Eshkol)*.

Naomi's intention was, 'Perhaps, my daughters-in-law, you do not part from me because you fear that if you desert me now — leaving

'Go, return, each of you to her mother's house. May HASHEM deal kindly with you, as you have dealt kindly with the dead and with me! ⁹ *May HASHEM grant that you may find security, each in the home of*

me destitute — all your previous kindness to me will be nullified; instead of being rewarded for the good you have done for so many years, you are afraid you will be punished for the final lapse. Fear not. You may return home to your mothers and God will reward you nonetheless (*Iggeres Shmuel*).

בַּאֲשֶׁר עֲשִׂיתֶם עִם הַמֵּתִים — *As you have dealt kindly with the dead*, i.e. by having been good to your husbands during their lifetimes, וְעִמָּדִי *and to me* (*Malbim*).

According to the *Midrash*: '*As you have dealt with the dead*' — in that you [went beyond what is *required* of a wife and] busied yourselves with their shrouds; '*and with me*' — in that you renounced the marriage settlement to which you were legally entitled ....

The *Midrash* thus understands the verse as referring to *posthumous* kindness ['busying themselves with their shrouds']. Had Naomi referred to kindness done during the lifetimes of their husbands, she would have said '*with your husbands*' instead of '*with the dead*' (*Torah T'mimah*).

Perhaps this is why Naomi addressed them in the Hebrew masculine gender [עִמָּכֶם, עֲשִׂיתֶם] as if to say: Your posthumous kindness to your husbands — in preparing their shrouds and funeral — was not a legal feminine obligation, but a masculine one (*Meishiv Nefesh*).

The *Targum* translates: 'The

kindness you have done to your husbands — *by refusing to remarry*; and to me, — *by feeding and sustaining me*.'

9. [Naomi elaborates on her blessing of the previous verse, specifying that the 'kindness' for which she prays is that God reward them at long last with domestic contentment].

יִתֵּן ה' לָכֶם —*May HASHEM grant that you.* [Lit. '*May HASHEM give to you*], i.e. over and above what you rightfully deserve (*Malbim*).

Ibn Ezra adds the word: בַּעַל, *a husband.*

וּמְצֶאןָ מְנוּחָה — *That you may find security,* [lit. '*rest*']. The *k'siv* [traditional written form] of the word is וּמְצֶאןָ, without the suffix, ה, i.e. in singular. [Naomi foresaw that] 'only one of you will find rest; not both' (*Midrash*).

Although Naomi foresaw that only Ruth was destined to be blessed, she nevertheless addressed them with the plural לָכֶם, *to you,* out of respect for Orpah's feelings. However the word וּמְצֶאןָ, *that you may find,* is indistinguishable in its spoken form from the singular to the plural (*Iggeres Shmuel*).

אִשָּׁה בֵּית אִישָׁהּ — *Each in the home of her husband.* [Lit. '*woman in the home of her man*']. From Naomi's blessing 'we see that a woman has no contentment except in her husband's house' (*Midrash*).

Witnessing the unhappiness of

אִישָׁה וַתִּשַּׁק לָהֶן וַתִּשֶּׂאנָה קוֹלָן
וַתִּבְכֶּינָה: וַתֹּאמַרְנָה־לָּהּ כִּי־אִתָּךְ נָשׁוּב
לְעַמֵּךְ: וַתֹּאמֶר נָעֳמִי שֹׁבְנָה בְנֹתַי לָמָּה
תֵלַכְנָה עִמִּי הַעוֹד־לִי בָנִים בְּמֵעַי וְהָיוּ
לָכֶם לַאֲנָשִׁים: שֹׁבְנָה בְנֹתַי לֵכְןָ כִּי
זָקַנְתִּי מִהְיוֹת לְאִישׁ כִּי אָמַרְתִּי יֶשׁ־לִי
תִקְוָה גַּם הָיִיתִי הַלַּיְלָה לְאִישׁ וְגַם יָלַדְתִּי

her daughters-in-law who became widowed after being barren for ten years, she wished them true domestic contentment in the future (*Iggeres Shmuel*).

וַתִּשַּׁק לָהֶן — *She kissed them.* A parting embrace (*Malbim*).

וַתִּבְכֶּינָה — *And they wept.* [The commentaries differ on whether the daughters-in-law cried on account of Naomi's imminent departure, or whether all three cried while reflecting on their sad state. The *Zohar Chadash* states that the spirits of their dead husbands stirred within them, evoking their tears].

10. וַתֹּאמַרְנָה לָּהּ — *And they said to her.* Now, they told her for the first time of their intention of returning with her (*Malbim*).

[The 'No!' in the translation is not in the Hebrew, but is implied in the context of the verse.]

לְעַמֵּךְ — *To your people.* At this point they expressed a desire not to accept the God of the Jews, but merely to settle among 'your people' in Eretz Yisrael (*Malbim*).

According to *Alshich*, however, Naomi understood these words as an implicit declaration that they wished to convert. Otherwise their

statement would have been self-contradictory: one cannot join the Jewish nation without accepting its God.

11. שֹׁבְנָה בְנֹתַי — *Turn back, my daughters.* [This was the second of Naomi's three attempts to dissuade the would-be converts; see verses 8 and 12.]

הַעוֹד־לִי בָנִים בְּמֵעַי — *Have I more sons in my womb?* Naomi was not seriously suggesting that her daughters-in-law wait for unborn sons to grow up and become their husbands! Rather, her statement was metaphorical: 'Have I any grown-up sons whom I have been keeping hidden, out of your sight, in my womb, and whom I could instantly produce to become your husbands?' (*Malbim*).

וְהָיוּ לָכֶם לַאֲנָשִׁים — *'Who could become husbands to you?'* 'Could then a man marry the widow of his brother [who became widowed] before he was born? [יִבּוּם, levirate marriage (see *Introduction*) would not apply to an as-yet unconceived child] (*Midrash*).

Since the law of levirate marriage could not apply, such a marriage would be forbidden by Torah law. Therefore, Naomi's words must be understood, not in the sense of יִבּוּם,

her husband.' She kissed them, and they raised their voice and wept. ¹⁰ And they said to her: 'No, we will return with you to your people.' ¹¹ But Naomi said: 'Turn back, my daughters. Why should you come with me? Have I more sons in my womb who could become husbands to you? ¹² Turn back, my daughters, go along, for I am too old to have a husband. Even if I were to say: there is hope for me, and even if I were to have a husband tonight — and even

---

levirate marriage, but rather as a loving gesture: 'Had I more sons in my womb, I would gladly give them to you in place of your dead husbands' *(Ibn Ezra)*.

12. שֹׁבְנָה בְנֹתַי לֵכְןָ — *Turn back, my daughters, go along.* 'Three times is it written שֹׁבְנָה, 'turn back,' corresponding to the three times that a would be convert is dissuaded. If he still persists, he is accepted' *(Midrash)*.

כִּי זָקַנְתִּי מִהְיוֹת לְאִישׁ — *For I am too old to have a husband.* i.e. to marry and bear children to be husbands to you *(Rashi)*.

Naomi adds to her argument, 'Even if you agreed to wait until I remarry, have children and raise them to marriageable age, there are still two reasons why this is impossible — first, כִּי זָקַנְתִּי מִהְיוֹת לְאִישׁ, *I am too old to have a husband;* secondly, you could not bear to wait so long — הֲלָהֵן תְּשַׂבֵּרְנָה, *would you wait for them? (Malbim)*.

כִּי אָמַרְתִּי יֶשׁ־לִי תִקְוָה — *Even if I were to say there is hope for me.* [The 'even' is not in the Hebrew, but the phrase is to be so understood according to the commentaries (e.g. *Rashi*)].

In a homiletic fashion *Rav*

Velvele Margolis interprets the verse as reflecting the social ills of society and the rationale for delaying marriage. Many people, wanting to climb the social ladder reject prospective suitors always hoping for someone better to come along. Thus, Naomi said: 'I am too old to have a husband because I wanted to become the wife of someone comparable to Elimelech, important and aristocratic; therefore I delayed remarriage כִּי אָמַרְתִּי יֶשׁ לִי תִקְוָה, because I always said: *There is hope for me,* I will find someone better, more suitable for me ' *(Ginzei Malchus)*.

גַּם הָיִיתִי הַלַּיְלָה לְאִישׁ — *And even if I were to have a husband tonight.* The *Malbim* explains: According to our sages, Naomi said: 'If I had a husband tonight I might have borne sons' *(Midrash)*. Now, according to the Sages, a woman who resigns herself to unmarried widowhood for ten years can no longer bear children afterward. Thus, the only two ways Naomi — ten years a widow — could have remained fruitful were if she had sustained the hope of remarriage throughout the period of widowhood; or if she would remarry *that very night*, the tenth anniversary of Elimelech's death.

פֶּרֶק א יג בָּנִים: הֲלָהֵן | תְּשַׂבֵּרְנָה עַד אֲשֶׁר יִגְדָּלוּ
יג הֲלָהֵן תֵּעָגֵנָה לְבִלְתִּי הֱיוֹת לְאִישׁ אַל
בְּנֹתַי כִּי־מַר־לִי מְאֹד מִכֶּם כִּי־יָצְאָה בִי

Thus, we can translate the verse: *Turn back, my daughters, go along, for I am too old to have a husband,* i.e. having remained widowed ten years, I should, under normal circumstances, not be able to remarry and bear children. *But,* said Naomi, *I said there is hope for me* — i.e. I sustained the hope of remarrying throughout the ten years of my widowhood, thus enabling me to have children even after this period — or on the other hand *if I had a husband tonight,* specifically *tonight,* the last night of the ten year period, *I might have children.* ... and so I ask you: *Would you wait for them* ... ? etc.' (Malbim).

וְגַם יָלַדְתִּי בָנִים — *And even bear sons.* 'Or even if I had already given birth to children' *(Rashi)*.

[Rashi apparently understands these words, not as the hypothetical result of *if I were to have a husband tonight,* but as an additional argument by Naomi, i.e. 'let us say I *had* given birth to sons ... *would you wait for them until they were grown?']*.

[The double use of גַם, *and* ('even'; 'furthermore') in this verse implies Naomi's resignation to an almost futile situation.]

13. הֲלָהֵן תְּשַׂבֵּרְנָה — *Would you wait for them?* i.e. for the hypothetical children to whom I might give birth? *(Iggeres Shmuel).*

הֲלָהֵן תֵּעָגֵנָה — *Would you tie yourselves down for them?* [The translation follows *Rashi* who holds that the root of תֵּעָגֵנָה is עוג, to en-

circle, to constrict. *Rashi* refutes those who translate the word as being related to עֲגוּנָה, *Agunah,* (a woman who is forbidden to marry because her husband is missing and she has no proof of his death.) The root of that word: עגן. Thus if תֵּעָגֵנָה stemmed from עגן (with the suffix נה, there would be a double נ in the word, or at the very least, the single נ with a *dagesh* (נּ) serving to take the place of the missing letter.)

In a lengthy grammatical discourse, the *Iggeres Shmuel* quotes the *Radak* as deriving the word from the root עגה, and translating it as *'delay'.* The *Iggeres Shmuel* then refutes this translation, and insists that it is derived from עגן, as in עֲגוּנָה, *Agunah,* which the Sages always use when referring to a married woman living without her husband. Therefore, explains the *Iggeres Shmuel,* the ג, *gimmel,* is vocalized with a *'tzere,'* (גֵ), for, were the word derived from the root עגה, the ג, *gimmel,* would be vocalized with a *'segol'* (גֶ). ...

The *Iggeres Shmuel* thus translates: *Would you remain as Agunahs* — in memory of your dead husbands?'

The *Talmud* translates the word as coming from the Hebrew עֹגֶן, *'an anchor'* — i.e. *would you remain anchored* ... ? *(Bava Basra 73a).*

לְבִלְתִּי הֱיוֹת לְאִישׁ — *And not marry anyone else?* [lit. *and not be to a man?*]. 'Would you delay and remain tied down, waiting for these children to grow up — with the end result that לְבִלְתִּי הֱיוֹת לְאִישׁ, *you*

*bear sons — 13 would you wait for them until they
were grown up? would you tie yourselves down for
them and not marry anyone else? No, my daughters!
I am very embittered on account of you; for the hand*

*will never marry anyone because
you will be too old to have
husbands? No, my daughters!...
(Iggeres Shmuel).*

אַל בְּנוֹתַי — *No, my daughters!* i.e.
do not come with me *(Ibn Ezra).*

The *Midrash* quotes Naomi as
saying, אַלְלַי בְּנוֹתַי, *'woe is to me, my
daughters* . . . [Had she meant an
absolute negation, an order that
they not accompany her based on
the irrefutable logic cited earlier, she
would have said לא. The word אַל,
on the other hand, indicates an
entreaty *(Torah T'mimah)*].

כִּי־מַר־לִי מְאֹד מִכֶּם — *I am very embittered on account of you.* [The
translation follows the majority of
the commentaries and the *Midrash*,
which renders: *'on account of
you.']*

Naomi blamed her bitterness and
the tragedies of her sons' death on
their marriage to gentile women,
rather than to their leaving Eretz
Yisrael because that had been done
at the command of their father *(Binyan Ariel).*

Although she had attempted to
discourage them by insisting that
there were no more unborn sons in
her womb, she made it clear that she
would not have allowed her
children to marry Ruth and Orpah
in any case *(Simchas haRegel).*

The *Chidah*, in his above-
mentioned *Simchas haRegel,* offers
an alternate interpretation of מִכֶּם:
Naomi felt that her sons had been
placed in an impossible situation by
their marriages to the Moabite

princesses. Machlon and Kilion
could not divorce or desert them
because of the political reper-
cussions. They could not return to
Eretz Yisrael with Moabite wives.
Naomi reasoned that her sons had
no alternative but to remain in
Moab *'because of them.'* As a result,
God had punished her sons.

Other commentaries interpret
מִכֶּם — *'more than you'* i.e. *'I am
more embittered than you* [for I
have suffered more tragedies than
you]' *(Rav Arama; Iggeres Shmuel;
Malbim).*

The *Vilna Gaon* interprets the
phrase: *'I am greatly distressed
witnessing your plight,* כִּי יָצְאָה בִי
יַד ה', *although the hand of God has
gone forth against me,* I am more
concerned with *your anguish.'*

According to the *Bach*, מִכֶּם is not
'additive' but *'causitive'* i.e. *'I am
embittered for your sake* — seeing
your bereavement, and remembering that because of you my sons
died.'

כִּי יָצְאָה בִי יַד ה' — *for the hand of
HASHEM has gone forth against me.*
*'Against me, against my sons, and
against my husband' (Midrash).*

Whatever God could possibly
have done to me, He has already
done *(Malbim).*

יָצְאָה — *Gone forth* [lit. *'went out']*
is used because God's wrath was so
severe in this case that it *'went out'*
beyond the bounds of its usual tem-
perance *(Iggeres Shmuel).*

יַד ה' — *The hand of God,* i.e. *afflict-
ion.* The reference to 'hand' is an-

יד יַד־יהוה: וַתִּשֶּׂנָה קוֹלָן וַתִּבְכֶּינָה עוֹד
וַתִּשַּׁק עָרְפָּה לַחֲמוֹתָהּ וְרוּת דָּבְקָה בָּהּ:

טו וַתֹּאמֶר הִנֵּה שָׁבָה יְבִמְתֵּךְ אֶל־עַמָּהּ
וְאֶל־אֱלֹהֶיהָ שׁוּבִי אַחֲרֵי יְבִמְתֵּךְ:

טז וַתֹּאמֶר רוּת אַל־תִּפְגְּעִי־בִי לְעָזְבֵךְ לָשׁוּב

thropomorphic; speaking in human terms (*Ibn Ezra.*)

The *Iggeres Shmuel* offers a novel interpretation: Naomi told her daughters-in-law not to think that she blamed them for her sons' death; 'בְּנוֹתַי' אַל', no my daughters, do not think *that my bitterness is because of you.* Definitely not! *The hand of G-d has gone forth against me* — in retribution for *my own sins.*'

14. *The Alshich* paraphrases verses 11-14:

Naomi, realizing that they wanted to convert and go to Eretz Yisrael, called them בְּנוֹתַי *my daughters,* — and said: 'If you desire to serve HASHEM, you can do that in Moab. If you wonder whom you could marry in Moab — all of them being idol worshipers — then realize that no Jew will marry you, because you are Moabites [and the law permitting marriage to female Moabites was not yet promulgated]). Don't rely on me for husbands; I am too old for marriage. Even if I were to marry, even tonight, who can say that I will give birth. If I do give birth, I might bear only daughters! And even if I were to have sons, would you wait for them?

'You might reply that you are content to accompany me to Eretz Yisrael with no thought of remarriage. No, my daughters: My state of bitterness is for you — I cannot

bear to see you in such a troubled state, for the hand of God has gone forth against *me;* you are sinless. It was for my sins that God has been punishing me, and you have been bearing my iniquity.

When Orpah and Ruth heard this, they cried. Orpah kissed her mother-in-law, but in Ruth's *clinging* to her; Naomi realized a רוּחַ קְדוּשָׁה, a spirit of holiness (*Alshich*)

וַתִּשֶּׂנָה קוֹלָן וַתִּבְכֶּינָה עוֹד — *They raised up their voice and wept again.* There is an א, aleph, missing [from וֹתשנה] teaching that תַּשַׁשׁ כֹּחָן, their strength diminished, as, weeping, they went on their way (*Midrash*)...

(i.e. the word וַתִּשֶּׂאנָה — with an א aleph, as in verse 9 — means *and they raised up.* Here, since וַתִּשֶּׂנָה omits the א, *aleph,* the *Midrash* homiletically links the word to תשש, 'to be weak.' The verse indicates that they wept continuously throughout their conversation with Naomi until even their strength to cry was weakened (*Iggeres Shmuel*).

וַתִּשַּׁק עָרְפָּה לַחֲמוֹתָהּ — *Orpah kissed her mother-in-law.* [The kiss was their parting. No words. Only a kiss. Scripture divulges no more, but the pain was intense. As Naomi watched Orpah walk towards Moab, she knew that the last vestige of her son Kilion was lost to her forever].

of HASHEM has gone forth against me.

14 They raised up their voice and wept again. Orpah kissed her mother-in-law, but Ruth clung to her. 15 So she said: 'Look, your sister-in-law has returned to her people and to her god; go follow your sister-in-law.' 16 But Ruth said: 'Do not urge me to leave

וְרוּת דָּבְקָה־בָּה — *But Ruth clung to her.* Ruth, too, remained silent. Her eyes showed her devotion to Naomi — her eyes and her refusal to go. But Naomi could not understand: wasn't Orpah right? *(Ima Shel Malchus).*

'Ruth and Orpah were of royal lineage, descended from Eglon king of Moab (*Nazir* 23b); it was a heroic sacrifice to forsake their country to accompany the impoverished Naomi. There, on a country road in the fields of Moab, *was enacted one of the great scenes of history.* Three times did Naomi urge Ruth and Orpah to desist from their kindliness and turn back. They refused to yield, but on the third time, Orpah weakened and returned to her land and her people. Ruth persisted in her resolve to go with Naomi... Generations later, David the descendant of Ruth, faced Goliath, the descendant of Orpah, on the battlefield' *(Behold a People).*

15. הִנֵּה שָׁבָה יְבִמְתֵּךְ — *Look, your sister-in-law has returned.* [Orpah's departure is not stated, but it is inferred from her 'farewell' kiss in the previous verse.]

The accent in Hebrew, notes *Rashi,* is under the שׁ of שָׁבָה, indicating that it is simple past tense, i.e. *she returned,* unlike the same word [in *Esther* 2:14] where the accent is under the ב and the tense is imperfect: בָּעֶרֶב הִיא שָׁבָה, *'in the evening she would return'.*

אֶל־עַמָּהּ וְאֶל־אֱלֹהֶיהָ — *To her people and to her god.* Rashba haLevi understands לְעַמֵּךְ, *to your people,'* in verse 10 as indicating their desire to convert. In contrast, he notes, the expression *'returned to her people and her god'* in this verse reveals that she renounced her previous intention to embrace Judaism.

[The *Ibn Ezra* and *Zohar Chadash,* in keeping with their interpretation that Ruth and Orpah had already converted when they got married, (see *Comm.* to v.4); deduce from this verse that Orpah now *'returned'* to her old faith. (See *Introduction* for full exposition of this interpretation)].

שׁוּבִי אַחֲרֵי יְבִמְתֵּךְ — *Follow your sister-in-law.* [i.e. *'return after your sister-in-law'*]. Naomi said: Your sister-in-law accompanied me because she was ashamed to leave. Now she finally succumbed and returned home. I grant you the same opportunity to depart gracefully and follow her *(Iggeres Shmuel).*

Naomi simply said, 'follow your sister-in-law; she carefully refrained from adding 'to her god' (Alshich).

16. אַל־תִּפְגְּעִי־בִי — *Do not urge me.* 'Do not persist so diligently in trying to dissuade me from joining you. Don't offer me excuses לְעָזְבֵךְ, *to leave you,* לָשׁוּב מֵאַחֲרָיִךְ, *and not follow you* in your return to

מֵאַחֲרַיִךְ כִּי אֶל־אֲשֶׁר תֵּלְכִי אֵלֵךְ וּבַאֲשֶׁר
תָּלִינִי אָלִין עַמֵּךְ עַמִּי וֵאלֹהַיִךְ אֱלֹהָי:
יז בַּאֲשֶׁר תָּמוּתִי אָמוּת וְשָׁם אֶקָּבֵר כֹּה
יַעֲשֶׂה יהוה לִי וְכֹה יוֹסִיף כִּי הַמָּוֶת
יח יַפְרִיד בֵּינִי וּבֵינֵךְ. וַתֵּרֶא כִּי־מִתְאַמֶּצֶת

Judaism — for no matter what, I am determined to convert' (Iggeres Shmuel).

'Better that my conversion should be at your hands than at those of another' (Midrash).

The Midrash [understanding תִּפְגְּעִי as a form of פגע, 'misfortune'] translates 'Do not turn your misfortune against me' — i.e. do not seek to turn me away by reciting your misfortunes to me (Yefe Anaf); — do not court misfortune through me, by repulsing me (Anaf Yosef); — do not sin and incur punishment by dissuading me from converting (Torah T'mimah).

כִּי אֶל־אֲשֶׁר תֵּלְכִי אֵלֵךְ — For wherever you go, I will go. [From this, the Sages infer,] 'If one desired to become a proselyte, he is acquainted with the various punishments [for neglect of the Commandments], so that if he wishes to withdraw, let him do so [Yevamos 47b]. (Or, following the approach of the Zohar Chadash/Ibn Ezra — that Ruth and Orpah had already converted upon marrying Machlon and Kilion [see Introduction] — Naomi was testing Ruth's resolve and commitment, now that her husband was dead, by acquainting her with the additional commandments.) From Ruth's responses we can deduce what Naomi must have told her ...

Naomi said: 'We are forbidden [to move on the Sabbath beyond the

2,000 cubits in each direction from one's town or resting place_known as] תְּחוּם שַׁבָּת, the Sabbath boundaries!' — [to which Ruth replied] Wherever you go, I will go (Yevamos 47b).

When Naomi heard Ruth's absolute resolve to convert, she began to unfold the laws to her, saying: 'My daughter, Jewish girls do not go to gentile theaters and circuses' [which had a well-deserved reputation for lewdness]; to which she replied: 'Wherever you go, I will go' (Midrash). ...

Do not ascribe to me a motive different from your own. It is my desire, also, to live in Eretz Yisrael so that I may fulfill the mitzvos that the Torah associates with that land (Malbim).

וּבַאֲשֶׁר תָּלִינִי אָלִין — Where you lodge, I will lodge. 'We are forbidden יְחוּד, seclusion between man and woman!' — 'Where you lodge,' Ruth responded, 'I will lodge' (Yevamos 47b).

'My daughter, Jewish girls do not live in a house which has no mezuzah,' — to which Ruth responded: 'Where you lodge, I will lodge' (Midrash).'I do not expect luxuries; I am prepared to be a mere lodger because there is only one object in my going' [as follows:] (Malbim).

עַמֵּךְ עַמִּי — Your people are my people. 'I will never forsake the Torah

you, to turn back and not follow you. For wherever
you go, I will go; where you lodge, I will lodge; your
people are my people, and your God is my God;
¹⁷ where you die, I will die, and there I will be buried.
Thus may HASHEM do to me — and more! — if
anything but death separates me from you.'
¹⁸ When she saw she was determined to go with

of the Jews and the Oneness of G-d'
(Ibn Ezra).

[Naomi said]: 'We have been
given 613 Commandments!' Ruth
answered, 'Thy people shall be my
people' [i.e. I am now part of your
people and I accept the mitzvos]
(Yevamos 47b).

וֵאלֹהַיִךְ אֱלֹהָי — Your God is my
God. 'We are forbidden idolatry!'
Said Ruth. 'Your God is my God'
(Yevamos 47b).

This refers to the acceptance of
all the mitzvos for, by accepting
the sovereignty of God, one accepts
all of His commandments. ...
Another interpretation: 'Your God
is my God ... who will repay me the
reward of my labor' (Midrash).

17. בַּאֲשֶׁר תָּמוּתִי אָמוּת — Where
you die, I will die. [According to the
Talmud and Midrash, Naomi
enumerated the four forms of
capital punishment to which Ruth
responded; By whatever mode you
die, I will die; i.e. I am prepared to
face death for capital offenses; and
there be buried].

She expressed her innermost
desire to die, the same מוֹת יְשָׁרִים,
death of the upright as would
Naomi (Malbim).

'I want to die in Eretz Yisrael,'
Ruth declared (Zos Nechemasi)

וְשָׁם אֶקָּבֵר — And there I will be
buried. For our sages tell us that he

who is buried in Eretz Yisrael is
likened to one who is buried under
the altar (Zos Nechemasi).

כֹּה יַעֲשֶׂה ה' לִי וְכֹה יוֹסִיף — Thus may
HASHEM do to me — and more.
[Ruth emphasized her loyalty to the
Jews by invoking God's name, in
this formula of an oath which is
common in the Bible. Usually,
however, the name אֱלֹקִים — God of
Judgment is used in such a context.]

Ruth insisted that she would wil-
lingly follow Naomi in her beliefs,
where she went, and where she
slept. But death is out of one's
hands. She prayed, therefore, that
she would die near enough to
Naomi to be buried alongside her
(Iggeres Shmuel).

This was the crux of Ruth's plea:
'My main reason for following you
was I realized that as close as we are
in life, if I remain in my heathen
state we will be separated in death —
you will return to HASHEM, and I
will wallow amidst idolators'
(Malbim).

18. מִתְאַמֶּצֶת הִיא לָלֶכֶת — She was
determined to go. The verb אמץ
suggests moral strength and determination — (Malbim).

[Once Ruth's genuine convic-
tions were demonstrated beyond any
doubt, Naomi stopped dissuading
her].

According to Zos Nechemasi, this

הִיא לָלֶכֶת אִתָּהּ וַתֶּחְדַּל לְדַבֵּר אֵלֶיהָ:
יט וַתֵּלַכְנָה שְׁתֵּיהֶם עַד־בּוֹאָנָה בֵּית לָחֶם
וַיְהִי כְּבֹאָנָה בֵּית לֶחֶם וַתֵּהֹם כָּל־הָעִיר
כ עֲלֵיהֶן וַתֹּאמַרְנָה הֲזֹאת נָעֳמִי: וַתֹּאמֶר
אֲלֵיהֶן אַל־תִּקְרֶאנָה לִי נָעֳמִי קְרֶאןָ לִי
כא מָרָא* כִּי־הֵמַר שַׁדַּי לִי מְאֹד: אֲנִי מְלֵאָה

יא' במקום ה'

verse refers to Naomi: i.e. when Naomi perceived that God had not stricken her down like her husband and children, she realized that she was endowed with a special strength לָלֶכֶת אִתָּהּ, *to accompany her* [i.e. *Ruth*] and that she should be the instrument for bringing Ruth into the fold. Everything that God had wrought was in preparation for this event; Naomi then stopped arguing with Ruth.

וַתֶּחְדַּל לְדַבֵּר אֵלֶיהָ — *She stopped arguing with her.*[lit. *she stopped 'talking' to her*].

From this verse the Rabbis (*Yevamos 47b*) deduced that 'A convert is not to be persuaded or dissuaded too much' (*Rashi*).

19. וַתֵּלַכְנָה שְׁתֵּיהֶם — *And the two of them went on.* [lit. 'And they went, the two of them].

See how precious proselytes are to God! Once she decided to convert, Scriptures ranked her equally with Naomi (*Midrash; Rashi*).

שְׁתֵּיהֶם, '*the two of them*' is mentioned to stress the determination of Ruth, who, although she was leaving her home, birthplace and kindred, marched on with the same strength of soul and purpose as Naomi. Also, *they went, the two of them;* just the two of them alone. They didn't even wait for a caravan (*Iggeres Shmuel*).

The *Alshich* deduces from the fact that שְׁתֵּיהֶם, *the two of them* ends with the masculine ם instead of the feminine ן, — that the two were afraid to travel the dangerous roads of Moab alone — and they disguised themselves as men — עַד בּוֹאָנָה בֵּית לָחֶם, *until they reached Bethlehem* at which time they discarded their disguises.

עַד־בּוֹאָנָה בֵּית לָחֶם — *Until they came to Bethlehem.* [The journey to Bethlehem was a profound emotional experience for Naomi. She recalled the scenery and paths that had once been her own and which she and Elimelech had renounced ten years earlier.]

וַתֵּהֹם כָּל הָעִיר עֲלֵיהֶן — *the entire city was tumultuous over them.* The fact that '*the entire city*' learned of their return so quickly, notes the *Iggeres Shmuel*, indicates that the townsfolk were gathered together. The *Midrash* offers several reasons for such an assembly:

That day was the reaping of the *Omer* [the measure of the barley which was offered on the second day of Passover], and all the inhabitants of the surrounding towns assembled to watch the ceremony; the wife of Boaz died on that day, and a multitude of Jews assembled to pay their respects. Just then Ruth entered with Naomi — Thus, one

I
19-20

her, she stopped arguing with her, ¹⁹ and the two of them went on until they came to Bethlehem.

And it came to pass, when they arrived in Bethlehem, the whole city was tumultuous over them, and the women said: 'Could this be Naomi?' ²⁰ 'Do not call me Naomi [pleasant one],' she replied,

Call me embittered'

'call me Mara [embittered one], for the Almighty has dealt very bitterly with me. ²¹ I was full when I went

---

[the wife of Boaz] was taken and the other [Ruth] entered (*Midrash*).

Naomi had always gone about surrounded with servants, and now, when the townsfolk gathered together to see two women — alone, hungry and barefoot — the pitiful sight threw all the citizens into a state of tumult and flurry (*Malbim*).

וַתֹּאמַרְנָה הֲזֹאת נָעֳמִי — *And the women said, 'Could this be Naomi?'* ["*The women'* is not explicit in the Hebrew but it is. to be inferred because תֹּאמַרְנָה , *they said,* is in the feminine form.]

The afflicted Naomi had so changed in appearance from her past glory that her former neighbors could hardly recognize her (*Alshich*).

When they first appeared, the *whole city was tumultuous* at their very arrival, but upon closer scrutiny of Naomi's appearance, it was *the women* who addressed her (*Gishmei Brachah*).

'Is this the one whose actions were fitting and נְעִימִים , *pleasant?* In the past, she used to go in a covered carriage, and now she walks barefoot; in the past, she wore a cloak of fine wool, and now she is clothed in rags; in the past, her appearance was full from food and drink, now it is shrunken from

hunger — *could this be Naomi?* (*Midrash*).

Did you see what befell her for Leaving Eretz Yisrael? (*Rashi*).

20. אַל תִּקְרֶאנָה לִי נָעֳמִי ... מָרָא —*Do not call me Naomi . . . call me Mara.* Naomi said, 'Don't think that I was righteous and my deed pleasant, and that God punished me unjustly; No! *call me 'Embittered One'* because my deeds were bitter, and *God justly dealt bitterly with me'* (*Alshich*).

Also, by calling me 'Naomi' you are reminding me of my former glory and thus making my pain even worse (*Pri Chaim*).

מָרָא —*Mara ends with an aleph* א instead of the usual *he* ה to accentuate the extent of her bitterness. There are two other instances of words usually ending in a *he* that are spelled with an *aleph,* in both cases to strengthen the connotation: *Numbers 11:20* זָרָא for זָרָה — *'very* loathsome; and *Daniel 11:44* חֵמָא for חֵמָה — *'great* anger' (*Rabbeinu Bachyai*).

21. אֲנִי מְלֵאָה הָלַכְתִּי — *I was full when I went away* — 'I went out full with sons and daughters! Another interpretation: 'I was pregnant' (*Midrash*).

פרק א
כב

הָלַכְתִּי וְרֵיקָם הֱשִׁיבַנִי יהוה לָמָּה
תִקְרֶאנָה לִי נָעֳמִי וַיהוה עָנָה בִי וְשַׁדַּי
הֵרַע־לִי: וַתָּשָׁב נָעֳמִי וְרוּת הַמּוֹאֲבִיָּה
כַלָּתָהּ עִמָּהּ הַשָּׁבָה מִשְּׂדֵי מוֹאָב וְהֵמָּה
בָּאוּ בֵּית לֶחֶם בִּתְחִלַּת קְצִיר שְׂעֹרִים:

כב

פרק ב
א־ב

וּלְנָעֳמִי מוֹדָע* לְאִישָׁהּ אִישׁ גִּבּוֹר חַיִל
מִמִּשְׁפַּחַת אֱלִימֶלֶךְ וּשְׁמוֹ בֹּעַז: וַתֹּאמֶר

א
ב

מוֹדַע ק'

'Full' — with wealth and children (Rashi; Ibn Ezra).

וְרֵיקָם הֱשִׁיבַנִי ה' — And empty has HASHEM brought me back' [Widowed, childless, and poverty-stricken].

לָמָּה תִקְרֶאנָה לִי נָעֳמִי —How can you call me Naomi: [lit. why do you call me Naomi]. How can you call me a name describing good fortune — a name which in retrospect, I was never really entitled to — seeing how afflicted I have become! (Malbim).

עָנָה בִי ה' — HASHEM has testified against me. [lit. 'and HASHEM answered in me'].

He testified against me that I sinned against Him (Rashi).

'You see from the gravity of my punishment how severely I sinned against God, for the punishment bears witness to the extent of my evil ways. To you, my sin was leaving Eretz Yisrael during a famine — an action which might be justified. But HASHEM, Who knows our innermost intentions, knew that we left to avoid feeding the poor and

that we stayed overlong in Moab' (Rashba haLevi).

וְשַׁדַּי הֵרַע־לִי — the Almighty has brought misfortune upon me! [lit. 'And the Almighty did bad to me.']

Here Naomi refers to God as שַׁדַּי, (Shaddai) Almighty God, the name which indicates that, despite His infinite power, He is the God שֶׁאוֹמֵר לְצָרוֹתַי דַי Who says 'enough [דַי] of my suffering.' Although He took my husband and sons, He stopped short of taking my life, limiting His punishment to having הֵרַע לִי, brought misfortune upon me (Alshich).

22. הַשָּׁבָה מִשְּׂדֵי מוֹאָב — Who returned from the fields of Moab.

The subject of 'who returned' is not clear: According to Ibn Ezra it refers to Naomi; Iggeres Shmuel comments that it refers to Ruth despite the fact that she could not have 'returned', having never been in Eretz Yisrael. Ruth entered Eretz Yisrael with the same burning desire as did Naomi, so Scriptures describes it as 'she returned' — as if she had lived there before and it had *away, but HASHEM has brought me back empty. How can you call me Naomi — HASHEM has testified against me, the Almighty has brought misfortune upon me!'*

²² And so it was that Naomi returned, and Ruth the Moabite, her daughter-in-law, with her — who returned from the fields of Moab. They came to Bethlehem at the beginning of the barley harvest.

Naomi had a relative through her husband, a man of substance, from the family of Elimelech, whose name was Boaz.

been her birthplace.

'People pointed to her (Ruth) saying: This is the first one who returned from the fields of Moab' *(Yerushalmi, Yevamos 8:3)* i.e., she is the first Moabite woman who שָׁבָה,'repented', and converted to Judaism. With her the law of 'Moabite not Moabitess' [see *Introduction*] was promulgated *(Torah T'mimah).*

Quite possibly no other Moabite woman had ever converted before, because it would have been her impression that she would not be permitted to marry a Jew; Ruth's sincerity was so great, however, that she converted without caring if she could ever remarry *(Iggeres Shmuel).*

[The *Midrash* seems to imply that the subject is Naomi: *This is the one who returned from the fields of Moab!* (i.e. people pointed a finger at Naomi, identifying her as the one who returned from Moab — *(Iggeres Shmuel)*].

בְּתְחִלַּת קְצִיר שְׂעֹרִים — *In the beginning of barley harvest.* The verse refers to the *Omer* harvest [i.e. Passover] *(Midrash; Rashi).*

This chronological detail serves as an introduction to the next chapter; it tells us that it was already the harvest season and too late to plant new crops in the fields belonging to the family of Elimelech. Hence they were poverty-stricken *(Malbim).*

II

1. וּלְנָעֳמִי מוֹדַע — *Naomi had a relative [Moda].* The word *'moda'* means *'kinsman,' 'relative'* *(Midrash)* — a familiar relative *(Ibn Ezra).*

He was the son of Elimelech's brother *(Rashi).*

Although Boaz was a close relative, Naomi avoided him even in her dire need. She did not ask him for

רוּת הַמּוֹאֲבִיָּה אֶל־נָעֳמִי אֵלְכָה־נָּא
הַשָּׂדֶה וַאֲלַקֳטָה בַשִּׁבֳּלִים אַחַר אֲשֶׁר
אֶמְצָא־חֵן בְּעֵינָיו וַתֹּאמֶר לָהּ לְכִי בִתִּי:
ג וַתֵּלֶךְ וַתָּבוֹא וַתְּלַקֵּט בַּשָּׂדֶה אַחֲרֵי

support because she still felt shame at having deserted her people during the famine, while Boaz stayed on and supported them. In addition, she was aware that Boaz was angry that she had brought a Moabite girl back with her. He avoided them both until God brought Ruth to his fields [verse 3] and he realized how virtuous she was (Alshich).

Scripture tells us of the strength of these two women. Even though she had a rich relative she did not thrust herself upon him — and Ruth, the daughter of the King of Moab was not too proud to shoulder the burden of support for herself and her mother-in-law (Alkabetz).

On the other hand, it should be mentioned that according to the Sages, Boaz's wife died on the day that Naomi and Ruth returned to Bethlehem (see Comm. 1:19 s.v. וַתֵּהֹם). Boaz, involved with the funeral and mourning, could not give them a proper welcome. When Ruth chanced upon his field, on the day he returned from mourning, he recognized her rare qualities. Seeing her glean, he assumed that she would not avail herself of charity, preferring to maintain herself with her own hands. Also, as a widower, he did not want to be suspected of ulterior motives regarding Ruth, so he refrained from overt acts of kindness toward her. As a result of his restraint in regard to Ruth, Naomi also did not benefit of his

beneficence (Rav Arama; Iggeres Shmuel).

אִישׁ גִּבּוֹר חַיִל — A mighty man of substance [usually translated 'a mighty man of valor.' Our translation follows Rashi in Exodus 18:21: 'men of substance, who need not flatter or show partiality'].

— A man endowed with the highest human qualities including magnanimity and dislike of ill-gotten gains (Malbim).

וּשְׁמוֹ בֹּעַז — And his name was Boaz.

In the case of wicked men, their names are given before the word שֵׁם, 'name', as it says: גָּלְיָת שְׁמוֹ, Goliath was his name; נָבָל שְׁמוֹ, Nabal was his hame; שֶׁבַע בֶּן בִּכְרִי שְׁמוֹ, Sheva son of Bichri was his name. But the names of the righteous are preceded by the word שֵׁם, 'name', as it says: וּשְׁמוֹ קִישׁ, his name was Kish; וּשְׁמוֹ שָׁאוּל, his name was Saul; וּשְׁמוֹ יִשַׁי, his name was Jesse; וּשְׁמוֹ מָרְדְּכַי, and his name was Mordechai; וּשְׁמוֹ אֶלְקָנָה, and his name was Elkanah; וּשְׁמוֹ בֹּעַז, and his name was Boaz. They thus resemble their Creator of whom it is written וּשְׁמִי ה', 'But by My Name HASHEM I made Me not known to them [Ex. 6:2] (Midrash).

Our Sages said [Bava Basra 91a] that Boaz was the judge Ivtzan [see Comm. to 1:1] (Ibn Ezra).

2. וַתֹּאמֶר רוּת הַמּוֹאֲבִיָּה — Ruth the Moabite said. Scripture praises the righteousness of Ruth, who according to the Sages, was the

2 *Ruth the Moabite said to Naomi: 'Let me go out to the field, and glean among the ears of grain behind someone in whose eyes I shall find favor.' 'Go ahead, my daughter,' she said to her.*

3 *So off she went. She came and gleaned in the field*

daughter of Eglon, King of Moab. The verse stresses the noble character of this princess who offered to glean like a common pauper to spare her mother-in-law the indignity of *her* going out and being subject to the humiliating gaze of those who knew her in her former affluence (*Malbim*).

אֵלְכָה־נָּא הַשָּׂדֶה — *Let me go out to the field* i.e. to the safety of the field; not to vineyards where poor people must be concerned with the danger of climbing trees in order to glean forgotten fruits (*Malbim*).

וַאֲלַקְטָה בַשִׁבֳּלִים — *And glean among the ears of grain* i.e. she limited herself to לֶקֶט, *gleaning* [the ears of grain that *fell* from the hands of harvesters to which the poor were entitled — Lev. 19:9; 13:22; Deut. 29:19] — because fields for *gleaning* were plentiful and she would not have to compete fiercely with the other poor, unlike the competition for פֵּאָה, *Pe'ah* [see ibid.] which was much more severe (*Malbim*).

אַחַר אֲשֶׁר אֶמְצָא־חֵן בְּעֵינָיו —*Behind someone in whose eyes I shall find favor.* i.e. where the owner will permit me to glean and not scold me (*Rashi*).

אַחַר, *'After* I find favor in his eyes' (*Targum*), i.e. 'I will not glean in a field until I am sure the owner allows it and that I won't be embarassed by the other gleaners (*Malbim*).

She stressed that she will glean

אַחַר, *'after,'* i.e. *'in back of,'* as a gesture of modesty (*Simchas ha-Regel*).

לְכִי בִתִּי — *Go ahead, my daughter.* 'It is not that I hold you in low esteem that I permit you to so degrade yourself by gleaning like a common pauper — I permit you only because of the circumstances and our dire needs which demand it' (*Iggeres Shmuel*).

'Even had you been בִתִּי, *my own daughter,* I would have let you go (*Alshich*).

[Naomi obviously consented very reluctantly, remembering only too painfully her former wealth and the circumstances which brought her to such depths, and which now forced her daughter-in-law to descend to pauperdom by gleaning to provide for their basic sustenance].

The term בִתִּי, *'my daughter'* in this particular instance is not neccessarily an indication of Ruth's youth. According to Rabbinic tradition, she was then forty years of age (*Midrash*).

3. וַתֵּלֶךְ וַתָּבוֹא — *So off she went; she came.* [lit. *'and she went and she came.'*]. 'She repeatedly went and came until she found decent people to accompany.' (*Shabbos* 113b).

The *Midrash* interprets this to mean that she went back and forth to 'mark off', i.e. familiarize herself, with the country lanes, so as not to lose her way on her return (*Rashi*).

According to *Malbim*, the prox-

הַקֹּצְרִים וַיִּקֶר מִקְרֶהָ חֶלְקַת הַשָּׂדֶה
ד־ו ד לְבֹעַז אֲשֶׁר מִמִּשְׁפַּחַת אֱלִימֶלֶךְ: וְהִנֵּה־
בֹעַז בָּא מִבֵּית לֶחֶם וַיֹּאמֶר לַקּוֹצְרִים
יהוה עִמָּכֶם וַיֹּאמְרוּ לוֹ יְבָרֶכְךָ יהוה:
ה וַיֹּאמֶר בֹּעַז לְנַעֲרוֹ הַנִּצָּב עַל־הַקּוֹצְרִים
ו לְמִי הַנַּעֲרָה הַזֹּאת: וַיַּעַן הַנַּעַר הַנִּצָּב עַל־

imity of these verbs suggest that as soon as she left she arrived — i.e. the field of Boaz to which she went was very near her home.

Rav Alkabetz sees in these words what must have been a brief account of her daily schedule: i.e. 'she would go and return daily until the harvest was over.'

Rav Arama interprets it simply: *'she went'* — i.e. she left her home, *'and she came'* — i.e. she arrived at the field.

וַתְּלַקֵּט בַּשָּׂדֶה אַחֲרֵי הַקֹּצְרִים — *And [she] gleaned in the field behind the harvesters.* Although it was morning, the time when other poor people were involved in the more productive gathering of פֵּאָה, *Pe'ah* [see *Leviticus* 19:9-10; *Deut.* 24:19], Ruth limited herself to לֶקֶט [leket] *gleaning,* and she was directly *'behind the harvesters,'* because there was no one else *gleaning* at the time *(Malbim).*

She limited her gleaning to the grain the harvesters left *behind* them — i.e. that which they definitely and undoubtedly discarded; also, she stayed in back of them out of modesty, so no one would glance at her *(Rav Gakkun).*

וַיִּקֶר מִקְרֶהָ — *her fate made her happen.* [This translation is in consonance with the profound philosophy of *Rav S.R. Hirsch* as

expressed in his *Commentary* on Genesis 24:12]: 'Nothing is farther from the Jewish concept of 'מִקְרֶה' [*'happening'*] than the idea of *'chance,'* with which it is associated. Rather, it refers to those moments of one's life that he himself did not direct but which directed him; they were only events which were not expected, not reckoned on, not intended, but which, all the more, could be the most intentional messages sent by the One Who directs and brings about all things.'

The *Malbim* notes that the fact that she was gleaning in the field of Boaz would seem to be nothing more than coincidence. The verse stresses, however, that it was מִקְרֶה, *'her'* fate i.e. the apparent coincidence was divinely arranged with *her* benefit in mind. By *'chancing'* upon the field of Boaz, she was implementing the heavenly plan to build the royal house of Israel.

אֲשֶׁר מִמִּשְׁפַּחַת אֱלִימֶלֶךְ—*Who was of the family of Elimelech,* who—prophetically—would prove ready to exercise his right as גּוֹאֵל, *redeemer,* and would יַבְּמָהּ, *marry her,* and ultimately father the Davidic dynasty *(Malbim).*

4. וְהִנֵּה־בֹעַז בָּא — *Behold, Boaz had arrived.* He had returned to his field after completion of the mourning

behind the harvesters, and her fate made her happen
upon a parcel of land belonging to Boaz, who was of
the family of Elimelech.

⁴ Behold, Boaz arrived from Bethlehem. He greet-
ed the harvesters, 'HASHEM be with you!' And
they answered him: 'May HASHEM bless you!' ⁵ Boaz
then said to his servant who was overseeing the
harvesters: 'To whom does that young woman

period for his wife (*Iggeres Shmu-el*).

The word וְהִנֵּה, '*behold,*' suggests something unusual. Boaz's coming to the field was unusual, and it was the guiding hand of Divine Providence that led him there on that particular day in order to meet Ruth. Also, Boaz is credited by the Sages with originating the custom of greeting one's neighbor in the Name of HASHEM so as to instill into the hearts of that lawless generation [see Comm. 1:1] the all-pervading presence of God as the Source of mankind's welfare. The custom was introduced that day with the sanction of the Sages in Bethlehem (*Malbim*), and with the intimated approval of the Heavenly Beth Din (*Midrash*).

יְבָרֶכְךָ ה' — *May HASHEM bless you.* '*May He bless you with an abundant harvest!*' (*Ibn Ezra*).

Boaz had just been widowed and the Sages consider הַשָּׁרוּי בְּלֹא אִשָּׁה — one who dwells without a wife, as שָׁרוּי בְּלֹא בְּרָכָה — one who dwells without 'blessing'. They greeted him, therefore, 'יְבָרֶכְךָ ה — 'may HASHEM 'bless' you with a worthy wife' (*Iggeres Shmuel*).

Rav Alkabetz observes that the workers did not *initiate* the greeting because one does not greet a

mourner; he greeted first and they responded.

5. לְמִי הַנַּעֲרָה הַזֹּאת — *To whom does that young woman belong?* i.e. '*is she fit to enter the Assembly of HASHEM?*'

The *Talmud* asks: 'Was it then Boaz's practice to inquire about young girls? [Surely he didn't inquire about *every* girl gleaning in the fields!] — Rav Eleazar answered: Her [*halachic*] knowledge and exemplary conduct caught his attention. She would glean two ears [of grain that fell from the harvesters' hands] but she would not glean three [in accordance with the law in *Mishnah Pe'ah* 6:5] (*Shabbos 113b*).

'When he noticed her modesty, he inquired about her. She would stand while gleaning the standing ears and sit while gleaning the fallen ears; the other women hitched up their skirts, and she kept hers down; the other women jested with the harvesters, while she remained reserved; the other women gathered from *between* the sheaves, while she gathered only from that which was definitely abandoned' (*Midrash*).

According to the *Malbim* who commented [verse 3] that Ruth was the only woman gleaning in the

הַקּוֹצְרִים וַיֹּאמַר נַעֲרָה מוֹאֲבִיָּה הִיא
הַשָּׁבָה עִם־נָעֳמִי מִשְּׂדֵי מוֹאָב: וַתֹּאמֶר
אֲלַקֳטָה־נָּא וְאָסַפְתִּי בָעֳמָרִים אַחֲרֵי
הַקּוֹצְרִים וַתָּבוֹא וַתַּעֲמוֹד מֵאָז הַבֹּקֶר
וְעַד־עַתָּה זֶה שִׁבְתָּהּ הַבַּיִת מְעָט: וַיֹּאמֶר

---

field at the time, her presence was obvious and Boaz readily noticed her. He assumed that she was related to one of the harvesters who had cleared the field of the other paupers so she could glean alone. This aroused his curiosity and he inquired about her identity.

Some commentators feel that Boaz was interested in finding out if she was married or single, but he was ashamed to pose the question explicitly lest he be suspected of harboring unseemly thoughts about her. Instead he asked seemingly innocent questions about the identity of a stranger who was obviously new to Bethlehem, confident that the reply would supply the information he sought (Iggeres Shmuel).

The Dubna Maggid points out that just as Ruth's 'coincidental choice' of Boaz's field [verse 3] and Boaz's unusual visit to his field on that particular day were acts of Divine Providence, so, too, was his notice of her and his inquiry about her upon his arrival — immediately after he greeted his men and before even asking about the progress of the harvest — also an act of Divine Providence.

6. וַיַּעַן הַנַּעַר הַנִּצָּב עַל־הַקּוֹצְרִים — The servant who was overseeing the harvesters replied. His position as overseer and trusted employee is repeated to emphasize that he responded to Boaz's inquiry in a most

familiar and intimate manner [see Midrash further] (Nachal Eshkol).

נַעֲרָה מוֹאֲבִיָּה הִיא — 'She is a Moabite girl' — 'and yet you say her conduct is praiseworthy and modest? Her mother-in-law instructed her well' (Midrash). i.e. 'her good manners are not her own,' the overseer responded. 'Her seemingly modest behavior was drilled into her by her mother-in-law' (Torah T'mimah).

The overseer tried, by many means to dissuade Boaz from showing interest in the girl. He replied that she is a נַעֲרָה, a young woman and was too young for Boaz [who was eighty years old at the time! Despite the fact that, according to the Midrash, she was forty years old, her beauty was that of a young girl.] Additionally, she was מוֹאֲבִיָּה, a Moabite, and as such not permitted in marriage (for the law of 'Moabite not Moabitess' was not yet widely known [see Introduction]). The overseer also suggested that she was still a Moabite at heart: her conversion had not been sincerely motivated out of love of God or desire to 'find shelter under His wings,' but rather out of love for Naomi (Iggeres Shmuel).

'Also,' the overseer added, 'her luck is bad — she buried her husband and is destitute' (Zos Nechemasi).

The overseer said: 'Furthermore

belong?' 6 'She is a Moabite girl,' the servant who was overseeing the harvesters replied, ' — the one that returned with Naomi from the fields of Moab; 7 and she had said: "Please let me glean, and gather among the sheaves behind the harvesters." So she came, and has been on her feet since the morning until now; except for her resting a little in the hut.'

(even if her marriage to a Jew were permitted), are there no *Jewish* girls for someone as important as Boaz to marry? — Girls *not* brought up amidst the miserliness of the Moabites?' (*Rashba haLevi*).

Alshich notes that the overseer probably did not dare verbalize these jibes at Ruth to his master; the propriety of the master-servant relationship would not have allowed it. Rather, from the wording and tone of the overseer's response Boaz inferred his displeasure.

הַשָּׁבָה עִם נָעֳמִי מִשְּׂדֵי מוֹאָב — *The one that returned with Naomi from the fields of Moab.* According to the *Malbim's* interpretation of the episode, the overseer responded: 'Don't wonder why I allow a foreign Moabite woman to glean in your field. *She is the one that returned with Naomi;* she converted, and as a Jew is entitled to glean.'

The *Iggeres Shmuel* stresses the positive in the overseer's response: '*She is a young Moabite woman,'* — she is young and capable of childbearing; '*a Moabitess*' — female and thus not under the ban of 'Moabite'; '*the one who returned with Naomi,*' — the sincerity of her conversion is beyond reproach, for she returned with an impoverished Naomi, leaving her country and royal ancestry behind.

7. וַתֹּאמֶר — *And she had said.* [This is a continuation of the overseer's response to Boaz.]. . .

אֲלַקֳטָה־נָא — *Please let me glean.* i.e. the *leket* [gleaning] of the sheaves (*Rashi*).

Note how even though gleaning was a legal right granted by the Torah to the impoverished, for which no permission is required, Ruth nevertheless displayed good manners and modesty by first asking permission (*Iggeres Shmuel*).

וְאָסַפְתִּי בָעֳמָרִים אַחֲרֵי הַקּוֹצְרִים — *And [I will] gather among the sheaves 'forgotten' stalks after the harvesters,* i.e. the שִׁכְחָה, i.e. a stalk overlooked or 'forgotten' by the harvesters (*Rashi*).

A different interpretation:
'I don't want charity; I'll even pay you for the privilege of gleaning by *helping the harvesters gather the sheaves*' (*Iggeres Shmuel*).

וַתָּבוֹא וַתַּעֲמוֹד — *So she came and has been on her feet.* — Diligently involved with her needs (*Ibn Ezra*).

'She has been working all along until this very moment, just prior to your arrival' (*Malbim*).

זֶה שִׁבְתָּהּ הַבַּיִת מְעָט — *Except for her resting a little in the hut.* [The translation of the very obscure Hebrew follows *Ibn Ezra* and *Malbim*].

According to the *Midrash*: 'She gathered a quantity — barely

בֹּעַז אֶל־רוּת הֲלֹוא שָׁמַעַתְּ בִּתִּי אַל־
תֵּלְכִי לִלְקֹט בְּשָׂדֶה אַחֵר וְגַם לֹא־
תַעֲבוּרִי מִזֶּה וְכֹה תִדְבָּקִין עִם־נַעֲרֹתָי:
ט עֵינַיִךְ בַּשָּׂדֶה אֲשֶׁר־יִקְצֹרוּן וְהָלַכְתְּ
אַחֲרֵיהֶן הֲלוֹא צִוִּיתִי אֶת־הַנְּעָרִים
לְבִלְתִּי נָגְעֵךְ וְצָמִת וְהָלַכְתְּ אֶל־הַכֵּלִים

---

enough for two — for her who was in the house [Naomi] since she was waiting for it.' [The language of the *Midrash*, too, is obscure. The above rendering follows *Mattanos Kehunah*.] The *Torah T'mimah* comments that according to the *Midrash*, the overseer misunderstood the question, and feared that Boaz was angry with him for allowing this stranger to enter the field. He defended himself by saying that she gleaned only a small amount and gave it to Naomi who had remained home, and for whom there was no other form of sustenance.

8. וַיֹּאמֶר בֹּעַז — *Then Boaz said.* [Having heard that the girl is Naomi's daughter-in-law, he displayed special interest in her, but apparently did not reveal that he was a relative].

הֲלֹוא שָׁמַעַתְּ בִּתִּי — *Hear me well, my daughter.* [Lit. 'have you not heard, my daughter?'].

Boaz said: You heard me discussing you with my overseer. Don't think I inquired about you because of any displeasure at your being here. To the contrary! I insist that you stay on and glean in my fields exclusively ...' (*Iggeres Shmuel*).

According to Pri Chaim (who holds that the overseer spoke positively about Ruth): 'You have

surely heard, my daughter, what the overseer said about you and how, impressed with your modest ways, he allowed you to glean here.'

בִּתִּי — *My daughter.* [A natural way for an elderly man to address a woman much younger than he. It also suggests that he would now treat her in a paternal fashion. (See *comment* end of verse 2, s.v. בִּתִּי]

A question arises:

Is this the same righteous Boaz lauded by the Sages? Ruth and Naomi were his closest kin; he should have offered them his home and supported them in dignity and comfort rather than just allowing Ruth the 'privilege' of exercising a pauper's legal right to glean the harvest!

—As soon as Boaz met Ruth he was told of her modest behavior and he was greatly impressed. But she was a foreigner and he wanted to assure himself, first hand, of her integrity, so he put her to the test. Had her conversion been insincere and had it been motivated by the knowledge that her relative, Boaz, would treat her royally, her reaction to his offer would have revealed her as a fraud. Instead she reacted superbly — like the righteous person she truly was [See also Commentary on 2:1] (*Rav Arama*).

אַל־תֵּלְכִי לִלְקֹט בְּשָׂדֶה אַחֵר — *Do not*

8 *Then Boaz said to Ruth: 'Hear me well, my daughter. Do not go to glean in another field, and don't leave here, but stay here close to my maidens. 9 Keep your eyes on the field which they are harvesting and follow them. I have ordered the young men not to molest you. Should you get thirsty,*

---

*go to glean in another field.' '*You may not be welcome by the owner' *(Malbim).*

Boaz said: 'A poor person leaves one field for another for two reasons: the crop is exhausted; or the inhospitality of the owner forces him to leave. Neither reason applies here, therefore: *Do not go to glean in another field ...' (Pri Chaim).*

The *Midrash,* interpreting the verse on a more lofty plane explains 'field' allegorically: '*Do not go to glean in another 'spiritual' field —* 'Thou shalt have no other gods before Me' [Exodus 20:3].

וְגַם לֹא־תַעֲבוּרִי מִזֶּה — *Also, don't leave here.* 'Even to another one of my own fields' *(Malbim).*

'Reside here and don't return home until the harvest is over' *(Rav Arama).*

וְכֹה תִדְבָּקִי עִם־נַעֲרֹתָי — *Stay here close to my maidens.* [Lit. 'and right here shall you cleave to my maidens']. 'Stay on the side of my field where the girls are working; not on the other side with the men' *(Malbim).*

9. עֵינַיִךְ בַּשָּׂדֶה — *Keep your eyes on the field.* [Lit. 'your eyes on the field!'] —Keep your eyes on the field that the girls are harvesting *(Malbim).*

Boaz recognized Ruth as a צִדְקָנִית, a righteous woman whose עַיִן טוֹב, 'generous eye' [antonym of

עַיִן הָרַע, 'evil eye'] will cause blessing to descend upon the object of her generosity as scripture says: טוֹב עַיִן הוּא יְבֹרָךְ, *He that has a generous eye shall bring blessing* [lit. 'shall be blessed'] *(Proverbs 22:9).* Knowing that Ruth would be a source of blessing to whatever field provided her sustenance, Boaz asked her to '*keep her eyes on the field during the harvest'* so that a blessing would descend on the crop *(Iggeres Shmuel).*

'*Keep your eyes on the field —* and as soon as it is harvested be the first to glean.' Boaz was planning to tell his men to deliberately discard sheaves for Ruth to glean [verse 16], and he wanted to make sure that she would benefit from his largesse by being on the scene first *(Kol Yaakov).*

וְהָלַכְתְּ אַחֲרֵיהֶן — *And follow them* [אַחֲרֵיהֶן — is feminine] i.e. 'follow the maidens.' [They will harvest, and you will glean after them] *(Malbim).*

לְבִלְתִּי נָגְעֵךְ — *Not to molest you.* Even if you are all alone in the field *(Rashba haLevi).*

[נָגְעֵךְ, 'molest you,' can also be understood in the more simple sense: 'not to interfere with you'].

— 'They have been so commanded by the Torah: וְאָהַבְתֶּם אֶת הַגֵּר, 'love the stranger' [Deut. 10:19] *(Midrash Lekach Tov)*

The *Midrash,* which has been

פרק ב
י-יא

י וְשָׁתִית מֵאֲשֶׁר יִשְׁאֲבוּן הַנְּעָרִים: וַתִּפֹּל
עַל־פָּנֶיהָ וַתִּשְׁתַּחוּ אָרְצָה וַתֹּאמֶר אֵלָיו
מַדּוּעַ מָצָאתִי חֵן בְּעֵינֶיךָ לְהַכִּירֵנִי וְאָנֹכִי
יא נָכְרִיָּה: וַיַּעַן בֹּעַז וַיֹּאמֶר לָהּ הֻגֵּד הֻגַּד לִי
כֹּל אֲשֶׁר־עָשִׂית אֶת־חֲמוֹתֵךְ אַחֲרֵי מוֹת
אִישֵׁךְ וַתַּעַזְבִי אָבִיךְ וְאִמֵּךְ וְאֶרֶץ
מוֹלַדְתֵּךְ וַתֵּלְכִי אֶל־עַם אֲשֶׁר לֹא־יָדַעַתְּ

allegorically explaining this verse as an admonition by Boaz for Ruth to be faithful to her new religion [see Comm. end of verse 8], translates לְבִלְתִּי נָגְעֵךְ — 'they will not discourage you.'

וְהָלַכְתְּ אֶל־הַכֵּלִים—Go to the jugs. 'If you get thirsty, don't hesitate to drink from the jugs of water fetched by the young men' (Rashi).

'Go yourself, and don't have the young men bring it to you. The less you associate with them, the better (Rav Yavetz).

מֵאֲשֶׁר יִשְׁאֲבוּן הַנְּעָרִים — From what the young men have drawn. 'And don't worry that the men might be angry; I already warned them לְבִלְתִּי נָגְעֵךְ not to bother you' (Iggeres Shmuel).

The well with the good drinking water was far from the fields and laborious to fetch from. Therefore, the men who brought the water would keep it for themselves. The poor would have to drink inferior water drawn from closer wells. Boaz told Ruth that if she became thirsty she should not hesitate to drink from the men's jugs, as they had been instructed by him personally not to interfere with her (Malbim).

10. ....וַתִּפֹּל עַל־פָּנֶיהָ — Then she fell

on her face ... bowing to the ground. In humble gratitude for his graciousness and cordiality towards her (Alshich).

At the same time she bowed down and praised God for His beneficence (Meishiv Nefesh).

מַדּוּעַ...וְאָנֹכִי נָכְרִיָּה Why ... though I am a foreigner. 'What did you see in me that made you take special notice and inquire about me though I am a נָכְרִיָּה, an ordinary stranger. Many other women who glean here also are strangers, but no one pays any special attention to them' (Iggeres Shmuel).

According to Pri Chaim, Ruth was not aware that Boaz was a relative. Her question was prompted by the fact that she thought it unusual for a stranger to be showered with such attention.

The Targum translates: 'How is it that I have found favor in your eyes? — I am of a foreign nation, a daughter of Moab, a nation not fit to enter into קְהַל ה', the Assembly of HASHEM.'

11. [Boaz responds that he has heard of her extraordinary and magnanimous deeds in the exemplary way she treated her mother-in-law, and her leaving

go to the jugs and drink from what the young men have drawn.'

10 Then she fell on her face, bowing down to the ground, and said to him: 'Why have I found favor in your eyes that you should take special note of me though I am a foreigner?'

11 Boaz replied and said to her: 'I have been fully

Boaz's generosity

informed of all that you have done for your mother-in-law after the death of your husband; how you left your father and mother and the land of your birth and went to a people you had never known before.

home and family to embrace Judaism.]

הֻגֵּד הֻגַּד לִי — *I have been fully told.* The verb הגד is doubled for emphasis. 'Your deeds are so widely discussed that *I have been hearing about them in the house and in the fields* i.e from all sides' (*Midrash*).

Ruth considered herself unworthy of Boaz's attention and she sincerely wanted him to explain the reason for his unexpected kindness; therefore, she posed the question to him. He responded that she — for her goodness — deserves much more kindness than he is capable of performing for her, and that whatever he did for her was miniscule compared to the rewards which would be bestowed upon her from God [see next verse] (*Alshich; Rashba haLevi*).

כֹּל אֲשֶׁר־עָשִׂית אֶת־חֲמוֹתֵךְ — *All that you have done for your mother-in-law.* Boaz told Ruth that his favorable attitude to her was a result of two things: Firstly, despite the fact that a woman usually has ill feelings toward her mother-in-law, Ruth treated Naomi in an exemplary manner — especially after

Naomi became widowed and forlorn — thus demonstrating a rare nobility of character; and secondly, for having left her parents and homeland to convert, etc. (*Malbim*).

אַחֲרֵי מוֹת אִישֵׁךְ — *After the death of your husband* — 'and certainly during his lifetime' (*Midrash*)

וַתַּעַזְבִי אָבִיךְ וְאִמֵּךְ וְאֶרֶץ מוֹלַדְתֵּךְ — *How you left your father and mother and the land of your birth.* i.e. 'Your conversion is remarkable because, in the face of coercion to remain in Moab, you freely left your parents' home and the country of your birth and, with no material considerations, you came to a strange country (*Alshich*).

אֲשֶׁר לֹא־יָדַעַתְּ תְּמוֹל שִׁלְשֹׁם — *Which you have never known before* [lit. 'which you have not known yesterday and the day before']. Boaz said; 'the law permitting female Moabite converts to marry Jews was popularized only in the last few days, and you could not possibly have been aware of it when you converted. Therefore, you could only have been motivated by the purest religious motivations with no ulterior motives' (*Rashba haLevi*).

יב תְּמוֹל שִׁלְשֹׁם: יְשַׁלֵּם יהוה פָּעֳלֵךְ וּתְהִי מַשְׂכֻּרְתֵּךְ שְׁלֵמָה מֵעִם יהוה אֱלֹהֵי יִשְׂרָאֵל אֲשֶׁר־בָּאת לַחֲסוֹת תַּחַת־כְּנָפָיו: יג וַתֹּאמֶר אֶמְצָא־חֵן בְּעֵינֶיךָ אֲדֹנִי כִּי נִחַמְתָּנִי וְכִי דִבַּרְתָּ עַל־לֵב שִׁפְחָתֶךָ

12. יְשַׁלֵּם ה' פָּעֳלֵךְ — *May HASHEM reward your actions.* [lit. *HASHEM will repay your actions*] The verse may be interpreted either as a prayer for divine reward or as a promise of it. One who performs acts of חֶסֶד, *kindliness*, with the poor is likened to one who lends money to God, and He assuredly repays all His debts (*Iggeres Shmuel*).

The *Malbim* differentiates between פּוֹעֵל, an artisan who is paid for a specific project, e.g. a tailor for a garment; and שׂוֹכֵר, a salaried employee who is paid for a period of time regardless of actual production. . .

Thus Boaz said: 'For the kindness you have shown your mother-in-law, *HASHEM will reward your actions* [פָּעֳלֵךְ] as an artisan is rewarded for whatever handiwork he has actually produced. But for accepting the Torah and the service of God as a שׂוֹכֵר, an employee, of HASHEM, so to speak, you have come under God's wings — under His perpetual protection and care — you will be paid your 'salary' [מַשְׂכֻּרְתֵּךְ] fully and regularly' (*Malbim*).

Only God can reward you, for no human act is capable of rewarding you commensurate with your deed (*Rav Arama*).

וּתְהִי מַשְׂכֻּרְתֵּךְ שְׁלֵמָה — *And may your payment be full* [lit. *and your

payment will be full*]. The *Iggeres Shmuel* interprets this verse as follows: *HASHEM will definitely reward your actions* in this world; *and your payment will be full,* boundless, *from HASHEM, the God of Israel,* in the world to come when you will bask directly in His radiance. And all of this will be *in reward for* having converted with a sincere heart, *to seek shelter under His wings. . .*

The *Iggeres Shmuel* further comments that Ruth's merits might be greater than those of Abraham. Of Abraham's merits, the Sages sometimes note that תָּמָה זְכוּת אָבוֹת, the merit of the Patriarchs [which act as a shield] is exhausted (*Shabbos 55a*); but of Ruth's merit Boaz blessed her that it be שְׁלֵמָה, *full,* i.e. eternally undiminishable. Abraham left his father's house only in response to God's call, לֶךְ לְךָ, *'Get thee out'* [Gen. 1:1] but Ruth left on her own initiative — without a divine call, and despite the dissuasion of her mother-in-law, — in order to come under the wings of HASHEM.

אֲשֶׁר־בָּאת לַחֲסוֹת תַּחַת־כְּנָפָיו — *Under whose wings you have come to seek refuge.* [Commenting on the anthropomorphic reference to the 'wings' of God, the Midrash enumerates the many anthropomorphic references to 'wings' in תנ"ך, the Scriptures]:

12 *May HASHEM reward your actions, and may your payment be full from HASHEM, the God of Israel, under whose wings you have come to seek refuge.'*
13 *Then she said: 'May I continue to find favor in your eyes, my lord, because you have comforted me, and because you have spoken to the heart of your*

Rav Abin said, We gather from Scriptures that there are wings to the earth (Isaiah 24:16); wings to the sun (Malachi 3:20); wings to the חַיּוֹת, *celestial beings* (Ezekiel 3:13); wings to the כְּרוּבִים, *cherubim* (I Kings 8:7); wings to the שְׂרָפִים, *seraphim* (Isaiah 6:2) . . .

'Come and see how great is the power of צַדִּיקִים, the righteous, and the power of צְדָקָה, righteousness, and charity, and how great the power of גּוֹמְלֵי חֶסֶד, those who do kindly deeds, for they find shelter neither in the shadow of the morning, nor of the sun, the *chayos*, the *cherubim*, or the *seraphim*, but *under the wings of Him at whose word the world was created'* (Midrash).

Boaz wished her that she should never have to rely on flesh and blood for sustenance, but on HASHEM alone *(Zos Nechemasi).*

The *Dubna Maggid* elaborates, in his *Kol Yaakov,* on the concept of reward for performing *mitzvos,* and sums up that the highest reward for any *mitzvah* is the satisfaction of the performance of that mitzvah which is a reward and incentive unto itself. Thus, Boaz told Ruth: Have no fear, my daughter, HASHEM will repay your actions: but may you reach a level of righteousness sufficient to appreciate that the most 'complete payment' from HASHEM, the God of Israel, is the very fact *that you have*

been inspired to seek shelter under His wings. '(Also *Vilna Gaon*)

Boaz's blessing was that in addition to rewarding Ruth for the performance of every *mitzvah* she would perform, God should also additionally reward her for the crucial decision upon which all her future good deeds ultimately hinged — the decision to 'come under His wings' *(Chidah, quoting his father).*

13. אֶמְצָא־חֵן בְּעֵינֶיךָ אֲדֹנִי — *May I continue to find favor in your eyes.* [The word *'continue'* is not in the Hebrew but is so understood by the commentators].

After he told her his reasons for favoring her, she expressed hope that she will continue to find favor in his sight *(Malbim).*

כִּי נִחַמְתָּנִי —*Because you have comforted me* — by your promise of care and divine compassion *(Vilna Gaon; Malbim).*

The *Targum* adds, 'and declared me fit to enter the congregation of HASHEM.'

Even if Boaz were to do nothing for her, his words of comfort were sufficient to win her gratitude *(Alshich).*

וְכִי דִבַּרְתָּ עַל־לֵב שִׁפְחָתֶךָ — *And because you have spoken to the heart of your maid-servant,* i.e. 'words which are receptive to the heart' *(Rashi* on Gen. 50:21).

Not merely אֶל לֵב, *to the heart,*

פרק ב

יד־טו

יד וְאָנֹכִי לֹא אֶהְיֶה כְּאַחַת שִׁפְחֹתֶךָ: וַיֹּאמֶר
לָהּ בֹּעַז לְעֵת הָאֹכֶל גֹּשִׁי הֲלֹם וְאָכַלְתְּ
מִן־הַלֶּחֶם וְטָבַלְתְּ פִּתֵּךְ בַּחֹמֶץ וַתֵּשֶׁב
מִצַּד הַקֹּצְרִים וַיִּצְבָּט־לָהּ קָלִי וַתֹּאכַל
טו וַתִּשְׂבַּע וַתֹּתַר: וַתָּקָם לְלַקֵּט וַיְצַו בֹּעַז
אֶת־נְעָרָיו לֵאמֹר גַּם בֵּין הָעֳמָרִים תְּלַקֵּט

but עַל לֵב, [lit. 'upon the heart'], i.e.
that your words prevailed over my
feelings (Rav S.R. Hirsch, ibid).

שִׁפְחֹתֶךָ — your maid-servant. [A
deferential term used in Scriptures
by women when addressing gentle-
men (comp. עַבְדְּךָ, 'your servant'
used by men.)]

וְאָנֹכִי לֹא אֶהְיֶה כְּאַחַת שִׁפְחֹתֶךָ —
Though I am not as worthy as one
of your maid-servants. [This translation follows Rashi, and Malbim.
Literally the words mean: 'And I
will not be as one of your maid-
servants.']

Ibn Ezra seems to translate: I am
not even worthy enough to be as
one of your maidservants.

You have indeed comforted me
by your kind words, for I have
never considered myself, to be as
worthy in your eyes as one of your
maid-servants (Iggeres Shmuel).

A different aproach is taken by
Mashal Umelitza: Ruth heard
Boaz's promise to her of divine
reward for her good actions. She
answered him: Thank you, my
lord, for your attempt to comfort
me with promises of reward, but it
is unnecessary, I am not like one of
your maid-servants who perform
good deeds for the sake of reward;
my intentions are only לְשֵׁם שָׁמַיִם,
"for the sake of Heaven."

14. לְעֵת הָאֹכֶל — At mealtime. By

this time their conversation had
stretched so long that dinner was
being served (Alschich).

He did not invite her earlier
because he was afraid she would
demur; he waited until everyone except her was eating, and then he invited her (Iggeres Shmuel).

גֹּשִׁי הֲלֹם — Come over here. i.e. to
Boaz's table (Pri Chaim).

According to the Midrash: 'Approach to royalty.' [prophetically
intimating to her the kings who
would one day descend from her]
(Midrash).

וְאָכַלְתְּ מִן־הַלֶּחֶם — And partake of
the bread. i.e. the bread of the
harvesters (Midrash). Share our
meal with us (Alschich).

וְטָבַלְתְּ פִּתֵּךְ בַּחֹמֶץ — And dip your
morsel in the vinegar. To refresh
yourself from the heat (Ibn Ezra).

Harvesters use vinegar to allay
the thirst, cool the body, and
stimulate the digestive system. Boaz
was afraid that, as a princess, Ruth
was not accustomed to spending so
many hours in the sun. He suggested vinegar to avoid sunstroke
(Rav Alkabetz).

וַתֵּשֶׁב מִצַּד הַקֹּצְרִים — So she sat
beside the reapers. Not in front of
them, so they should not glance at
her; not in back of them so she
should not watch them; but
alongside them (Alschich; Midrash).

maid-servant—though I am not even as worthy as one of your maid-servants.'

14 At mealtime, Boaz said to her, 'Come over here and partake of the bread, and dip your morsel in the vinegar.' So she sat beside the harvesters. He handed her parched grain, and she ate and was satisfied, and had some left over.

15 Then she got up to glean, and Boaz ordered his young men, saying: 'Let her glean even among the

---

Boaz invited her to גְּשִׁי הֲלם, *come over here*, and sit with him at the head of the table, but obviously she modestly preferred to station herself *beside the reapers (Malbim).*

וַיִּצְבָּט־לָהּ קָלִי — *He handed her parched grain*. [i.e. Boaz to Ruth] This is the only place in Scripture where this word (וַיִּצְבָּט, *and he handed*) occurs *(Rashi; Ibn Ezra).*

Seeing that she was *sitting beside the reapers* and that she modestly refrained from taking any food, Boaz himself handed the food to her like a gracious host *(Iggeres Shmuel).*

'The verse teaches us that if a man is about to perform a good deed, he should do it with all his heart. For had Boaz known that Scripture would record of him *'he handed her parched grain,'* he would have fed her fatted calves...

'In the past when a man performed a good deed the prophet recorded it, but nowadays when a man performs a good deed who records it? — Elijah records it and the Messiah and the Holy One blessed be He affix His seal to it *(Midrash).*

וַתֹּאכַל וַתִּשְׂבַּע וַתֹּתַר — *And she ate and was satisfied and had some left over.*

According to the *Midrash* [connecting the word קָלִי, *'parched grain'* with קָלִיל, *'a little'*] Boaz gave her just a 'pinch of parched grain between his two fingers', and Ruth's stomach was blessed for she was satisfied with such a small morsel and even had some left over.

Other commentaries, [*Ralbag, Malbim, Rav Alkabetz*], however, interpret this verse that Boaz displayed unusual generosity: he graciously prepared her a portion so abundant that she ate her fill and still had a great deal left over.

Alshich notes that this was the first filling meal she had eaten in a long while.

15. וַתָּקָם לְלַקֵּט — *Then she got up to glean*. Having eaten, she returned to her task with increased vigor *(Alshich.)*

וַיְצַו בֹּעַז אֶת־נְעָרָיו — *Boaz gave orders to his young men*. Boaz's invitation to Ruth was meant as a signal to her that he was ready to support her at his table. He assumed that she would no longer wish to demean herself by gleaning in the fields like a common pauper. But when he saw that she was determined to continue gleaning, he acquiesced to her wishes. Simultaneously, however, he informed his employees that he

טז וְלֹא תַכְלִימוּהָ: וְגַם שֹׁל־תָּשֹׁלּוּ לָהּ מִן־
הַצְּבָתִים וַעֲזַבְתֶּם וְלִקְּטָה וְלֹא תִגְעֲרוּ־
יז בָהּ: וַתְּלַקֵּט בַּשָּׂדֶה עַד־הָעָרֶב וַתַּחְבֹּט
אֵת אֲשֶׁר־לִקֵּטָה וַיְהִי כְּאֵיפָה שְׂעֹרִים:
יח וַתִּשָּׂא וַתָּבוֹא הָעִיר וַתֵּרֶא חֲמוֹתָהּ אֵת
אֲשֶׁר־לִקֵּטָה וַתּוֹצֵא וַתִּתֶּן־לָהּ אֵת אֲשֶׁר־
יט הוֹתִרָה מִשָּׂבְעָהּ: וַתֹּאמֶר לָהּ חֲמוֹתָהּ
אֵיפֹה לִקַּטְתְּ הַיּוֹם וְאָנָה עָשִׂית יְהִי

expected them to treat her especially well (*Pri Chaim*).

גַם בֵּין הָעֳמָרִים תְּלַקֵּט — *Let her glean even among the sheaves*. [i.e. give her a completely free hand]. '*Even if she gleaned from between the sheaves* — which the poor are not legally entitled to — *nevertheless*,' Boaz ordered, '*do not embarrass her*' (*Ralbag*).

וְלֹא תַכְלִימוּהָ — *Do not embarrass her* [Quietly encourage her, and be sympathetic to her situation].

16. שֹׁל־תָּשֹׁלּוּ לָהּ מִן־הַצְּבָתִים — *And even deliberately pull out some for her from the heaps*. Pretend you forgot them (*Rashi*) [He knew that her pride would not permit her to take charity] — 'Rav Yochanan used to deliberately drop coins in order that Rav Shimon bar Abba (who was extremely poor) might 'find' them. Rav Yehudah used to leave lentils about in order that Rav Shimon ben Chalafta might acquire them' (*Midrash*).

Rav Alkebetz stresses the word לָהּ, *for her*, to indicate that Boaz made it clear that when they deliberately pulled out stalks and 'forgot' them, the stalks should be dropped where Ruth could reach them before anyone else.

וְלֹא תִגְעֲרוּ בָהּ — *And don't rebuke her*. [Even though you might not understand my intent, and my request causes you extra work, don't vent your anger at her].

With this Boaz explicitly stated his noble intention to fully sustain her (*Malbim*).

She is a convert — and thus deserving of our compassion (*Nachal Eshkol*).

17. וַתְּלַקֵּט בַּשָּׂדֶה עַד הָעָרֶב — *So she gleaned in the field until evening*.

The verse stresses '*gleaned*' because although the harvesters were deliberately dropping large amounts for her as Boaz ordered, Ruth limited herself to the meager gleanings she was entitled to by law [i.e. a maximum of two stalks at a time], and avoided Boaz's charity. Nevertheless, the verse tells us, her efforts were greatly blessed, because she worked hard and managed to gather over an *ephah* of barley (*Iggeres Shmuel*).

For this reason she had to glean '*until evening*'; had she availed herself of Boaz's charity she could have finished much earlier (*Ibn Yachya*).

sheaves; do not embarrass her. ¹⁶ And even
deliberately pull out some for her from the heaps and
leave them for her to glean; don't rebuke her.'

¹⁷ So she gleaned in the field until evening, and she
beat out what she had gleaned — it came to about an
ephah of barley. ¹⁸ She carried it and came to the
city. Her mother-in-law saw what she had gleaned,
and she took out and gave her what she had left over
after eating her fill.

¹⁹ 'Where did you glean today?' her mother-in-law
asked her. 'Where did you work? May the one that

וַתַּחְבֹּט אֵת אֲשֶׁר לִקֵּטָה — *And she
beat out what she had gleaned* — to
make it easier to carry. The burden
of carrying home the ears still attached to the stalks would have
been too much for her (*Midrash
Lekach Tov*).

The *Iggeres Shmuel* also suggests
that Ruth was afraid to travel the
roads alone. Had she not beaten the
stalks into flour, she would have
had to make two or three trips carrying stalks. This she wanted to
avoid.

וַיְהִי כְּאֵיפָה שְׂעֹרִים — *And it came to
about an ephah of barley.* Very
heavy to carry (*Ibn Ezra*).

An *ephah* equals three *seahs* [see
Exodus 17:36 where an *ephah*
equals ten *omers*. (An omer is a
day's food for one person). Thus,
Ruth's yield from her first day of
gleaning was sufficient to feed
Naomi and herself for five days — a
rather impressive amount].

18. וַתִּשָּׂא וַתָּבוֹא הָעִיר — *She
carried it and came to the city.* She
went directly home without stop-
ping or detouring (*Midrash Lekach
Tov*).

She went to Naomi that day to
ask permission to accept Boaz' invitation and remain henceforth with
his maidens (*Rav Arama*).

וַתֵּרֶא חֲמוֹתָהּ אֵת אֲשֶׁר לִקֵּטָה — *Her
mother-in-law saw what she had
gleaned.* Ruth had worked so quickly, that darkness had not yet
descended, and Naomi was still able
to see Ruth approaching by
daylight (*Iggeres Shmuel*).

Ruth did not go about pompous-
ly displaying her gleanings; her
mother-in-law looked into her
packages to see (*Rav Alkebetz*).

אֵת אֲשֶׁר הוֹתִרָה מִשָּׂבְעָהּ — *what she
had left over after eating her fill.* Iggeres Shmuel stresses 'her' fill — i.e.
someone else might have eaten
more; Ruth purposely left food for
her mother-in-law.

19. אֵיפֹה לִקַּטְתְּ הַיּוֹם — *Where did
you glean today?* Seeing such an
abundant load, Naomi knew that
the gleaning had to have been done
in the field of a particularly friendly
owner (*Alkabetz*).

וְאָנָה עָשִׂית — *And where did you
work?* Besides the gleanings, Ruth

מַכִּירֵךְ בָּרוּךְ וַתַּגֵּד לַחֲמוֹתָהּ אֶת אֲשֶׁר־
עָשְׂתָה עִמּוֹ וַתֹּאמֶר שֵׁם הָאִישׁ אֲשֶׁר
כ עָשִׂיתִי עִמּוֹ הַיּוֹם בֹּעַז: וַתֹּאמֶר נָעֳמִי
לְכַלָּתָהּ בָּרוּךְ הוּא לַיהוָה אֲשֶׁר לֹא־עָזַב
חַסְדּוֹ אֶת־הַחַיִּים וְאֶת־הַמֵּתִים וַתֹּאמֶר

also brought back leftovers from the afternoon meal to which Boaz had invited her. Naomi therefore asked *'where did you glean today, yielding such a large produce; and where did you work,* even bringing back left-over food?' (*Iggeres Shmuel*).

The quality of the leftovers made it obvious that Ruth could not have merely spent the day gleaning, but must have performed some extra work to have earned so sumptuous a meal; on the other hand, the sheer abundance of her gleanings bespoke a full day of toil in the field. Therefore, in bewilderment, Naomi asked her both questions: *'where did you glean today and where did you work? —* a kind person must have befriended you' (*Malbim*).

The *Iggeres Shmuel* notes that it was unusual for the gleaners to beat the stalks while still in the field; usually the landowner would not allow it, and they would have to carry the stalks home and beat it there. Seeing Ruth coming home with beaten grain, Naomi was prompted to ask her: *'Where did you work?* Which owner was kind enough to allow you to beat the stalks in his field?'

יְהִי מַכִּירֵךְ בָּרוּךְ — *May the one that gave you such generous notice be blessed.* [Lit. 'May he that recognized you be blessed']. 'May blessing alight upon the head of the

field-owner who so generously permitted you to glean in his field!' (*Rashi*).

'I hope that this man's intentions are blessed and that it was not lust which prompted him to be so extraordinarily kind to you' (*Iggeres Shmuel*).

An alternate interpretation: Naomi said: The large amount you gleaned in one day is quite impressive; how did you manage it? יְהִי מַכִּירֵךְ בָּרוּךְ! — I am certain that the *'man who will come to know you'* some day as his wife *'will indeed be blessed'* — having such an industrious wife as you! (*Vilna Gaon*)

Ruth modestly *'told her mother-in-law all that had occurred'* — that it was not her zeal which allowed her to glean so much; but the kindness of Boaz (*Alshich*)

וַתַּגֵּד לַחֲמוֹתָהּ — *And she told her mother-in-law.* וַתַּגֵּד, 'told' has a harsher connotation than וַתֹּאמֶר, *said.* Ruth was angered by Naomi's suggestion that the land-owner's intentions were not honorable, so she detailed all that had happened and revealed his name (*Iggeres Shmuel*).

Ruth explained that the special kindness was not for any labor performed by her, but rather because the landowner was impressed with the stories circulating about her (*Malbim*).

שֵׁם הָאִישׁ ... בֹּעַז — *The name of the man with whom I worked is Boaz.*

*took such generous notice of you be blessed.' So she
told her mother-in-law whom she had worked by,
and said: 'The name of the man by whom I worked
today is Boaz.'*

*²⁰ Naomi said to her daughter-in-law: 'Blessed be
he of HASHEM, for not failing in his kindness to the
living or to the dead! 'The man is closely related to*

'As the judge of Israel, Boaz was greatly impressed with the rumors about my special relationship with you and my conversion, so he rewarded me with extra food (*Malbim*).

[Apparently, Ruth was making a simple revelation, still not aware that Boaz was related to them. Naomi, however, was especially delighted at hearing Boaz's name. She felt that Boaz, as a cousin and as a recent widower, might feel obligated to enter into a levirate marriage with Ruth thus perpetuating the name of Machlon.]

אֲשֶׁר עָשִׂיתִי עִמּוֹ — *By whom I worked.* [Lit. 'with whom I wrought']. The *Midrash* comments in a homiletical fashion: The verse does not read אֲשֶׁר עָשָׂה עִמָּדִי, *who has wrought for me*; but אֲשֶׁר עָשִׂיתִי עִמּוֹ, *I have wrought for him.* This teaches us that יוֹתֵר מֵאֲשֶׁר בַּעַל הַבַּיִת עוֹשֶׂה עִם הֶעָנִי, more than the householder does for the poor man, עוֹשֶׂה הֶעָנִי עִם בַּעַל הַבַּיִת, the poor man does for the householder [i.e. the householder benefits more — spiritually — from the charity he dispenses, than the poor man gains — temporally — from the charity he receives from the householder.]

20. בָּרוּךְ הוּא לַה' — *Blessed be he of HASHEM.* When Naomi heard that the man was Boaz she said: This

righteous man has no need of *my* blessing. בָּרוּךְ הוּא לַה' *He is blessed of HASHEM.*

[In the preceding verse she merely blessed him. Now that he was identified as Boaz, she blessed him in God's Name].

אֲשֶׁר לֹא עָזַב חַסְדּוֹ אֶת הַחַיִּים וְאֶת הַמֵּתִים — *For not failing in his kindness to the living or to the dead.* [There is a difference of opinion among the commentators whether the subject of this ambiguous phrase is God or Boaz. The translation follows *Ibn Ezra* and the majority of the commentators according to whom the subject is Boaz].

Naomi blessed Boaz who always sought to do kindness with the living and the dead. The kindness he did with the living (Ruth and Naomi) is obvious; the *kindness he did with the dead* is the gratification that the dead receive beyond the grave when benefits are bestowed upon their living relatives (*Iggeres Shmuel*).

'To the living' — by sustaining us; and *to the dead* — for he will ultimately perform יִבּוּם, *levirate marriage*, with you and he will thus do kindness to the memory of your dead husband' (*Alshich; Pri Chaim*).

According to *Rav Arama*, Naomi said: 'I have been wondering all

כא לָהּ נָעֳמִי קָרוֹב לָנוּ הָאִישׁ מִגֹּאֲלֵנוּ הוּא: **פֶּרֶק ב**
וַתֹּאמֶר רוּת הַמּוֹאֲבִיָּה גַּם כִּי־אָמַר אֵלַי כא-כב
עִם־הַנְּעָרִים אֲשֶׁר־לִי תִּדְבָּקִין עַד אִם־
כב כִּלּוּ אֵת כָּל־הַקָּצִיר אֲשֶׁר־לִי: וַתֹּאמֶר
נָעֳמִי אֶל־רוּת כַּלָּתָהּ טוֹב בִּתִּי כִּי תֵצְאִי

along how this man, famous for his kindness, has ignored us so since our arrival here. But now, seeing 'that he has not failed in his kindness to us, the living, or to the memory of our dead husbands, I truly bless him.'

The subject of the phrase, 'who has not failed in his kindness, may be God. Thus, Naomi blessed him: *May he be blessed of HASHEM who has not failed in His kindness to the living* — in this world; *or to the dead* — in the world to come (*Iggeres Shmuel*).

קָרוֹב לָנוּ הָאִישׁ מִגֹּאֲלֵנוּ הוּא — *This man is closely related to us, he is one of our redeeming kinsmen.* The גּוֹאֵל, *redeemer,* is the next of kin who is obligated to redeem the property which his impoverished relative was compelled to sell (see *Leviticus 25:25*).

'I no longer question this man's motives — he is our close relative and he is fulfilling the verse — מִבְּשָׂרְךָ לֹא תִתְעַלָּם, *'do not hide yourself from your own flesh'* [*Isaiah 58:7*] (*Ibn Yachya*).

The *Iggeres Shmuel* quotes a homiletic interpretation: מִגֹּאֲלֵנוּ הוּא — from him will eventually descend our Redeemer, a reference to the Messiah.

21. גַּם כִּי־אָמַר אֵלַי — *What's more, he even said to me.* 'You blessed him for what he did on my behalf.

He deserves your additional blessing for having also invited me to *'stay close to his workers'* (*Rav Yavetz*).

Rav Yehudah Ibn Shushan notes that at first Ruth did not mention Boaz's offer for her to stay with his maidens for fear that Naomi might suspect Boaz of dishonorable, ulterior motives. Once Naomi revealed that Boaz was a close kinsman, however, Ruth was reassured that Boaz was sincere so she confidently related his additional kind offer.

עִם־הַנְּעָרִים אֲשֶׁר־לִי תִּדְבָּקִין — *Stay close to my workers* [lit. 'cleave to my young men.' Our translation follows *Rav Alkabetz*; see below].

[There is a great discrepancy here between Boaz's actual words (*'stay here close to my maidens* — verse 8), and Ruth's version (*stay close to my young men'*). Various interpretation are offered:

The *Midrash,* noting that in this verse her title *'Moabite'* was restored, comments, 'In truth she was still *'a Moabite,'* for Boaz said to her *'stay here close to my maidens,'* while she said, *'to my young men...'*

The *Torah T'mimah* explains the *Midrash* in two possible ways: *'She was still a Moabite'* — and still imbued with the immorality of her upbringing. At the very least, it was very indelicate of her to describe

*us,' Naomi then said to her; 'he is one of our redeem-
ing kinsmen.'*

²¹ *And Ruth the Moabite said: 'What's more, he
even said to me: Stay close to my workers, until they
have finished all my harvest.' ²² Naomi said to her
daughter-in-law Ruth: 'It is fine, my daughter, that
you go out with his young women, so that you will*

Boaz as asking her to keep company
with his young *men*. Scripture
refers to her as a Moabite, as an
implied rebuke as if to say, "Spoken
like a descendent of the nation that
was born in incest." Or, as a
Moabite, Ruth was not intimately
familiar with the Hebrew differ-
entiation between the masculine
and feminine forms. In the Moabite
language, like English, most nouns
do not have separate male and
female forms. Ruth mistakenly used
the masculine form without in-
tending to be suggestive, because,
as the *Midrash* interprets, "*she was
a Moabite!*" Naomi tactfully corrected her mistake [next verse].

Rav Alkabetz feels that Ruth
simply used נְעָרִים as a general term
for *'workers'* without making a distinction between male and female
workers.

The *Simchas haRegel* suggests
that Ruth had become aware of the
recently publicized law permitting
her, as a female Moabite to 'enter
the Assembly of God.' She was, of
course, anxious to tell this to her
mother-in-law, but, out of modesty,
she alluded to it by hinting that
Boaz told her she could now '*cleave
to one of his young men*' i.e. is
henceforth permitted to marry an
Israelite. [See comment of *Simchas
haRegel* next verse].

The *Besuras Eliyahu* notes, that
in any case, the phrase גַם כִּי־אָמַר
אֵלַי *'what's more, he said to me'* is
obscure. He suggests that Ruth's intention was to convey the idea to
Naomi that she held Boaz and his
men in such high esteem that she
remarked, 'I would listen to him,
גַם כִּי אָמַר אֵלַי, *even if her were to
tell me* עִם הַנְּעָרִים אֲשֶׁר לִי תִּדְבָּקִין,
'stay close to my young *men*.'

22. אֶל־רוּת כַּלָּתָהּ טוֹב בִּתִּי — *.. To
Ruth, her daughter-in-law ... fine,
my daughter.* [Note how Naomi's
motherly response is accented in
this verse by the contrasting use of
'mother-in-law' and 'daughter'].

According to the interpretation of
Simchas haRegel [see his comm.
end of previous verse], Naomi
answered: 'Fine, I am overjoyed to
learn that you are now permitted to
marry within the fold. As for the
practical matter of how to respond
to Boaz, yes, you may dwell with his
maidens.'

כִּי תֵצְאִי עִם נַעֲרוֹתָיו — *That you go
out with his young women.* 'I am
sure that if Boaz invited you to associate with his young men he
knows them well and they are
צַדִּיקִים, righteous, and above
reproach. Nevertheless, my motherly advice is '*go out with his young
women*' (*Rashba haLevi*).

עִם־נַעֲרוֹתָיו וְלֹא יִפְגְּעוּ־בָךְ בְּשָׂדֶה אַחֵר:

כג וַתִּדְבַּק בְּנַעֲרוֹת בֹּעַז לְלַקֵּט עַד־כְּלוֹת
קְצִיר הַשְּׂעֹרִים וּקְצִיר הַחִטִּים וַתֵּשֶׁב
אֶת־חֲמוֹתָהּ:

א וַתֹּאמֶר לָהּ נָעֳמִי חֲמוֹתָהּ בִּתִּי הֲלֹא
ב אֲבַקֶּשׁ־לָךְ מָנוֹחַ אֲשֶׁר יִיטַב־לָךְ: וְעַתָּה
הֲלֹא בֹעַז מֹדַעְתָּנוּ אֲשֶׁר הָיִית אֶת־

וְלֹא יִפְגְּעוּ־בָךְ בְּשָׂדֶה אַחֵר — *So that
you will not be annoyed in another
field.* [lit. 'and they will not annoy
you in another field'].

[Boaz had cautioned his men
against molesting her in any way
(verse 16) and Ruth was thus safe in
Boaz's fields; she had no such as-
surances in other fields.].

[It is perhaps possible to translate
וַיִּפְגַּע — 'be met,' i.e. 'so that you
will not be met in another field and
appear to be בְּפוּיָה טוֹב, ungracious
of his hospitality].

The *Malbim* adds: 'and come under suspicion.'

23. וַתִּדְבַּק בְּנַעֲרוֹת בֹּעַז לְלַקֵּט — *So
she stayed close to Boaz's young
women to glean.* Most commentators feel that she spent the entire
harvest period with Boaz's young
women away from Naomi.

According to *Iggeres Shmuel*, the
verse specifies 'to glean' — only during gleaning time, i.e. Ruth stayed
close to the young women only during the day, when she gleaned. She
did not sleep away from Naomi for
the duration of the harvest; she
went home every night so as not to
leave her mother-in-law alone.

עַד־כְּלוֹת קְצִיר הַשְּׂעֹרִים וּקְצִיר הַחִטִּים
— *Until the end of the barley
harvest and of the wheat harvest.* A
total period of three months
(*Midrash*).

The *Malbim* notes that this
period of time is equal to the יְמֵי
הַבְחָנָה, the ninety day waiting-
period a new convert must wait
before she can marry. After this
period was up, she began considering יִבּוּם, levirate remarriage .

וַתֵּשֶׁב אֶת־חֲמוֹתָהּ — *She stayed* [lit.
'sat'] *with her mother-in-law.*
Although the verse mentions that
Ruth *cleaved* [וַתִּדְבַּק], to the young
women, nevertheless, her deep love
for and 'cleaving' to [compare 1:14]
Naomi never subsided. As soon as
the harvest was over she resumed
living with her mother-in-law,
because Ruth's love for Naomi sur-
passed all other considerations (*Iggeres Shmuel; Malbim*).

Also, the verse ends with וַתֵּשֶׁב
אֶת־חֲמוֹתָהּ, 'she stayed with her
mother-in-law,' to emphasize that
although Ruth was away in the
fields gleaning, her thoughts were
with Naomi *as if she were living
with her* (*Iggeres Shmuel*).

not be annoyed in another field.'

²³ *So she stayed close to Boaz' young women to glean, until the end of the barley harvest and of the wheat harvest. Then she stayed (at home) with her mother-in-law.*

Naomi, her mother-in-law, said to her: 'My daughter, I must seek security for you, that it may go well with you. ² Now, Boaz, our relative, with

III

Prefatory Remarks

[When reading this chapter, we must attempt to approach it by comprehending fully the purity and innocence with which the Sages — in the context of Biblical times — understood the episode as being fully לְשֵׁם שָׁמַיִם, for the sake of Heaven. 'Two women sacrificed themselves for the sake of the tribe of Judah,' — declares the Yalkut Shimoni, — 'Tamar and Ruth.'

During the harvest, while Ruth spent her time gleaning in Boaz's field and had at least limited access to him, Naomi dreamt and hoped that Boaz would bestir himself and 'redeem' Ruth, thus perpetuating Machlon's memory.

But now the harvest was over and Boaz had made no such move. The future prospect of Ruth's meeting Boaz was remote, and Naomi feared that since Boaz had not taken the initiative when Ruth was so at hand, he could hardly be expected to respond to more conventional suggestions of marriage when Ruth was out of sight. For all they knew, Boaz might even be offended at the mere suggestion of his marrying Ruth. After all, Naomi was destitute, Ruth was of foreign, Moabite stock, and Boaz was a man of substance, the Judge and leader of the generation. Could she expect to approach him and simply ask him to redeem and marry this girl?

Naomi became convinced that the condition of stalemate could not continue. Things had to be brought to a head one way or the other.

It must be remembered that the prohibition of יְחוּד פְּנוּיָה, the seclusion of a man with an unmarried woman — later forbidden by the court of King David — had not yet been proclaimed. Naomi therefore decided that the best course of action — however daring and unconventional — was for Ruth herself to approach Boaz under the most intimate and personal circumstances and remind him of his responsibility to the family of his dead uncle, Elimelech. In a personal confrontation — convinced that her motives were sincere — his compassion for her bitter plight might be evoked. (See Introduction.) — M.Z.]

1. וַתֹּאמֶר לָהּ נָעֳמִי חֲמוֹתָהּ — *Naomi, her mother-in-law, said to her.* Naomi and Ruth both interpreted Boaz's actions towards Ruth in his field as if he was considering marriage with her. They waited until the harvest was over and Boaz was free of business worries. Still, he made no move in that direction. Naomi therefore sought out ways to

expedite the matter. She was convinced that a direct action was needed (*Kol Yehuda; Akeidas Yitzchak*).

בִּתִּי — *My daughter.* [The word בִּתִּי, 'my daughter,' is treated differently throughout the Book, according to its context; see *Comm.* on 2:2; 2:8; and 2:22.] In this case, the Commentaries observe, *'my daughter,'* is stressed because human nature is such that when one's daughter-in-law is left widowed, the mother-in-law begrudges her remarriage. However, when a daughter is widowed, her mother encourages quick remarriage. Therefore, Naomi addressed Ruth as follows:

'Although I am your mother-in-law, I feel as if you are my own daughter, and I seek only the very best security in marriage for you, that it may go well with you. If you counter: Boaz is an old man [he was 80 at the time! — (Midrash)] and how 'good' could such a marriage be?' — Yes! Earthly pleasures might not be plentiful, but the Heavenly reward for being married to such a צַדִּיק, righteous man, as he — and the righteous children that would result from such a marriage — is abundant! *(Nachal Eshkol; Iggeres Shmuel).*

הֲלֹא אֲבַקֶּשׁ־לָךְ מָנוֹחַ — *I must seek security for you* [lit. 'shall I not find 'rest' for you?']. A woman has no security ['rest'] until she marries *(Rashi)* — [compare Naomi's blessing in 1:9 וּמְצֶאןָ מְנוּחָה, *'that you may find security'].*

On an esoteric level, the *Zohar Chadash* explains the use of the term *'rest'* as a synonym for marriage: The first husband's 'spirit' continues to stir within his widow's body until she remarries and replaces it with a new spirit. Naomi, therefore, suggested to Ruth that she must seek to quiet the spiritual turmoil within herself — the rem-

nants of Machlon — by marriage, to as near a kin as possible and thereby find *'rest'.*

אֲשֶׁר יִיטַב לָךְ — *That it may go well with you.* 'I am not concerned with the memory of my son; your welfare is foremost in my mind' *(Meishiv Nefesh).*

[The phrase may also be interpreted in the spiritual sense: 'Your marriage to this צַדִּיק, righteous man, though he is old, will bring you spiritual happiness.' As the *Talmud* interprets לְמַעַן יִיטַב לָךְ, *that it may go well with you* [*Deut. 5:16*] — 'in the world to come *(Kiddushin 39b)*].

[The word יִיטַב which we have translated *'it' may go well,* can also be translated *'he' may do good.* The *'he'* could conceivably apply to the new husband who will *'treat you well'].*

2. הֲלֹא בֹעַז מֹדַעְתָּנוּ אֲשֶׁר הָיִית אֶת־נַעֲרוֹתָיו — *Now, Boaz, our relative, with whose maidens you have been.* Naomi, afraid that Ruth would possibly have a negative attitude towards marrying this octogenarian, enumerates his qualities: 'His name *Boaz* is known and familiar to all; *he is our relative,* from the same aristocratic family as your late husband, and he is a "redeemer" of ours; you are personally familiar with his righteousness and kindnesses *having been with his maidens ...'* *(Iggeres Shmuel).*

אֲשֶׁר הָיִית אֶת־נַעֲרוֹתָיו — *With whose maidens you have been.* [A

*whose maidens you have been, will be winnowing
barley tonight on the threshing floor. ³ Therefore,
bathe and annoint yourself, don your finery, and go
down to the threshing floor, but do not make*

reference to verses 22 and 23 of the preceding chapter.]

הַלַּיְלָה — *Tonight.* [Naomi was certain that Boaz would spend the night there because] 'the generation was crime-ridden, and he would sleep on the threshing floor to guard his grain from thieves' (*Rashi*).

Now that the harvest was over, and it was the most productive one in many years, Naomi knew that Boaz would certainly be well-disposed toward taking a new wife to share his good fortune (*Meishiv Nefesh*).

The *Malbim* comments that there must have been workers at the threshing floor during working hours. If any of them were to see Ruth going to the threshing floor that particular night, they would assume she was going to visit the girls with whom she had worked previously, and to rejoice with her relative Boaz over his abundant harvest.

3. וְרָחַצְתְּ — *Bathe* [lit. 'wash']. Since the verse does not specify hands or face, but simply 'bathe,' in a general sense, and since Naomi would not have to instruct Ruth to do such a basic thing, the *Midrash* interprets this verse in the spiritual sense: וְרָחַצְתְּ, *wash yourself,* 'clean yourself from your idolatry,' [i.e. take a ritual bath] (*Torah T'mimah*).

The *Bach* quotes a *Midrash haNe'elam* that a convert is not free of the remnant of his impurity until three months following conversion. The three months were now ended [see *Comm.* to verse 1], and Naomi thus instructed her to take a ritual bath and cleanse herself entirely.

Rav Breuer notes that Naomi specified these Sabbath-like preparations to ready Ruth for her holy mission because she was preparing for a solemn, holy occasion.

וָסַכְתְּ — *And anoint yourself.* With perfume — as was the custom of Jewish nobility, both men and women (*Ibn Ezra*).

The *Midrash* interprets anoint yourself 'with good deeds and righteous conduct.'

וְשַׂמְתְּ שִׂמְלֹתַיִךְ עָלַיִךְ — *Don your finery.* [Lit. 'place your dress upon yourself*].

'Was she then naked? — It must refer to Sabbath garments. It was from this verse that Rav Chaninah said: A man should have two sets of garments, one for weekdays and one for Sabbath (*Yerushalmi: Pe'ah 8:6*)

According to the *Akeidas Yitzchak* and *Malbim,* Naomi did not advise Ruth to go down to the threshing floor *wearing* her Sabbath finery. The verse says וְשַׂמְתְּ, *place,* not וְלָבַשְׁתְּ, *wear, dress.* Rather, Naomi advised Ruth to *place her dress* on her, i.e. take along her Sabbath clothes and change into them at the threshing floor after everyone else was gone and she was in hiding.

The *k'siv* [traditional spelling] of the word is in first person: ושמתי, 'I

לָאִישׁ עַד כַּלֹּתוֹ לֶאֱכֹל וְלִשְׁתּוֹת: וַיְהִי
בְשָׁכְבוֹ וְיָדַעַתְּ אֶת־הַמָּקוֹם אֲשֶׁר יִשְׁכַּב־
שָׁם וּבָאת וְגִלִּית מַרְגְּלֹתָיו וְשָׁכָבְתִּי*
וְהוּא יַגִּיד לָךְ אֵת אֲשֶׁר תַּעֲשִׂין: וַתֹּאמֶר
אֵלֶיהָ כֹּל אֲשֶׁר־תֹּאמְרִי * אֶעֱשֶׂה. וַתֵּרֶד
הַגֹּרֶן וַתַּעַשׂ כְּכֹל אֲשֶׁר־צִוַּתָּה חֲמוֹתָהּ:
וַיֹּאכַל בֹּעַז וַיֵּשְׁתְּ וַיִּיטַב לִבּוֹ וַיָּבֹא

ד

ה

ו

ז

*וְשָׁכַבְתְּ ק'

*אֵלַי קרי ולא כתיב

---

will dress you,' to imply that Naomi intimated 'my זְכֻיּוֹת, merits, will enhance your appearance' *(Shoresh Yishai).*

וְיָרַדְתְּ הַגֹּרֶן — *And go down to the threshing floor.* [The *k'siv* is first person: וירדתי, *'I will go down,'* which the *Midrash* interprets: 'my merits will descend with you.'— i.e. 'through my merits the plan will work, and Boaz will not be angry with you' *(Nachal Eshkol).*

'*Go down*' is used, because the threshing floor was situated below the city *(Midrash).*

אַל־תִּוָּדְעִי לָאִישׁ — *Do not make yourself known to the man.* 'The' man — i.e. to Boaz *(Rashi).*

Remain hidden *(Ralbag),* and the workers will assume that you left before them *(Malbim).*

4. וַיְהִי בְשָׁכְבוֹ — *And when he lies down,* i.e. when you see him preparing to retire, note his sleeping place. Then later, in the dark of night when he is fast asleep, you can easily locate him *(Targum; Iggeres Shmuel).*

וְגִלִּית מַרְגְּלֹתָיו — *Uncover his feet.* The *Malbim* suggests that Naomi was proposing a method of reminding Boaz, as a redeemer, of his moral obligation to marry Ruth.

A brother who refuses to enter into יִבּוּם, *a levirate marriage,* undergoes a ceremony of *chalitzah* which involves the removal of his shoe [see *Deut. 25:5-10*]. For Naomi to directly suggest that Boaz marry Ruth would have been a gross impropriety. Therefore she asked Ruth to *'uncover his feet,'* a gesture reminiscent of *chalitzah,* in the hope that it would make Boaz aware of his moral obligation to her.

וְשָׁכָבְתְּ — *And lie down.* [Here, too, the *ksiv* [traditional spelling] of the imperative verb 'lie down' is written as if it were a first person verb— וְשָׁכַבְתִּי, *I will lie down,* as if to say that Naomi's merit will accompany her (see preceding verse) and Naomi thus identified herself with the deed].

וְהוּא יַגִּיד לָךְ... — *He will tell you what you are to do.* Whether you or he should undertake to approach a closer redeemer *(Malbim).*

The *Besuras Eliyahu* takes הוּא, *'he'* to refer to God, i.e. Naomi said: 'I can't possibly know what Boaz will say or how you should respond. Follow my directions and God will inspire you to say the right thing.'

5. כֹּל אֲשֶׁר־תֹּאמְרִי [אֵלַי] אֶעֱשֶׂה — *All that you say to me I will do.* The

III
4-7

yourself known to the man until he has finished
eating and drinking. ⁴ *And when he lies down, note*
the place where he lies, and go over, uncover his feet,
and lie down. He will tell you what you are to do.'
⁵ *She replied, 'All that you say to me I will do.'*

⁶ *So she went down to the threshing floor and did*
everything as her mother-in-law instructed her.
⁷ *Boaz ate and drank and his heart was merry. He*

---

word אֵלָי *'to me'* is read, but it does
not appear in the written Hebrew
text. This, and all textual readings,
as transmitted by the Soferim, are
Halachah from Moses at Sinai
(*Nedarim* 37b). [i.e. the 'contradiction' between the written and
read versions is apparent but not
real. Each is valid; the discrepancy
is to teach us the deeper meaning
implied in the text. The Commentaries offer serveral interpreta-
tions]:

The absence of אֵלָי, *'to me'*, in the
Hebrew, suggests that Ruth cast her
whole dependence upon Naomi,
and removed *'herself'* for all decision making. Ruth vowed to do not
only what Naomi had *specifically*
instructed her to do, but even what
she only *alluded* to, indirectly
through others. Moreover, 'even
those instructions which were not
אֵלָי, *"to me,"* i.e. for my own
benefit, I will still do' (*Iggeres*
Shmuel).

According to *Akeidas Yitzchak*,
אֵלָי, *to me*, is read but not written to
convey that although the advice
seemed improper *'to her,'* nevertheless Ruth would obey because
Naomi had given it.

M'lo ha'Omer suggests that the
omitted אֵלָי demonstrates the extent
to which Ruth left matters בִּידֵי
שָׁמַיִם, in the hands of Heaven — as

if she excluded *herself*, and had no
personal stake in their resolution;
she left everything to God's beneficence.

'Although you tell me that Boaz
will instruct me, I will first consult
you, and *all that you say to me I will*
do (Alshich; Malbim).

6. ...וַתֵּרֶד הַגֹּרֶן וַתַּעַשׂ — *So she went*
down to the threshing floor and did
everything her mother-in-law told
her. Ruth didn't follow her bidding
in every detail. She feared that by
going to the threshing floor per-
fumed and festively attired she
would attract curious glances making it impossible to carry out her
mission discreetly. Therefore, the
verse tells us first וַתֵּרֶד הַגֹּרֶן, *she*
went down to the threshing floor —
and then *did everything her*
mother-in-law told her Only after
arriving at the threshing floor did
Ruth follow Naomi's bidding by
perfuming and dressing in her best
finery (*Rashi; Malbim*).

אֲשֶׁר־צִוַּתָּה חֲמוֹתָהּ — *As her mother-*
in-law instructed her. Although
Ruth didn't quite understand or fully agree with the plan, she did it
blindly and respectfully, *because*
her mother-in-law instructed her
(*Besuras Eliyahu*).

7. וַיִּיטַב לִבּוֹ — *And his heart was*
merry. Having recited the grace

פֶּרֶק ג
לִשְׁכַּב בְּקְצֵה הָעֲרֵמָה וַתָּבֹא בַלָּט וַתְּגַל
ח־ט ח מַרְגְּלֹתָיו וַתִּשְׁכָּב: וַיְהִי בַּחֲצִי הַלַּיְלָה
וַיֶּחֱרַד הָאִישׁ וַיִּלָּפֵת וְהִנֵּה אִשָּׁה שֹׁכֶבֶת
ט מַרְגְּלֹתָיו: וַיֹּאמֶר מִי־אָתְּ וַתֹּאמֶר אָנֹכִי
רוּת אֲמָתֶךָ וּפָרַשְׂתָּ כְנָפֶךָ עַל־אֲמָתְךָ כִּי

after meals (Midrash) and having added a special prayer thanking God for heeding his prayers and putting an end to the famine [see Comm. 1:6] (Targum).

His heart was merry — because he studied Torah (Rashi).

The Sages note the difference between a צַדִּיק, righteous man, and a רָשָׁע, wicked man. Boaz' heart was merry, and the presence of a pure, beautiful and festively attired woman was a great temptation. Nevertheless, he mastered his impulses and did nothing in the least immoral. Of the wicked Ahasuerus, on the other hand, we find that when 'his heart was merry' [Esther 1:10] he ordered his queen to appear before his guests unclothed (Iggeres Shmuel).

בְּקְצֵה הָעֲרֵמָה — At the end of the grain pile. To guard his grain from that immoral generation (Midrash) [see Comm. verse 2, s. v. הַלַּיְלָה, 'tonight']. Also because they are so scrupulous about earning their money honestly, the righteous are zealous about their property (Sotah 12a).

וַתָּבֹא בַלָּט — And she came stealthily 'בְּנַחַת, quietly' (Rashi). Radak derives the word from לוּט, wrapped, and translates: 'She came with her face covered.

8. בַּחֲצִי הַלַּיְלָה — In the middle of the night when he got up to study Torah. . . (Iggeres Shmuel)

וַיֶּחֱרַד הָאִישׁ — The man was startled. 'He could easily have cursed her but God put it in his heart to bless her, as it is said [verse 10] בְּרוּכָה אַתְּ לַה', Be blessed of HASHEM' (Midrash)

וַיִּלָּפֵת — And turned about. [So Ibn Ezra; according to Rashi]: He thought she was a demon and he wanted to scream so she 'placated' him.

The Talmud, deriving the word from לֶפֶת, turnip, translates: 'His skin hardened like a turnip' [from fright] (Sanhedrin 19b)

וְהִנֵּה אִשָּׁה — A woman. 'Purest of women' (Midrash).

He touched her head and realized it was a woman (Rashi)

Perhaps she whispered: 'Don't be afraid!' and he recognized it as a woman's voice, or he distinguished a womanly form by the light of the moon (Ibn Ezra).

'How few words are used to express the 'fear' Boaz must have felt during this incident! The leader of that generation, involved all his life in elevating the morals of his people, spends a night in his threshing floor to guard against robbers in that lawless generation, wakes up in the middle of the night and finds a woman lying at his feet! What audacity she must have had; how embarrassing for him, what an awkward position to be put in to!

Under normal circumstances he should have cursed her and

went to lie down at the end of the grain pile, and she came stealthily, uncovered his feet, and lay down. **8** *In the middle of the night the man was startled, and turned about — there was a woman lying at his feet!*

9 *'Who are you?' he asked. And she answered: 'I am your handmaid, Ruth. Spread your robe over your handmaid; for you are a redeemer.'*

banished her for her unseemly act. But the sincerity of Ruth and the determination of Naomi caused Providence to inspire Boaz with a compassion for Ruth. Recognizing her sincerity, he did not curse her — instead he blessed her. This is but another one of the many miracles wrought for the Jews in the middle of the night throughout their history.

As interpreted by the Sages, this is the incident King David referred to when generations later he would get up at midnight and recount all the miracles wrought for the Jews throughout history: חֲצוֹת לַיְלָה — *'At midnight I rise to thank You for Your righteous judgments. (Psalms 119;62)* And among the miracles he recounted was the miracle wrought for his great-grandparents, that midnight on the threshing floor. As the *Midrash* states: *'And the righteousness which you have wrought for my great-grandfather and great-grandmother,* for had Boaz hastily cursed her but once, from where would I have come?' *(Nachalas Yosef)*

9. וַיֹּאמֶר מִי־אָתְּ — *'Who are you?' he said.* 'A woman,' she answered. 'Married or unmarried?' She answered, 'unmarried.' *(Midrash)*.

וּפָרַשְׂתָּ כְנָפֶךָ עַל־אֲמָתְךָ — *Spread your robe over your handmaid.*

[כְנָפֶיךָ can be understood as *'your wings'*; i.e. *'protection'*.]

The 'wing' is a metaphor borrowed from birds — who shield each other with their wings during mating. Therefore it is used as a symbol of marriage *(Malbim)*.

Most commentators, however, understand the word in the sense of 'corner' of a garment, i.e. *'place the corner of your garment over me as a token of marriage'* *(Rashi)*.

'Take me as your wife, with a proper wedding ceremony' *(Iggeres Shmuel)*.

'Cursed be the wicked' says the *Midrash* [noting the difference between the behavior of Ruth and others]. In the case of Potiphar's wife and Joseph it is said [Gen. 312] *'Lie with me'*, but here Ruth said: *'Spread your robe over your handmaid'*

כִּי גֹאֵל אָתָּה — *For you are a redeemer,* and, as such, it is incumbent upon you to redeem the estate of my husband in accordance with Lev. 25. Ruth explained to Boaz that she and her mother-in-law are forced to sell their inheritance, and as a redeemer, it is his obligation to buy the property so that it would remain in the family. She then made an additional request: 'Take possession of me, too, so that the name of the deceased will be perpetuated on his property. If you marry me, peo-

גָּאֵל אָתָּה: וַיֹּאמֶר בְּרוּכָה אַתְּ לַיהוה י
בִּתִּי הֵיטַבְתְּ חַסְדֵּךְ הָאַחֲרוֹן מִן-הָרִאשׁוֹן
לְבִלְתִּי-לֶכֶת אַחֲרֵי הַבַּחוּרִים אִם-דַּל
וְאִם-עָשִׁיר: וְעַתָּה בִּתִּי אַל-תִּירְאִי כֹּל יא
אֲשֶׁר-תֹּאמְרִי אֶעֱשֶׂה-לָּךְ כִּי יוֹדֵעַ כָּל-
שַׁעַר עַמִּי כִּי אֵשֶׁת חַיִל אָתְּ: וְעַתָּה כִּי יב
אָמְנָם כִּי אִם גֹּאֵל* אָנֹכִי וְגַם יֵשׁ גֹּאֵל

ple will say: She was the wife of Machlon' whenever I visit the field (Rashi).

'And it is your duty to 'redeem' the soul of Machlon and marry me...' (Alshich)

The Bach states, esoterically, that she hinted: 'Only from both of us together will the Davidic dynasty descend, not from only one of us.'

10. בְּרוּכָה אַתְּ לַה' בִּתִּי — Be blessed of HASHEM, my daughter. [The Sages stress Boaz's righteousness and superhuman self control. He recognized her mission as a difficult one and wholly devoted לְשֵׁם שָׁמַיִם, for the sake of Heaven. No evil thoughts came to his mind. He was moved, and he blessed her.]

'He might easily have cursed her, but God put it in his heart to bless her' (Midrash).

Boaz compared this incident in his mind with the incidents of Lot's daughters and Judah and Tamar. He said, 'You, my daughter, are more blessed than Lot's daughters and Tamar, because your actions do not involve serious prohibitions such as theirs did (Kol Yehuda).

הֵיטַבְתְּ חַסְדֵּךְ הָאַחֲרוֹן מִן-הָרִאשׁוֹן — You have made your latest act of kindness greater than the first. For a woman in the prime of life to give up the opportunity to marry a young man in favor of marrying a very old one is a great sacrifice. Yet you are prepared to do this solely to perpetuate the name of your late husband. This, your latest act of kindness, is even greater than your earlier kindness to your mother-in-law. [According to Bach it is also greater than the kindness you did your soul by embracing Judaism...] (Ralbag; Rav Arama; Iggeres Shmuel; Alshich)

לְבִלְתִּי-לֶכֶת אַחֲרֵי הַבַּחוּרִים — In that you have not gone after the young men. With your beauty you could have whoever you want, and yet you honor your husband's memory by choosing me, though I am old, because I am a close relative (Ibn Ezra; Malbim).

אִם-דַּל וְאִם-עָשִׁיר — Be they poor or rich. 'Rav Shmuel b. Isaac said. A woman usually prefers a poor young man to an old rich man' (Midrash).

11. כֹּל אֲשֶׁר-תֹּאמְרִי אֶעֱשֶׂה-לָּךְ — Whatever you say I will do for you! Boaz reassured her that he was not merely putting her off with soothing words (Meishiv Nefesh).

'I will even do anything you request of me in the future, but at the

¹⁰ *And he said: Be blessed of HASHEM, my daughter; you have made your latest act of kindness greater than the first, in that you have not gone after the younger men, be they poor or rich.* ¹¹ *And now, my daughter, do not fear; whatever you say, I will do for you; for all the men in the gate of my people know that you are a worthy woman.* ¹² *Now while it is true that I am a redeemer; there is also another*

moment we face an obstacle: there is a redeemer closer than I' *(Iggeres Shmuel).*

Knowing he could not marry her immediately, he reassured her in this way because he did not want her to be discouraged for having approached him *(Alshich).*

כִּי יוֹדֵעַ כָּל־שַׁעַר עַמִּי — *For all the men in the gate of my people know.* [Lit. 'the gate of my people knows — i.e. those who assemble at the gate, the gathering point of the city.]

'Those who sit at the gate of the Great Sanhedrin' *(Targum).*

It now became manifestly clear to Boaz why the law of 'Moabite not Moabitess' 'happened' to be the topic of discussion of the Sanhedrin and was 'revealed' to them immediately prior to Ruth's arrival *(Nachal Eshkol).*

Boaz said: My intentions are compatible with yours. But don't worry, even though you think that the wise men at the gate will try to dissuade me, saying it is below my dignity to marry a Moabite girl, have no fear. 'The people at the gate *know* you are a worthy woman' *(Malbim).*

The *Iggeres Shmuel* offers a different interpretation of these verses: '*Do not fear, my daughter; I want to marry you. And things will*

probably work out. '*I' will be the one to do whatever you say. Only I* and the people of my gate [i.e. Sanhedrin] are aware that as a female Moabite you are now permitted to me — everyone else thinks you are still prohibited. The other redeemer definitely does not know the law and he will demur, but, *in the event he does decide to redeem you, then it is for the best. I promise you, however, that if he does not accept the responsibility of redeeming you with a good heart, I myself will redeem you.*

כִּי אֵשֶׁת חַיִל אָתְּ — *That you are a worthy woman* — and fit for a גִּבּוֹר חַיִל, '*man of substance*' [2:1, i.e. Boaz] *(Midrash Lekach Tov).*

12. כִּי גֹאֵל אָנֹכִי — *I am a redeemer.* The written text has כִּי אִם גֹאֵל אָנֹכִי — 'For if I am a redeemer; but according to the *Masorah* the word אִם *if,* is כְּתִיב וְלֹא קְרִי, 'written but not read': This occurs several times in Scripture and is a *halachah* from Moses at Sinai *(Nedarim 37b)* [see Comm. beginning of verse 5].

The word אִם is not read because it implies uncertainty, while in fact there *was* definitely another גּוֹאֵל *(Midrash Lekach Tov; Rashi).*

Commenting on why the אִם is written, *Rav Alkabetz* suggests that

יג קָרוֹב מִמֶּנִּי: לִינִי|הַלַּיְלָה וְהָיָה בַבֹּקֶר אִם־יִגְאָלֵךְ טוֹב יִגְאָל וְאִם־לֹא יַחְפֹּץ לְגָאֳלֵךְ וּגְאַלְתִּיךְ אָנֹכִי חַי־יהוה שִׁכְבִי עַד־הַבֹּקֶר: וַתִּשְׁכַּב מַרְגְּלוֹתָו עַד־הַבֹּקֶר יד וַתָּקָם בְּטֶרֶום יַכִּיר אִישׁ אֶת־רֵעֵהוּ וַיֹּאמֶר אַל־יִוָּדַע כִּי־בָאָה הָאִשָּׁה הַגֹּרֶן: טו וַיֹּאמֶר הָבִי הַמִּטְפַּחַת אֲשֶׁר־עָלַיִךְ

[עיין מנחת ש״י].
*מַרְגְּלוֹתָיו ק׳
*יתיר ו׳

it implies a doubt that Boaz left un-stated. Boaz was impressed by Ruth's noble act and was flattered at the suggestion that he 'redeem' Ruth and raise up the memory of her husband but he was doubtful whether he could function in that capacity and have children due to his advanced age [he was eighty!].

וְגַם יֵשׁ גֹּאֵל קָרוֹב מִמֶּנִּי — *There is also another redeemer closer than I.* A brother of Elimelech; whereas Boaz was only a nephew. [see Comm. next verse] (*Rashi*).

[Boaz did not believe that the closer redeemer would exercise his right, but he was obliged to first consult him and give him the op-portunity of so doing.]

13. לִינִי הַלַּיְלָה — *Stay the night.* Without a husband (*Rashi*).

'This night you will spend without a husband, but you will not be without a husband for another night' (*Midrash*).

When Ruth heard, now for the first time, that there was a redeemer closer than Boaz, she grew dis-couraged and got up to leave. Boaz then asked her not to lose heart, but to remain the night, and then he swore to her that he is quite ready to

marry her if the other redeemer would not (*Rav Alkabetz*).

*[The *Minchas Shai* observes that in some texts the ל, *lamed* of לִינִי is enlarged, in some the נ, *nun* is enlarged, and in many manuscripts none are enlarged.]

אִם־יִגְאָלֵךְ טוֹב יִגְאָל — *If he will redeem you, fine! let him redeem.*

The *Midrash* states that Salmon, Tov, and Elimelech were brothers. Many commentators [e.g. *Alshich; Bach, Rav Arama, Malbim*) main-tain therefore that the word טוֹב, 'Tov, is the name of the closer redeemer, the 'Ploni Almoni' refer-red to later. According to their in-terpretation, the verse translates thus: אִם־יִגְאָלֵךְ טוֹב, *if Tov will redeem you*, יִגְאָל, *let him redeem...'*

Ibn Ezra, however, disagrees: If Scripture, here identifies the redeemer as Tov, why should he be referred to as 'Ploni Almoni' later? Rather the meaning is: *If he will redeem you fine*, he is a good man, etc.

The redeemer was not learned, and Boaz knew that if, by some chance, he would agree to redeem, it would be the result of shame, not of conviction. Therefore, the transla-tion is 'If he will redeem you from the goodness of his heart, let him

III
13-15

redeemer closer than I. 13 Stay the night, then in the morning, if he will redeem you, fine! let him redeem. But if he does not want to redeem you, then I will redeem you "Chai HASHEM"! Lie down until the morning.'

14 So she lay at his feet until the morning and she arose before one man could recognize another, for he said: 'Let it not be known that the woman came to the threshing floor.' 15 And he said, 'Hold out the shawl you are wearing and grasp it.' She held it, and he

redeem; if he does not so desire, then I will redeem' *(Shoresh Yishai).*

חַי־ה' — *Chai HASHEM!* [Lit. 'As HASHEM lives! A Biblical form of oath]. Ruth accused him of paying lip-service to her request, so he jumped up and swore to her that he was sincere. Some Sages say he was addressing his יֵצֶר הָרָע, evil inclination *(Rashi).*

שִׁכְבִי עַד־הַבֹּקֶר — *lie down until the morning,* i.e., early in the morning, so you can leave at the crack of dawn and not be discovered *(Iggeres Shmuel).*

14. וַתִּשְׁכַּב מַרְגְּלוֹתָו עַד־הַבֹּקֶר — *So she lay at his feet until the morning.* [Some commentators see in the fact that מַרְגְּלוֹתָו is spelled defectively חסר, (it should be spelled מַרְגְּלוֹתָיו with a *yud*) that she did not lay close to his feet. Instead, out of modesty, she moved away].

בְּטֶרֶם — *Before one man could recognize another.* [רֵעֵהוּ, lit. 'his friend'] The word בְּטֶרֶם, *before,* is spelled here with a

superfluous ו, *vav,* teaching that she spent six hours with him, the numerical equivalent of the letter ו, *vav. (Midrash);* and we can further appreciate from this length of time the extent of their self control *(Torah T'minah).*

וַיֹּאמֶר אַל־יִוָּדַע כִּי־בָאָה הָאִשָּׁה הַגֹּרֶן — *And he said, let it not be known that the woman came to the threshing floor.* The *Midrash* comments that he was addressing himself to God: "All that night Boaz lay stretched out upon his face and prayed, 'Lord of the Universe, it is revealed and known to you that I did not touch her; so may it be Your will that it not be known that the woman came *into* the threshing-floor, that the name of Heaven be not profaned through me.' "

He wasn't concerned for his own reputation; he was known as a צַדִּיק, *a righteous man,* and he was old — he would not be accused of unbecoming conduct. It was Ruth's reputation he was concerned with; after all *she* went out in the middle of the night! He therefore specified *that it not be known that the woman came to the threshing-floor (Alshich).*

פרק ג

טז־יח

וְאֶחֱזִי־בָהּ וַתֹּאחֶז בָּהּ וַיָּמָד שֵׁשׁ־שְׂעֹרִים
טז וַיָּשֶׁת עָלֶיהָ וַיָּבֹא הָעִיר: וַתָּבוֹא אֶל־
חֲמוֹתָהּ וַתֹּאמֶר מִי־אַתְּ בִּתִּי וַתַּגֶּד־לָהּ
יז אֵת כָּל־אֲשֶׁר עָשָׂה־לָהּ הָאִישׁ: וַתֹּאמֶר
שֵׁשׁ־הַשְּׂעֹרִים הָאֵלֶּה נָתַן לִי כִּי אָמַר
* אַל־תָּבוֹאִי רֵיקָם אֶל־חֲמוֹתֵךְ:
יח וַתֹּאמֶר שְׁבִי בִתִּי עַד אֲשֶׁר תֵּדְעִין אֵיךְ

*אֵלַי קרי ולא כתיב

15. וַיָּמָד שֵׁשׁ־שְׂעֹרִים — *And he measured out six measures of barley* [lit. 'and he measured six barleys']. The exact measure is not stated. The Talmud discusses this: 'What are 'six barleys' Shall we translate it literally [i.e. six grains of barley] — But would [the magnanimous] Boaz give only six grains? On the other hand, if it means six se'ah's [the measure usually used on the field and in the threshing-floor (Rashi)], a woman cannot carry such a heavy weight! — Rather he symbolically alluded to her [by giving her a token six barley grains] that six righteous men each possessing six outstanding virtues, are destined to descend from this marriage: David, the Messiah, Daniel, Hananiah, Mishael and Azariah' (*Sanhedrin 93a-b*).

Rav Einhorn, in his Commentary to the Midrash points at that since it says 'measured' and later וַיָּשֶׁת עָלֶיהָ, *he laid it on her*, it must refer to a quantity larger than six grains! He resolves the apparent contradiction by suggesting that first he gave her the symbolic six grains, then he measured out a larger quantity which she carried home.

The *Malbim* maintains that שֵׁשׁ does not mean 'six' in this verse but

that 'Shesh' was a standard measure, one-sixth of a *se'ah*. Half a *shesh* is considered enough for one meal for one person. Thus, Boaz gave her enough to provide a meal for herself and Naomi. The implication of this gesture was that by the time that meal was finished she would be 'redeemed' and won't have to worry about the next meal.

According to *Rav Alkabetz*, the reason he gave her the barley [in addition to having given it as a gift for Naomi as Ruth states in the verse 17], was so that if anyone would see her leaving the threshing floor early in the morning, he would assume that she was carrying home barley gleanings.

וַיָּבֹא הָעִיר — *Then he went into the city.* 'Surely it should have stated that *she* went into the city, yet it says, 'he went to the city'? — it teaches that he accompanied her lest she be molested (*Midrash*)

16. וַתָּבוֹא אֶל־חֲמוֹתָה — *She came to her mother-in-law.* [Imagine the anxiety Naomi must have experienced through the night, waiting for Ruth and wondering whether her hazardous plan had succeeded].

III
16-18
measured out six measures of barley, and set it on her; then he went into the city.

16 *She came to her mother-in-law who said: 'How do things stand with you, my daughter?' So she told her all that the man had done for her,* **17** *and she said: 'He gave me these six measures of barley for he said to me, Do not go empty-handed to your mother-in-law.'*

18 *Then she said, 'Sit patiently, my daughter, until*

מִי־אַתְּ בִּתִּי — *How do things stand with you my daughter?* [lit. 'who are you, my daughter?'] The translation follows the *Midrash*: Did she then not recognize her? — Yes, but she meant: 'Are you still a maiden or a married woman?' She answered, 'A maiden', *and she told her all that the man had done for her. Midrash Lekach Tov* offers the above commentary, and also suggests that perhaps it was still dark and Naomi did not recognize her.

אֶת כָּל־אֲשֶׁר עָשָׂה־לָהּ הָאִישׁ — *All that the man had done for her.* The question demanded more than a 'yes' or 'no' answer. Ruth went into elaborate detail so Naomi would know exactly where matters stood (*Alshich*).

17. כִּי אָמַר [אלי] — *For he said to me.* [The word אלי 'to me' is read, but it does not appear in the written Hebrew text. This is *Halachah* from Moses at Sinai (*Nedarim 37b*); see *Comm. on 2:5*]

By omitting אלי, *to me*, Ruth intimated that Boaz in his modesty, did not even look directly at her during their conversation (*Iggeres Shmuel*).

אַל־תָּבוֹאִי רֵיקָם אֶל־חֲמוֹתֵךְ — *Do not go empty-handed to your mother-in-law.* It is not recorded that Boaz actually told her this. However, the large amount of grain he had given her, could not have been intended for Ruth alone, so Ruth 'stretched the truth' a bit for the sake of שָׁלוֹם בַּיִת *domestic tranquility*, and to flatter her lonely, widowed mother-in-law. Perhaps this is why אֵלַי, is not written, because in actuality Boaz had not said it; she, in her wisdom, added it on her own (*Iggeres Shmuel*).

Ruth also wanted to impress upon her mother-in-law that the barley was intended for her, and not as a gift to Ruth for loose conduct on the threshing floor (*Rav Alkabetz*). Nor did she want Naomi to think that it was a farewell gift and that Boaz had forsaken them (*Ibn Shushan*).

18. וַתֹּאמֶר שְׁבִי בִתִּי — *Sit patiently, my daughter.* i.e. Be prepared (*Alshich*).

We can do nothing but wait. We have done ours, God will now do His (*Zos Nechemasi*).

אֵיךְ יִפֹּל דָּבָר — *How the matter will*

פֶּרֶק ג יִפֹּל דָּבָר כִּי לֹא יִשְׁקֹט הָאִישׁ כִּי אִם־
כִּלָּה הַדָּבָר הַיּוֹם:

פֶּרֶק ד א וּבֹעַז עָלָה הַשַּׁעַר וַיֵּשֶׁב שָׁם וְהִנֵּה הַגֹּאֵל
א־ב   עֹבֵר אֲשֶׁר דִּבֶּר־בֹּעַז וַיֹּאמֶר סוּרָה שְׁבָה־
ב   פֹּה פְּלֹנִי אַלְמֹנִי וַיָּסַר וַיֵּשֵׁב: וַיִּקַּח עֲשָׂרָה
אֲנָשִׁים מִזִּקְנֵי הָעִיר וַיֹּאמֶר שְׁבוּ־פֹה

turn out. If your destined husband is Boaz or Tov *(Zos Nechemasi)*.

Since all decrees issue from Heaven *(Ibn Ezra)*.

כִּי אִם־כִּלָּה הַדָּבָר הַיּוֹם — *Unless he settles the matter today.* Rav Huna said in the name of Rav Shmuel b. Yitzchak: The yes of the righteous is yes, and their no, no.' *(Midrash).* [If Boaz said he will act on the matter, rest assured he will not delay].

IV

1. וּבֹעַז עָלָה הַשַּׁעַר — *Boaz, meanwhile, had gone up to the gate.* To fulfill his promise to Ruth [3:13] *(Zos Nechemasi)*.

Boaz was the head of the Sanhedrin, and in that capacity he stationed himself there *(Iggeres Shmuel)*.

[The gate, like the gates around the Old City of Jerusalem today, was a fairly large edifice. The Sanhedrin convened there, Torah was taught, and disputes settled.]

וַיֵּשֶׁב שָׁם — *And sat down there.* Knowing that there was nothing more he could do, and confident that God would arrange something for him *(Iggeres Shmuel)*.

וְהִנֵּה הַגֹּאֵל עֹבֵר — *Just then, the redeemer passed by.* The *Midrash*, noting the striking coincidence of the redeemer's passing by just at that very moment, asks: 'Was he waiting behind the gate? — Rav Shmuel bar Nachman answered, Had he been at the opposite end of the earth God would have caused him to fly, so to speak, to be there, in order to relieve the righteous Boaz of the anxiety of waiting ...'

The *Midrash* continues: 'Boaz played his part, Ruth played hers, Naomi played hers, whereupon the Holy One, blessed be He, said: I, too, must play Mine.'

The word וְהִנֵּה, *just then*, suggests something unusual [see Comm. of *Malbim* on 2:4]. The redeemer did not usually pass by the *you know how the matter will turn out, for the man will not rest unless he settles the matter today.'*

IV
1-2

Boaz, meanwhile, had gone up to the gate, and sat down there. Just then, the redeemer of whom Boaz had spoken passed by. He said, 'come over, sit down here, 'Ploni Almoni,' and he came over and sat down. ² He then took ten men of the elders of the

gate. Divine Providence guided him that day אֲשֶׁר דִּבֶּר בֹּעַז, *as Boaz had spoken*, i.e. to enable the righteous Boaz to fulfill his promise to Ruth (*Malbim*).

סוּרָה שְׁבָה־פֹּה — *Come over, sit down here.* [Lit. 'turn away'] from your planned destination and sit here (*Malbim*).

פְּלֹנִי אַלְמֹנִי — *Ploni Almoni.* —[A pseudonym. Sometimes translated 'So and so'. Compare *I Samuel 21:3*, and *II Kings 6:8*].

His real name was withheld because he did not discharge his duty as redeemer. The meaning of *Ploni* is 'hidden;' *Almoni* — 'nameless.' Another interpretation: *Almoni* — mute and devoid of Torah. He should have known the law of 'Moabite not Moabitess' but instead he asserted '*lest I imperil my own inheritance*' [verse 6] (*Rashi; Midrash*).

Rav Shmariah Halkriti explains the word אַלְמֹנִי — 'fit for an אַלְמָנָה, [widow].

Boaz probably addressed him by his real name, Tov; it is Scripture

that disguised his name to avoid his embarrassment (*Rav Alkabetz*).

According to *Ima Shel Malchus*, it was only proper that he was not called by his real name, Tov; he did not deserve to be called *Tov* — 'good', because he ignored his familial obligation.

וַיֵּשֶׁב — *And he sat.* Even though *Ploni Almoni* was Boaz's uncle [see Comm. 2:17 s.v. אִם יִגְאָלֵךְ], he did not take a seat until told to do so by Boaz, who was the head of the Sanhedrin.

He sat and waited, because Boaz did not tell him why he wanted him until the quorum of ten assembled (*Alshich*).

2. וַיִּקַּח עֲשָׂרָה אֲנָשִׁים מִזִּקְנֵי הָעִיר — *He then took ten men of the elders of the city.* 'Rav Eleazar ben Rav Yose said: From here we learn that the blessing of the bridegroom [i.e. a wedding ceremony] requires a מִנְיָן, quorum of ten. Rav Yuden ben Pazzi said: Not only the marriage of a bachelor to a maiden, but even the marriage of a widower to a widow

ג וַיֵּשֵׁבוּ: וַיֹּאמֶר לַגֹּאֵל חֶלְקַת הַשָּׂדֶה אֲשֶׁר
לְאָחִינוּ לֶאֱלִימֶלֶךְ מָכְרָה נָעֳמִי הַשָּׁבָה
מִשְּׂדֵה מוֹאָב: וַאֲנִי אָמַרְתִּי אֶגְלֶה אָזְנְךָ ד
לֵאמֹר קְנֵה נֶגֶד הַיֹּשְׁבִים וְנֶגֶד זִקְנֵי עַמִּי
אִם־תִּגְאַל גְּאָל וְאִם־לֹא יִגְאַל הַגִּידָה לִי

[as Boaz and Ruth] requires a quorum of ten (Midrash).

According to others in the Talmud, the presence of ten elders was required to publicly confirm the halachah permitting a female Moabite into the community of Israel. [This auspicious public gathering made the law clear to all, and thus Boaz could marry Ruth the Moabite] (Kesubos 7b).

According to the Malbim, Boaz wanted to make sure he would not be subject to accusations of partiality toward Ruth in promulgating the law allowing her to enter the Assembly of God. He therefore expounded the law while the responsibility of redemption still lay upon Ploni Almoni.

שְׁבוּ פֹה וַיֵּשֵׁבוּ — 'Sit here,' and they sat down. Boaz was head of the Sanhedrin, and though they were older than he, they did not sit until he asked them to because 'an inferior has no right to take a seat until his superior grants him permission' (Midrash; Zos Nechemasi).

He bid them to remain there and be present for a wedding ceremony which, regardless of who the redeemer turned out to be, was sure to take place (Malbim).

3. חֶלְקַת הַשָּׂדֶה — The parcel [lit. 'portion] of land. Possibly, there was a large field, a part of which belonged to Elimelech (Ibn Ezra).

Perhaps the reason[*] why it is referred to as חֶלְקַת הַשָּׂדֶה, the part of the land is that the three brothers:Elimelech, Tov and Salmon inherited a large field from their father and divided it among themselves. Boaz inherited a portion of land from his father, Salmon [see 2:3], Tov had his, and Naomi was administering her late husband's portion. Boaz had therefore advised the kinsman that he should purchase the piece adjacent to both their properties so that a non-relative should not intrude on the family property (Iggeres Shmuel).

לְאָחִינוּ לֶאֱלִימֶלֶךְ — To our brother, Elimelech. [The Talmud and Midrash note that Elimelech was not Boaz's brother, but his uncle — the brother of Boaz's father, Salmon — but he called him 'brother' in a general sense, as the Midrash puts it, 'because one does not refrain from calling his uncle 'brother'.]

מָכְרָה נָעֳמִי — Is being offered for sale by Naomi. [The literal translation of the Hebrew is 'Naomi has sold,'but the context of the verse, according to most of the commentators demands our translation, because Naomi had not in fact sold the field, as it appears from verse 5. Rather, מָכְרָה נָעֳמִי here means 'Naomi was determined to sell.' The commentators discuss the halachic status of such a sale and suggest that in a *city, and said: 'Sit here,' and they sat down.*

³ Then he said to the redeemer: 'The parcel of land which belonged to our brother, Elimelech, is being offered for sale by Naomi who has returned from the fields of Moab. ⁴ I resolved that I should inform you to this effect: Buy it in the presence of those sitting here and in the presence of the elders of my people. If you are willing to redeem, redeem! But if it will not be

classic sense 'redemption' would imply that the field had *already* been either sold or was in the process of being sold to someone else, and it is the duty of the near-of-kin to 'redeem' its sale. In the strict *halachic* sense, however, had the property already been sold to another, there would have to be a two-year waiting period between sale and redemption (which certainly was not the case here). Therefore, in the final analysis, most commentators (*Rashi, Ramban, Ibn Ezra, Alkabetz, Alshich*) agree that in this case, a prior sale had not taken place.]

הַשָּׁבָה מִשְּׂדֵה מוֹאָב — *Who has returned from the field of Moab.* Destitute, hungry and barefoot (*Iggeres Shmuel*).

4. וַאֲנִי אָמַרְתִּי — *I resolved* [lit. *'I said'*]. Since I wanted to avoid having the field fall into the hands of strangers — and you precede me — I decided to give you the first option to act as redeemer (*Malbim*).

אֶגְלֶה אָזְנְךָ לֵאמֹר — *I should inform you to this effect.* I personally, not via an intermediary (*Midrash Lekach Tov*).

קְנֵה נֶגֶד הַיֹּשְׁבִים... — *Buy it in the presence of those sitting here ...*

Note that here Boaz uses the word קְנֵה, *buy*, and later in the verse גָּאַל, *redeem. There is a difference: One who buys* looks for a bargain, and tries to purchase at the lowest possible price. A גָּאַל, *redeemer,* however, is more magnanimous; to keep his family estate intact he will graciously pay more. Boaz, therefore, said: '*In the presence of the elders*, etc., *I officially advise you to 'buy'*; but, between ourselves, my advice is *'redeem it'* i.e. act more magnanimously, because if you won't, I will' (*Iggeres Shmuel*).

Boaz was apprehensive that before their departure to Moab, Machlon and Kilion might have sold their estates. He therefore insisted that this transaction take place *'in the presence of those sitting here and in the presence of the elders of my people', i.e. in public,* to prevent the possibility of an unknown purchaser arising later and laying claim to the field (*Meishiv Nefesh*).

אִם־תִּגְאַל גְּאָל — *If you are willing to redeem, redeem.* 'Immediately, and without delay' (*Alshich*) [as it is your primary right and obligation to do according to *Leviticus 25:25*].

וְאִם־לֹא יִגְאַל — *But if it will not be redeemed.* [The phrase literally

וְאֵדְעָ֖* כִּ֣י אֵ֤ין זוּלָֽתְךָ֙ לִגְא֔וֹל וְאָנֹכִ֖י אַחֲרֶ֑יךָ
וַיֹּ֖אמֶר אָנֹכִ֥י אֶגְאָֽל׃ וַיֹּ֨אמֶר בֹּ֜עַז בְּיוֹם־ ה
קְנוֹתְךָ֧ הַשָּׂדֶ֛ה מִיַּ֥ד נָעֳמִ֑י וּ֠מֵאֵ֠ת ר֣וּת
הַמּוֹאֲבִיָּ֤ה אֵֽשֶׁת־הַמֵּת֙ קָנִ֔יתָ* לְהָקִ֥ים
שֵׁם־הַמֵּ֖ת עַל־נַחֲלָתֽוֹ׃ וַיֹּ֣אמֶר הַגֹּאֵ֗ל לֹ֤א ו
אוּכַל֙ לִגְאָוֹל־* לִ֔י פֶּן־אַשְׁחִ֖ית אֶת־נַחֲלָתִ֑י

°וְאֵדְעָה ק'

°קָנִ֫ית

°יתיר ו'

means: 'But if he will not redeem'
According to the Midrash, Boaz
said this phrase directly to the
elders.]

כִּי אֵין זוּלָתְךָ לִגְאוֹל — For there is no
one else to redeem it but you. i.e. no
one else from among our relatives
(Rashi). — just the two of us
(Alshich).

And according to the Torah, you,
as the closest relative, are given the
first option (Akeidas Yitzchak).

וַיֹּאמֶר אָנֹכִי אֶגְאָל — And he said, I am
willing to redeem. He consented
because he was aware only of his
obligation to redeem Naomi's field.
— At that time, he knew nothing of
Ruth (Malbim).

According to the Midrash, he assumed that he had no obligation
vis-a-vis Ruth's portion of the estate (Yefe Anaf).

5. בְּיוֹם־קְנוֹתְךָ הַשָּׂדֶה מִיַּד נָעֳמִי — The
day you buy the field from Naomi.
When Boaz heard the kinsman was
accepting his obligation, he told him
of the condition attached to the
redemption: he must also, at the
same time, marry Ruth (Midrash
Lekach Tov).

'When you buy Naomi's field,
don't think you thereby have fulfilled your obligation. Naomi owns
only half the estate; [according to
the Zohar Chadash (that Ruth con-

verted when she married Machlon)
— see Introduction] the other half
belongs to Ruth — and it is absolutely essential that when you
redeem Naomi's portion you must
also redeem Ruth's (Pri Chaim).

וּמֵאֵת רוּת הַמּוֹאֲבִיָּה אֵשֶׁת־הַמֵּת
קָנִיתָ — You must also buy from
Ruth the Moabite, the wife of the
deceased. [The translation of this
obscure Hebrew phrase follows
Rashi, who continues: 'and she is
not willing [to sell] unless you marry her'].

'And just as we cannot leave the
redemption of the field to an outsider, so can we not allow a
righteous woman like Ruth to be
married to an outsider'(Zos
Nechemasi).

The Iggeres Shmuel notes that
Boaz stressed מוֹאֲבִיָּה, the Moabite
[even though female Moabites had
already been officially permitted]
and he also mentioned אֵשֶׁת־הַמֵּת,
wife of the deceased, invoking the
memory of the dead, in a further attempt to discourage the kinsman.
Boaz hoped to keep the mitzvah of
the redemption for himself.

[My father, Harav Aron Zlotowitz שליט"א, pointed out that the
Shaarei Teshuvah on Orach Chaim
484:1, quotes this Iggeres Shmuel
to support a halachah: Although
misleading someone is prohibited —

redeemed, tell me, that I may know; for there is no one else to redeem it but you, and I after you.' And he said: 'I am willing to redeem it.'

⁵ Then Boaz said: 'The day you buy the field from Naomi, you must also buy it from Ruth the Moabite, wife, of the deceased, to perpetuate the name of the deceased on his inheritance.' ⁶ The redeemer said, 'Then I cannot redeem it for myself, lest I imperil my

in financial matters — however in matters pertaining to the performance of a *mitzvah*, in a case where no one has *specifically* been appointed to perform that particular *mitzvah*, that *mitzvah* is considered open to all who wish to fulfill it. One should strive as much as possible, by whatever means, to perfect his soul and acquire that *mitzvah* for himself.]

The כְּתִיב, traditional spelling is קָנִיתִי, 'I bought,' because Boaz prophetically foresaw that it was *he* who would ultimately consummate the transaction *(Torah T'mimah)*.

לְהָקִים שֵׁם־הַמֵּת עַל נַחֲלָתוֹ — *To perpetuate the name of the deceased on his inheritance.* Boaz made clear that the main purpose of this entire transaction was *'to perpetuate the name of the deceased on his inheritance;* acquisition of the field itself was secondary *(Vilna Gaon).*

6. לֹא אוּכַל לִגְאָל־לִי — *'Then I cannot redeem it for myself.'* 'Machlon and Kilion died only because they took them [Ruth and Orpah — Moabite women] as wives; shall *I* then go and take her?' *(Midrash).*

I cannot allow myself to take on a second wife and destroy the harmony of my home *(Targum).*

The *Iggeres Shmuel* stresses לֹא אוּכַל as meaning *'I am unable'* — i.e. 'my merits are insufficient to effect a redemption of Machlon's soul; his sin was great and he needs זְכוּיוֹת merits, like, yours, Boaz, to effect true redemption.' The *Malbim* stressing לִי, *for myself,* translates: 'I cannot redeem because it will not remain לִי, *in my name,* but rather in the name of the deceased, and *I will thus destroy my own inheritance.'*

פֶּן אַשְׁחִית אֶת נַחֲלָתִי — *Lest I imperil my own inheritance.* [The *Midrash* takes נַחֲלָה to mean *'children'* (comp. *Psalms 127:3,* נַחֲלַת ה' בָּנִים, *'the heritage of God is children').*]

'Heaven forfend that I should take her; I will not contaminate my seed — even if I myself will not die for the sin [of marrying a Moabite woman], my children may suffer. I will not cause my children to become disqualified.'' But, the *Midrash* continues, he was unaware of the law newly publicized 'Moabite but not Moabitess' [see *Introduction*].

The *Chidah* discusses this *Midrash* and asks the obvious question: If he was unaware, why didn't they tell it to him? Furthermore, they had just finished confirming it [see *Comm.* to 4:2], Didn't he hear? — Rather, he was unlearned in Torah and could not comprehend

גְּאַל־לְךָ אַתָּה אֶת־גְּאֻלָּתִי כִּי לֹא־אוּכַל
לִגְאוֹל: וְזֹאת לְפָנִים בְּיִשְׂרָאֵל עַל־
הַגְּאֻלָּה וְעַל־הַתְּמוּרָה לְקַיֵּם כָּל־דָּבָר
שָׁלַף אִישׁ נַעֲלוֹ וְנָתַן לְרֵעֵהוּ וְזֹאת

how the law could have been unknown for so long until it was just
now repromulgated. He thought
they were mistaken in their ruling —
therefore he used the uncertain term
פֶּן, 'lest.' He was uncertain himself,
and he refused to put his progeny in
jeopardy, hence he 'made himself
unaware.'

The *Bach* questions how the
kinsman could have been so brazen
as to disagree with a ruling of the
Sanhedrin, an act which is rebellious and, under some circumstances, punishable by death! Also,
if according to the kinsman the ruling permitting a female Moabite
was improper, how dare he suggest
that Boaz take her? — Rather, he
acknowledged the ruling as valid,
but he considered himself insignificant to execute it, for were the ruling ever disputed [as it was when
Doeg later attempted to disqualify
David!; see *Introduction*] — his seed
would be disqualified, and he would
have been of insignificant stature to
combat the slur. Therefore he stressed לִי, *for myself*, i.e. I, a commoner
cannot take this awesome responsibility upon myself. He felt that
such a precedent-setting act must
be done by a great man, a leader and
judge such as Boaz himself. גְּאַל־לְךָ
אַתָּה, 'You redeem for yourself' he
said to Boaz, 'because as a man of
great stature *your* deeds are less
prone to be disputed.

According to *Rav Velvele Brisker*
[pointed out to me by my friend

Harav David Cohen] *Ploni Almoni*
mistakenly thought that this law
was *interpreted* by the Sanhedrin —
and as such, open to possible later
reinterpretation. He was not aware
that it was a never-before-invoked
*tradition from Moses at Sinai, and
hence uncontestable.*

גְּאַל־לְךָ אַתָּה אֶת־גְּאֻלָּתִי — *Take over
my right of redemption for
yourself.* [Lit. 'Redeem for yourself
my redemption']. 'Boaz, you are a
man of merits; you accept the
responsibility' (*Iggeres Shmuel*).

'You don't have a wife and
children; you do it!' (*Alshich*).

'I feel a female Moabite is
prohibited and I don't want to contaminate my seed thereby. If you
permit it *take over my right of
redemption yourself*, because under
the circumstances *I am unable to
redeem* (*Pri Chaim*).

The greater the selfishness of the
egoist, the more generous the
measure of altruism he allows to
others' (*Rav Breuer*).

7. וְזֹאת לְפָנִים בְּיִשְׂרָאֵל — *Now this
was formerly done in Israel* — i.e. in
ancient times (*Ibn Ezra*).

Since the next verse goes on to
tell us that Boaz removed his shoe to
consummate the transaction. This
verse introduces the custom, explaining that, although it is not
Biblical in origin, it is nevertheless
an ancient and well founded one
(*Iggeres Shmuel*).

own inheritance. Take over my redemption respon-
sibility on yourself for I am unable to redeem.'

7 *Formerly this was done in Israel in cases of*
redemption and exchange transactions to validate all
matters: one would draw off his shoe, and give it to

Rav Alkabetz notes that this ancient form of acquisition, once very much in mode, fell into disuse for some time, and Boaz reinstituted it on that occasion. Therefore the author found it appropriate to explain the custom as being old, and וְזֹאת הַתְּעוּדָה בְּיִשְׂרָאֵל, *having the strength of Torah-law* עֵדוּת, *testimony, ratification.*

עַל־הַגְּאוּלָה וְעַל־הַתְּמוּרָה — *In cases of redemption and exchange transactions. 'Redemption'* — i.e. sales; *'exchange transactions'* — חֲלִיפִין' (*Rashi*).

[This verse parenthetically discusses קִנְיָן , the mode of acquisition of property which was in vogue at that time. According to *halachah*, whenever a transaction occurs, the transaction may be consummated — even before money changes hands — by a symbolic barter, an example of which is חֲלִיפִין, *'exchange'*. In our times it is called קִנְיָן סוּדָר, lit. *'acquisition of a scarf'* during which a garment is symbolically grasped by both parties to the transaction .]

[According to the *Rambam*: 'Real estate ... may be acquired by symbolic barter. This act is called *Kinyan*. The fundamental principal of this mode of acquisition is that the transferee should give the transferor an article of some utility no matter how small its value and say to him, "Acquire this article in exchange for the yard ... you sold me for so much and so much." If

this is done, then the moment the vendor lifts the article and takes possession of it, the purchaser acquires title to the land ... though he has not paid its price. Then neither party may renege.']

שָׁלַף אִישׁ נַעֲלוֹ וְנָתַן לְרֵעֵהוּ *One would draw off his shoe and give it to the other.* A shoe was used because it was always convenient and available; a shirt or other necessary garment could not very well be removed leaving the purchaser bare! *(Ibn Ezra).*

The *Targum*, without further elucidation translates נַעַל, *'shoe'* as *'glove.'*

[It must be made clear that the transference of a shoe described in this verse is not to be confused with the act of *chalitzah (Deut. 29:9)* where a similar symbolic action takes place. *Chalitzah* is applicable only in the case of a sister-in-law, where the brother of the deceased does not want to perform יִבּוּם, *levirate marriage.* Thus procedure *'frees her to marry whomsoever'* she desires. Note, also, that in reference to *chalitzah (Deut., ibid.)* the Torah uses the word חָלַץ for *'removal'* instead of its synonym שָׁלַף used in this verse, suggesting a different procedure]. Therefore, the verse describes this procedure as one accompanying *every* exchange and sales transaction, so as not to confuse it with *chalitzah (Meishiv Nefesh).*

ח הַתְּעוּדָה בְּיִשְׂרָאֵל: וַיֹּאמֶר הַגֹּאֵל לְבֹעַז
ט קְנֵה־לָךְ וַיִּשְׁלֹף נַעֲלוֹ: וַיֹּאמֶר בֹּעַז
לַזְּקֵנִים וְכָל־הָעָם עֵדִים אַתֶּם הַיּוֹם כִּי
קָנִיתִי אֶת־כָּל־אֲשֶׁר לֶאֱלִימֶלֶךְ וְאֵת כָּל־
אֲשֶׁר לְכִלְיוֹן וּמַחְלוֹן מִיַּד נָעֳמִי: וְגַם אֶת־
י רוּת הַמֹּאֲבִיָּה אֵשֶׁת מַחְלוֹן קָנִיתִי לִי
לְאִשָּׁה לְהָקִים שֵׁם־הַמֵּת עַל־נַחֲלָתוֹ
וְלֹא־יִכָּרֵת שֵׁם־הַמֵּת מֵעִם אֶחָיו וּמִשַּׁעַר

וְזֹאת הַתְּעוּדָה בְּיִשְׂרָאֵל — *This was the process of ratification in Israel.* תְּעוּדָה stems from עֵדוּת, 'testimony' (Ibn Ezra); and the transference of the shoe, once completed, was 'testimony' hallowed by Biblical tradition, that the transaction was complete and irrevocable (Ralbag; Alshich).

[The *halachos* stemming from this verse are fully treated in *Choshen Mishpat* 195].

8. קְנֵה־לָךְ — *Buy it for yourself.* The *Bach* observes that (in verse 6) the kinsman renounced his right of redemption, but Boaz did not immediately respond. He was apprehensive that the kinsman would later regret it and lay claim to the redemption. Only after the kinsman, noting Boaz's silence *specifically* said *'buy it for yourself'* — before the elders and the entire community — did Boaz formalize his acceptance by drawing off his shoe.

וַיִּשְׁלֹף נַעֲלוֹ — *He drew off his shoe.* 'Whose shoe, Boaz's or the kinsman? — It is more likely Boaz's shoe, for according to the established *halachah*, it is the purchaser who gives the pledge

(Bava Metzia 47a; Midrash). The Talmud [Bava Metzia 47a] records a minority opinion that it was the kinsman who drew off his shoe and gave it to Boaz as if to say 'As I hand you the shoe, I hand over the rights of redemption' (Ibn Ezra).

9, וְכָל־הָעָם — *And all the people* [Obviously, a crowd had assembled by this time, to witness the events.]

עֵדִים אַתֶּם הַיּוֹם — *You are witnesses this day.* This phrase is repeated twice (in this and the next verse). The *Malbim* explains that he summoned two groups of witnesses: one for the purchase of the land, and the other for the marriage of Ruth.

Boaz thus took every possible precaution to ensure the legality of the proceeding (Nachlas Yosef).

לְכִלְיוֹן וּמַחְלוֹן — *Kilion and Machlon.* Their names are recorded here in seemingly reverse order from the other places where they are mentioned. They are listed in this verse in the order of their death and the succession of their inheritance (Vilna Gaon; Bach; Iggeres Shmuel).

According to Alshich, Boaz men-

*the other. This was the process of ratification in
Israel. * * So, when the redeemer said to Boaz: 'Buy it
for yourself,' he drew off his shoe.*

*⁹ And Boaz said to the elders, and to all the people:
'You are witness this day, that I have bought all that
was Elimelech's and all that was Kilion's and
Machlon's from Naomi.*

*¹⁰ And, what it more important, I have also 'ac-
quired' the wife of Machlon as my wife, to
perpetuate name of the deceased on his inheritance,
that the name of the deceased not be cut off from*

---

tioned Kilion first to stress that his
property had also been redeemed so
that no descendent of his widow
Orpah would ever be able to dispute
Boaz's absolute right of ownership.
One must be concerned with the inferior members of the family. Hence
he mentioned him first (*Zos
Nechemasi*).

מִיַּד נָעֳמִי — *from the hand of Naomi.*
i.e. with Naomi's consent (*Zos
Nechemasi*).

These commentators point out
that according to *halachah*, the estates of Machlon and Kilion would
not have reverted to Naomi. What
then is the significance of מִיַּד נָעֳמִי
from the hand of Naomi? — Several
explanations are given. According
to the *Bach* it was given back to
Naomi as a *gift*; the *Chidah* suggests that it remained part of the
marriage settlement in her care.

10. וְגַם אֶת־רוּת הַמֹּאֲבִיָּה. . . קָנִיתִי לִי
לְאִשָּׁה — *And, what is more, I have
also 'acquired' Ruth the Moabite
wife of Machlon.* The act of taking
Ruth as his wife was separate from
the redemption of the field. For this

event he enlisted them as separate
witnesses (*Malbim*).

[Boaz mentions the 'acquisition'
of Ruth with great delicacy. The acquisition of a wife and property are
referred to with the same legalisms,
but there the similarity ends. A
Jewish wife is a respected and
beloved partner in the sacred text of
building a home. Therefore, Boaz
mentions his marriage separately to
make it clear that he does not lump
Ruth with his newly acquired land.]

He referred to her as הַמֹּאֲבִיָּה, *the
Moabite,* to stress to the populace —
who might not as yet have heard the
ruling permitting female Moabites
— that although she was a Moabite,
she was nevertheless permitted to
him (*Shaar Bas Rabim*).

אֵשֶׁת מַחְלוֹן — *wife of Machlon.* She
is still considered Machlon's 'wife'
because as the *Zohar* states her husbands 'spirit' still stirred within her
[see Comm. on 3:1] (*Malbim*).

לְהָקִים שֵׁם־הַמֵּת — *And thereby
perpetuate the name of the deceased.*
[Here again Boaz emphasizes the
sincerity with which he embarked
on this transaction. His purpose

יא מְקוֹמוֹ עֵדִים אַתֶּם הַיּוֹם: וַיֹּאמְרוּ כָּל־
הָעָם אֲשֶׁר־בַּשַּׁעַר וְהַזְּקֵנִים עֵדִים יִתֵּן
יהוה אֶת־הָאִשָּׁה הַבָּאָה אֶל־בֵּיתֶךָ כְּרָחֵל |
וּכְלֵאָה אֲשֶׁר בָּנוּ שְׁתֵּיהֶם אֶת־בֵּית
יִשְׂרָאֵל וַעֲשֵׂה־חַיִל בְּאֶפְרָתָה וּקְרָא־שֵׁם
יב בְּבֵית לָחֶם: וִיהִי בֵיתְךָ כְּבֵית פֶּרֶץ אֲשֶׁר־
יָלְדָה תָמָר לִיהוּדָה מִן־הַזֶּרַע אֲשֶׁר יִתֵּן
יג יהוה לְךָ מִן־הַנַּעֲרָה הַזֹּאת: וַיִּקַּח בֹּעַז
אֶת־רוּת וַתְּהִי־לוֹ לְאִשָּׁה וַיָּבֹא אֵלֶיהָ

was not selfish, but to 'perpetuate Machlon's memory — not with *actual* levirate marriage, for that did not apply here, but symbolically]. . .

'By his wife going about the field doing her business all who see her will say, she was the wife of Machlon. His name is thereby perpetuated because of her' (Rashi).

11. כָּל־הָעָם — *All* [The blessing was a spontaneous response offered in unison by all present].

They witnessed the proceedings and also blessed him in three ways: a. הָאִשָּׁה, *the woman* — despite the fact that she is of foreign stock and upbringing, by virtue of her *coming into your house*, the house of a righteous man like yourself, she will become like *Rachel and Leah* — also foreigners, daughters of Laban the Aramean, who married Jacob and *built up the House of Israel*. So will Ruth, too, merit righteous and royal descendants; b. *Boaz* himself should *prosper as an Ephrathite*, i.e. his distinguished family name, bringing further glory to his family, [see Comm. 1:2 s.v. אֶפְרָתִים) *and be famous in Bethlehem*, i.e. may your own accomplishments bring such

praise to Bethlehem that all will say 'The great man Boaz was born here!'; and c. [next verse] *your house* i.e. the children you will have from this marriage may be considered as if they were the children of Machlon because you are taking Ruth in the spirit of levirate marriage (see Introduction), nevertheless, just *as the home of Peretz whom Tamar bore* [Gen. Chapter 38] was ascribed to *Judah*; so may your 'house' be honored and distinguished through the offspring which HASHEM will give *you* by this young woman' (Malbim).

וַעֲשֵׂה־חַיִל בְּאֶפְרָתָה — *And be famous in Bethlehem*. The *Alshich* offers: May she no longer be called 'Ruth the Moabite' but 'Ruth of Bethlehem.'

כְּרָחֵל וּכְלֵאָה — *like Rachel and like Leah*. Although those present were of the tribe of Judah, descendent of Leah, they agreed that Rachel was the mainstay of the house, and they mentioned Rachel first (Rashi).

The *Gishmei Brachah* suggests that the people compared Ruth to Rachael and Leah because they too came from non-righteous parents.

among his brethren, and from the gate of his place.
You are witnesses today.'

11 Then all the people who were at the gate, and the
elders, said: 'We are witnesses! May HASHEM make
the woman who is coming into your house like
Rachel and like Leah, both of whom built up the
House of Israel. May you prosper in Ephrath and be
famous in Bethlehem; 12 and may your house be like
the house of Peretz, whom Tamar bore to Judah,
through the offspring which HASHEM will give you
by this young woman.'

Holy
seeds
unite

13 And so, Boaz took Ruth and she became his
wife; and he came to her. HASHEM let her conceive,

Sarah and Rivka were not mentioned because each of them had one evil son — Yishmael and Esav — whereas Rachel and Leah had only righteous children; also Ruth, like Rachel and Leah deserted their parents' home to cleave to God and a righteous husband.

12. וִיהִי בֵיתְךָ כְּבֵית פֶּרֶץ — *May your house be like the home of Peretz whom Tamar bore unto Judah.* By evoking Tamar's memory, they meant to allay any guilt Boaz might have felt about the propriety of the circumstances leading to his marriage to Ruth (*Gishmei Brachah*).

13. בֹּעַז אֶת־רוּת — *And so, Boaz took Ruth and she became his wife.* This was not a true levirate marriage. Boaz first 'took' her as his wife, formally, with קִידוּשִׁין, 'sanctification', and only *then* וַיָּבֹא אֵלֶיהָ *did he consummate the marriage* (*Malbim*). [see *Rambam*: 'According to *Scriptual Law*, there need be no marriage ceremony for

Levirate marriage, since she is his wife already, married to him by Heaven'] The verse makes it clear that Boaz did not act in accordance with the custom [see *Rambam*] of יִבּוּם, levirate marriage.

On that very night, Boaz died (*Yalkut Shimoni*).

[With Ruth's marriage and the birth of her child, her place in Jewish history is secure. Ruth's name is no longer mentioned in the *Megillah*. The Sages maintain she enjoyed unusual longevity. She lived to see her royal descendent Solomon on the throne (*Bava Basra 91b*).]

וַיִּתֵּן ה' לָהּ הֵרָיוֹן — *HASHEM let her conceive* [lit. HASHEM gave her conception]. God, in His Providence allowed her to conceive immediately, although with her first husband — who had been a young man — she never conceived (*Malbim*).

The numerical value of הֵרָיוֹן, conception, equals 271; the amount of days which, according to the Sages [*Niddah, 38b*], a pregnant woman carries (*Nachal Eshkol*).

יד וַיִּתֵּן יהוה לָהּ הֵרָיוֹן וַתֵּלֶד בֵּן: וַתֹּאמַרְנָה
הַנָּשִׁים אֶל־נָעֳמִי בָּרוּךְ יהוה אֲשֶׁר לֹא
הִשְׁבִּית לָךְ גֹּאֵל הַיּוֹם וְיִקָּרֵא שְׁמוֹ
בְּיִשְׂרָאֵל: וְהָיָה לָךְ לְמֵשִׁיב נֶפֶשׁ וּלְכַלְכֵּל
טו אֶת־שֵׂיבָתֵךְ כִּי כַלָּתֵךְ אֲשֶׁר־אֲהֵבָתֶךְ
יְלָדַתּוּ אֲשֶׁר־הִיא טוֹבָה לָךְ מִשִּׁבְעָה
טז בָנִים: וַתִּקַּח נָעֳמִי אֶת־הַיֶּלֶד וַתְּשִׁתֵהוּ
יז בְחֵיקָהּ וַתְּהִי־לוֹ לְאֹמֶנֶת: וַתִּקְרֶאנָה לוֹ
הַשְּׁכֵנוֹת שֵׁם לֵאמֹר יֻלַּד־בֵּן לְנָעֳמִי
וַתִּקְרֶאנָה שְׁמוֹ עוֹבֵד הוּא אֲבִי־יִשַׁי אֲבִי

וַתֵּלֶד בֵּן — *and she bore a son.* Rav Alkabetz comments that 'unto him' is not mentioned because Boaz was already dead when the child was born.

14. אֲשֶׁר לֹא הִשְׁבִּית לָךְ גֹּאֵל — *who has not left you without a redeemer.* i.e. the child will 'redeem' you from dying childless as he carries the soul of your son Machlon. Also, since Boaz died on the night of his marriage, had the child not been conceived that very night, Naomi would truly have been cut off completely (*Alshich*).

הַיּוֹם — *Today.* This phrase is seemingly superfluous, and the *Midrash* interprets it as an additional blessing: 'Just as the day [i.e. the sun] holds dominion in the skies, so may your seed produce one [the Messiah from the House of David] who will hold sway over Israel forever. . .

Rav Chunya said: 'It was the result of the blessings of these women that the line of David was not cut off entirely in the days of

Ataliah [see *II Kings*]' (*Midrash*).

וְיִקָּרֵא שְׁמוֹ בְּיִשְׂרָאֵל — *And may his name be famous in Israel.* (lit. 'may his name be called in Israel) He will be righteous, and people will name their children after him (*Iggeres Shmuel*).

Pri Chaim observes that had this child been born during Machlon's lifetime — before Ruth's conversion [according to those who maintain that Ruth's conversion took place after her husband's death (see *Introduction*)] — the child would have been considered a non-Jew following the nationality of his mother; now, after Machlon's death and Ruth's conversion, 'his name is called' in Israel i.e. he is a full-fledged Jew.

15. וְהָיָה לָךְ לְמֵשִׁיב נֶפֶשׁ — *He will become your life-restorer* [lit. 'as one who refreshes the soul']. [i.e. a comforter, after so many years of trials and suffering].

The *Malbim* explains that his birth, in a sense, 'revived' the soul of her son Machlon.

and she bore a son. 14 *And the women said to Naomi,
'Blessed be HASHEM who has not left you without a
redeemer today! May his name be famous in Israel.*
15 *He will become your life-restorer, and sustain your
old age; for your daughter-in-law, who loves you,
has borne him, and she is better to you than seven
sons.'*

16 *Naomi took the child, and held it in her bosom,
and she became his nurse.* 17 *The neighborhood
women gave him a name, saying: 'A son is born to
Naomi.' They named him Oved; he was the father of*

Ruth—
mother of
monarchy

וּלְכַלְכֵּל אֶת־שֵׂיבָתֵךְ — *And sustain
your old age.* As a son of Ruth, who
so selflessly sustained you in her
youth, he will certainly sustain you
in your old age (*Alshich*).

He will sustain you in your old
age with delicacies (*Targum*).

אֲשֶׁר־הִיא טוֹבָה לָךְ מִשִּׁבְעָה בָּנִים — *and
she is better to you than seven sons.*
The *Midrash* differs on whether this
refers to the seven sons of Jesse
(enumerated in I *Chron.* 2:13) or to
the seven generations listed in
verses 18-21).

16. וַתְּהִי־לוֹ לְאֹמֶנֶת — *And became
his nurse.* The *Alshich* explains that
Naomi was miraculously enabled to
nurse the child. It became manifestly clear to all that Machlon's
memory had been perpetuated
through the child and, in a spiritual
sense, a *child had* truly *been born* to
Naomi.'

17. וַתִּקְרֶאנָה לוֹ הַשְּׁכֵנוֹת שֵׁם — *The
neighborhood women gave him a
name.* Seeing the miracle God
wrought for Naomi, allowing her to
nurse the child, they realized that a
continuity of Machlon's soul had
been implanted in the child; it was

truly Naomi's child (*Zos
Nechemasi*).

יֻלַּד־בֵּן לְנָעֳמִי — *A son is born to
Naomi.* The *Talmud* remarks: 'Was
it then Naomi who bore him? Surely it was Ruth who bore him! — But
Ruth bore and Naomi brought him
up; hence he was called after
Naomi's name' (*Sanhedrin 19b*).

It was through her counsel that
the marriage came about, and so it
was proper that the child should be
called after her (*Nachlas Yosef*).

'The neighbors described the
child as a son born to Naomi,' with
reference to the legitimacy of the
child, which some questioned, for
he had been born from a Moabitess.
That is to say, it is not the name of
the Moabite mother which is called
on this child, but the name of
Naomi — a granddaughter of
Nachshon son of Aminadov, a
prince among his people. And Ruth
had also become to Naomi like her
own child from birth — how dare
anyone slur this noble child! (*Sefer
haToda'ah*).

וַתִּקְרֶאנָה שְׁמוֹ עוֹבֵד — *They called his
name Oved.* i.e. as a blessing that
this child will 'serve [עוֹבֵד] God

יח דָוִד: וְאֵלֶּה תּוֹלְדוֹת פָּרֶץ פֶּרֶץ הוֹלִיד
יט אֶת־חֶצְרוֹן: וְחֶצְרוֹן הוֹלִיד אֶת־רָם וְרָם
כ הוֹלִיד אֶת־עַמִּינָדָב: וְעַמִּינָדָב הוֹלִיד
אֶת־נַחְשׁוֹן וְנַחְשׁוֹן הוֹלִיד אֶת־שַׂלְמָה:
כא וְשַׂלְמוֹן הוֹלִיד אֶת־בֹּעַז וּבֹעַז הוֹלִיד אֶת־
כב עוֹבֵד: וְעֹבֵד הוֹלִיד אֶת־יִשַׁי וְיִשַׁי הוֹלִיד
אֶת־דָּוִד:

with a full heart (Iggeres Shmuel).

אֲבִי דָוִד — The father of David. According to Iggeres Shmuel this phrase refers back to Oved, i.e. it was not merely by the merit of Jesse that David was born; by the merit of Oved were Jesse and David born. He was the 'father of Jesse' and the 'father of David.'

'This story was the cause of severe harassment to the house of David. "How long," said David to God, "will they speak angrily and say: Is he not of unworthy lineage? Is he not descended from Ruth the Moabite? (Ruth Rabbah 8:1)...A man-made story would have attributed the privilege of David's birth to an aristocratic Israelite mother, in accordance with the dignity of Boaz, the descendant of the illustrious Nachshon ben Aminadov. The gentile monarchs had their lineage traced to gods or celestial bodies (the sun or the stars), and this was taught to the people as a religious principle. But this is another monument to the truthfulness of the prophetic books, *wherein the voice of prophecy spoke without fear of man*. It was only because of the prestige of prophecy in Israel that this narrative was able to be told and was preserved' (Behold A People).

18. Having detailed David's descent from Ruth the Moabite, the author now traces his lineage to Judah (Rashi).

וְאֵלֶּה תּוֹלְדוֹת פָּרֶץ — Now these are the generations of Peretz: [The son of Judah]. Judah was avoided here, and the listing of generations begins with Peretz to avoid evoking the memory of the Judah-Tamar incident which is embarrasing to many (Iggeres Shmuel; Meishiv Nefesh). [See Comm. of Gishmei Bracha on verse 12.].

IV
18-22

Jesse, the father of David.

18 *Now these are the generations of Peretz: Peretz begot Chetzron; *19*and Chetzron begot Ram, and Ram begot Aminadav; *20* and Aminadav begot Nahshon, and Nahshon begot Salmah; *21* and Salmah begot Boaz, and Boaz begot Oved; *22* and Oved begot Jesse, and Jesse begot David.*

חֶצְרוֹן — *Chetzron.* [Mentioned, in *Gen.* 46:12].

19. וְחֶצְרוֹן הוֹלִיד אֶת־רָם — *Chetzron begot Ram.* The *Midrash* points out that Yerachmiel, not Ram, was the elder son. Having married a Canaanite woman *(I Chron. 11:26)*, Yerachmiel was unworthy to be an ancestor of the house of David.

[Ram is not mentioned in the Torah. In I Chron. 2:9 he is identified as the second son of Chetzron].

עַמִּינָדָב — *Aminadav.* [One of the greatest personalities of the tribe of Judah during the slavery in Egypt. His daughter, Elisheva was the wife of Aaron the *Kohen (Exodus 6:23).]*

20. נַחְשׁוֹן — *Nachshon* [the leader of the tribe of Judah. The Sages credit him with being the first one to plunge into the Red Sea. According to *Seder Olam Rabba* he died in the second year in the Desert.]

שַׂלְמָה — *Salmah.* [Sometimes called *Salmon.* He was the brother of Elimelech and Tov].

21. וּבֹעַז הוֹלִיד אֶת עוֹבֵד — *And Boaz begot Oved.* 'Who served [עָבַד, *(avad)]* the Master of the Universe with a perfect heart *(Targum).*

22. וְיִשַׁי הוֹלִיד אֶת דָּוִד — *And Jesse begot David.*

So said the Holy One blessed be He to David: 'What need have I to record the geneology of Peretz, Hezron, Ram, Aminadav, Nachshon, Salmon, Boaz, Oved, Jesse? Only on account of you; מָצָאתִי דָוִד עַבְדִּי, *I have found my servant David'* [(Psalms 89:21)] *(Midrash).*

תם ונשלם שבח לאל בורא עולם

Bibliography—
Biographical Sketches

Bibliography
of Authorities Cited in the Commentary

Italics are used to denote the name of a work. **Bold italics** *within the biography indicate the specific book of that particular author cited in the commentary.*

An asterisk (*) precedes the names of contemporary figures

Alkabetz, Rav Shlomo haLevi:

[b. 1505-Salonica; d. 1576 Safed]
One of the greatest Kabbalists and mystical poets of his day. Author of the Piyyut 'L'cha Dodi' recited every Friday evening. He was a contemporary and friend of Rav Yosef Karo, author of *Shulchan Aruch*.

His commentary on Ruth, **Shoresh Yishai**, published in 1561 is quoted by nearly every commentator on Ruth after him.

He is cited constantly in *Iggeres Shmuel*, who refers to him in various ways: 'Rashba haLevi'; Rav Shlomo haLevi;' Harav ibn Alkabetz haLevi'.

He wrote commentaries on most of the Bible, the Passover Hagaddah, on *Kabbalah*, and was a noted Paytan.

In his Piyyut, 'L'cha Dodi,' he speaks of the sufferings of the Jewish people and their aspirations for Redemption. Probably no other Piyyut has reached the popularity of 'L'cha Dodi'; it is recited every Friday evening by all Jewish congregations throughout the world.

Alshich, Rav Moshe:

[Also spelled Alshekh]

Rav, Posek and Bible Commentator. Born in Andrionople in 1508; studied Torah there in Yeshiva of Rav Yosef Karo. Settled in Safed where he spent most of his life and was ordained there by Rav Karo with the full *Semichah* reintroduced by Rav Yaakov Berav. Among his pupils was Rav Chaim Vital, whom he ordained in 1590.

He died in Damascus, where he was travelling, before 1600.

He wrote Commentaries on most of the Bible, and published a collection of 140 of his *halachic* Responsa.

His **Eynei Moshe** on Ruth was published in 1615.

Alter, Rav Yitzchak Meir

(1789-1866)

Gerrer Rebbe; founder of the Gerrer Chassidic dynasty. Rav Yitzchak Meir was a disciple of the Maggid of Koznitz, and later of Rav Simcha Bunem of Pshyscha, and of Rav Menachem Mendel of Kotzk.

After the Kotzker's death in 1859, Rav Yitzchak Meir was acknowledged Rebbe by the majority of Kotzk Chassidim

His influence was far-reaching. Although his leadership lasted only seven years, he had a formative influence on the development of Chassidus in Poland. Gerrer Chassidus became a powerful element in Orthodox Polish Jewry.

He is most famous for *Chiddushei haRim*, novellae on the Talmud and *Shulchan Aruch*, and was frequently referred to by the name of his work, "The Chiddushei haRim."

Alter, Rav Yehudah Aryeh Leib:

(1847-1903)

Gerrer; known by his work 'Sefas Emes'.

His father, Rav Avraham Mordechai, a great but chronically ill man, died when Yehudah Leib was only 12 years old. His upbringing fell to his grandfather, the illustrious Chidushei haRim. Yehudah Aryeh would study eighteen hours a day as a youth. It became widely known that a fitting successor was being groomed for the Chiddushei haRim.

He was 19 years old when his grandfather died and, despite the pleas of the chassidim, insisted he was unworthy to become Gerrer Rebbe. Several years later, after the death of Rav Henach of Alexandrow, he acceded to their wishes and molded Ger into the largest chassidus in Poland.

A prodigious and diligent scholar, he nevertheless found time to counsel tens of thousands of disciples every year and to become an effective leader in Torah causes. His discourses were distinguished for profundity and originality.

Although he never wrote for publication, his writings were posthumously published as **Sefas Emes**, separate volumes of novellae on Talmud, and chassidic discourses on Torah and festivals.

Anaf Yosef

see *Rav Chanoch Zundel ben Yosef.*

Arama, Rav Yitzchak b. Moshe:

(1420-1494)

Spanish Rav, philospher and preacher. He was Rav of Calatayud where he wrote most of his works. After the expulsion of the Jews from Spain in 1492, he settled in Naples where he died.

He is best known for his book **Akeidas Yitzchak**, a collection of allegorical commentaries on the Torah. First published in 1522, it has been reprinted many times and has exercised great influence on Jewish thought.

Because of this work he is often referred to as the 'Baal Akeidah' ['author of the *Akeidah*.]

He also wrote a **Commentary on the Five Megillos** which was printed together with his *Commentary to the Torah* in Salonica, 1573.

He wrote *Yad Avshalom,* a commentary on *Proverbs,* in memory of his son-in-law Avshalom, who died shortly after his marriage.

Ashkenazi, Rav Shmuel Jaffe:

16th Century Rav in Constantinople.

Not being satisfied with any commentary to the *Midrash,* Rav Shmuel devoted himself to writing a comprehensive commentary to *Midrash Rabba* and to the *Aggados* in the *Talmud.*

His first published work was *Yefe Mar'eh* on the *Aggados* in the Jerusalem *Talmud* (1597); *Yefe To'ar* to *Midrash Rabba: Genesis, Exodus, and Leviticus* (1606); **Yefe Anaf** to *Ruth, Esther,* and *Lamentations* (1691); and *Yefe Kol* to *Song of Songs* (1739).

His commentary to *Ecclesiastes,* and his *halachic* writing are still in manuscript form.

Avodah Zarah

Talmudic tractate on *Seder Nezikin.*

Azulai, Rav Chaim Yosef David:

Known by his Hebrew acronym CHIDA.

Born in Jerusalem in 1724; died in Leghorn in 1806. Halachist, Kabbalist, and bibliographer-historian, he possessed great intellectual powers and many-faceted talents.

He went abroad as an emissary and he would send large sums of money back to Israel. He ended his mission in 1778 in Leghorn where he spent the rest of his life.

His fame as a *halachist* rests on his glosses to *Shulchan Aruch,* contained in his *Birkei Yosef,* a work constantly cited by later authorities.

He was the author of the famous bibliographic work Shem haGedolim. Among his many works was the homiletical **Nachal Eshkol** on the *Five Megillos,* and **Simchas haRegel** on *Ruth.*

Baal haTurim:

see *Rav Yaakov ben Asher.*

Bach:

see *Sirkes, Rav Yoel.*

Bachrach, Rav Yehoshua.

Contemporary Bible scholar on Israeli scene.

Educated in Lithuanian Yeshivos, the first of which was the Yeshivah of Rav Shimon Shkop in Grodno.

He is senior lecturer in *Neviim Rishonim* at the Jerusalem College for Women (Michlalah). He published a monumental study of David and Saul; a book on Jonah and Elijah; and a commentary on *Esther*. His commentary on Ruth, *Ima Shel Malchus* ("Mother of Royalty"), is a poetically profound synthesis of *p'shat* (plain meaning) and *d'rash* (homiletical interpretation).

Bamidbar Rabba:

The *Midrash Rabba* to *Numbers*. See *Midrash Rabba*.

Bava Basra:

Talmudic tractate in *Seder Nezikin*.

Bava Kamma:

Talmudic tractate in *Seder Nezikin*.

Behold a People:

see **Miller, Rav Avigdor*.

Besuras Eliyahu:

see *Rav Eliyahu Shlomo Avraham ha-Kohen*.

Binyan Ariel:

see *Rav Shaul ben Aryeh Leib of Amsterdam*.

Breuer, Rav Raphael:

(1881-1932)

Grandson of Rav S.R. Hirsch; son of Rav Shlomo Breuer; and late brother of Rav Joseph Breuer, shlita, of Washington Heights.

Rav Breuer was born in Papa, Hungary. He was district Rabbi at Aschaffenburg, Bavaria.

He published a commentary (in German) on many books of the Bible. His *Commentary on Ruth* was published as part of his commentary to the *Five Megillos* between the years 1908-12.

Rav Chanoch Zundel Ben Yosef

(d. 1867).

Rav Chanoch lived in Bialystock, Poland, where he devoted his life to writing commentaries on the *Midrash* and the *Ein Yaakov*.

He published two commentaries which appear side-by-side in the large editions of the *Midrash Rabba* and *Ein Yaakov*: *Eitz Yosef*, in which he strives to give the plain meaning of the text; and *Anaf Yosef* which is largely homiletical.

Rav Chanoch also published a commentary to *Pirkei Avos*, but his commentaries to *Yalkut Shim'oni* and the *Mechilta* are still in manuscript.

Chidah:

See *Azulai, Rav Chaim Yosef David*.

Chidushei haRim:

see *Alter, Rav Yitzchak Meir*.

Chafetz Chaim:

See *Rav Yisrael Meir haKohen*.

Rav Yehudah Leib Chasman:

(1869-1935)

Born in Lithuania, he studied in Slobodka, Volozhin, and Kelm. He was strongly influenced by three of the *Mussar* giants of the era: Rav Simcha Zisel Ziev of Kelm; Rav Yitzchak Lazar of St. Petersburg — both of whom were among the foremost disciples of Rav Yisrael Salanter; and Rabbi Nosson Zvi Finkel of Slobodka.

Rav Chasman held several positions as Rav and lecturer of Talmud. He found his place in Shtutzin, Lithuania, where, after assuming the rabbinate in 1909, he established a Yeshivah that grew to 300 students. However, the destruction and dislocation brought about by World War I, destroyed the Torah life of the city.

After the War, Rav Chasman was a vital activist in rebuilding Torah life in Europe.

The call to become 'Mashgiach' (Spiritual Guide) of the Hebron Yeshivah in Eretz Yisrael, gave him the opportunity to become a seminal figure in the development of the Torah Yishuv.

Ohr Yohel, published posthumously by his students, is a collection of his lectures and writings.

Chayes, Rav Zvi Hirsch:

(1807-1856).

Born in the Galician region of Poland. Even at the age of 5 he was known as a prodigy, having mastered the entire *T'nach* by heart.

He was ordained at 21 by Rav Ephraim Zalman Margolias of Brody. Rav Chayes's most famous rabbinical position was Kalisch. He wrote extensively and originally in addition to glosses on the Talmud and halachic responsa. Noteworthy was his *M'vo haTalmud* (Introduction to the Talmud), printed in most editions of the Talmud; Responsa; *Imre Binah; Darkei Horaah.*

Among his most basic writings were a series of monographs called **Toras haNevi'im,** in which he dealt with and clarified many obscure topics in the Torah and post-Biblical tradition.

Derech Hashem:

see *Luzatto, Rav Moshe Chaim*

Dessler, Rav Eliyahu Eliezer:

(1891-1954).

One of the outstanding personalities of the Mussar movement. He was born in Homel, Russia.

In 1929 he settled in London. He excercised a profound influence on the teaching of Mussar, not only because of the profundity of his ideas, but also on

account of his personal, ethical conduct.

In 1941 he became director of the Kollel of Gateshead Yeshiva in London.

In 1947, at the invitation of Rav Yosef Kahaneman, he became Mashgiach of Ponovez Yeshiva in Bnei Brak, Israel, and there remained until his death.

His teachings reflect a harmonious mixture of Mussar, Kaballah, and Chassidus. Some of his ideas were published by his pupils in **Michtav me-Eliyahu** (3 vols. 1955-64).

Dubna Maggid:

See *Kranz, Rav Yaakov.*

Eidels, Rav Shmuel Eliezer ben Yehuda haLevi:

1555-1631.

(Known as Maharsha — Moreinu ha-Rav Shmuel Eliezer.)

One of the foremost Talmud commentators, whose **commentary** is included in almost every edition of the Talmud.

Born in Cracow, he moved to Posen in his youth. In 1614 he became Rav of Lublin, and in 1625 of Ostrog, where he founded a large Yeshivah.

Einhorn, Rav Zev Wolf:

Rav in Vilna, end of 19th century.

Author of **Peirush Maharzu,** comprehensive and well-detailed commentary to *Midrash Rabba* appearing in the Romm edition.

Rav Eleazar b. Yehudah of Worms:

[*Heb.* Eleazar of Germizah.] Also known as *Baal haRokeach*].

1160-1237.

Scholar in the field of Halachah, Kaballah, and Paytan in medieval Germany. Student of Rav Yehudah haChassid the author of *Sefer Chassidim.*

Rav Eleazar is known primarily for his authoritative halachic work **Sefer**

Rokeach, which is quoted extensively in the *Shulchan Aruch.*

His students were many, among them Rav Yitzchak of Vienna, author of *Or Zarua.* Among his exegetical works are **Shaarei Binah.**

Rav Eliyahu Shlomo Avraham haKohen:

(d. 1729).

Born in Smyrna, he spent most of his life there as *Dayyan* and *Rav.*

His most famous works are *Shevet Mussar* on Ethics and homiletics; *Midrash halttamari,* a homiletical work on ethical subjects. Because of this work, he became known as 'Rav Eliyahu halttamari'. He also wrote *Midrash Talpiyos,* novellae on various subjects arranged alphabetically; and *D'na Pashra* [abbreviated: *Perush SHir Hashirim, Ruth, Esther*] commentary on three *Megillos:* — *Song of Songs, Ruth* and *Esther.*

The commentary on *Ruth* is entitled **B'suras Eliyahu.**

Rav Eliyahu ben Shlomo Zalman of Vilna [Vilna Gaon]:

Also known by his acronym haGRA = haGaon Rav Eliyahu.

(Born, first day Passover 1720; died third day of Chol haMoed Sukkos 1797).

One of the greatest spiritual leaders of Jewry in modern times. A child prodigy and man of phenomenal genius, his knowledge of every facet of Torah learning was without equal. His glosses and commentaries encompassed nearly every one of the important classical writings.

The GRA also familiarized himself with astronomy, algebra, and geography in order to better understand certain Talmudic laws and discussions.

According to his sons, he did not sleep more than two hours a night, and never for more than half an hour at a time. He would often study with his feet in cold water to prevent himself from falling asleep.

More than 70 of his works and commentaries have been published. His **Commentary to Ruth** has been reprinted several times.

His influence was immense. According to the testimony of one of his contemporaries, 'without his knowledge, no important activity can be carried out.'

Epstein, Rav Baruch haLevi:

(1860-1940).

Born in Bobruisk, Russia. He received his early education from his father, Rav Yechiel Michel Epstein, author of *Aruch haShulchan.*

Rav Baruch later studied under his uncle, Rav Naftali Zvi Yehudah Berlin [the 'Netziv'].

He was the author of several works, but he is best known for a brilliant commentary to Chumash **Torah T'mimah,** in which he quotes and explains the Halachic and Aggadic passages on the various verses. He also wrote **Gishmei Bracha** on the *Five Megillos.*

Eshkol haKofer:

See *Sava, Rav Avraham ben Yaakov.*

*Feinstein, Rav Moshe:

Contemporary Posek and Rosh Yeshivah, Harav Feinstein is considered by many to be the *Gadol Hador* — Torah leader of the generation.

Born in Russia in 1895, Harav Feinstein was known as a child prodigy. He came to America in 1937 and became Dean of Mesivtha Tifereth Jerusalem on New York's lower East side. Harav Feinstein responds to Halachic inquiries from around the world daily. Author of 'Igrose Moshe' — 5 volumes of his Halachic responsa; and an ongoing series of *Dibrose Moshe* — his novellae on Talmud.

Gans, Rav David.

(1541-1516).

Chronicler and mathematician.

Rav David was a student of the RAMA (Rav Moshe Isserles) and the MAHARAL of Prague (Rav Yehudah Loew), where he mastered his Talmudic studies.

He spent most of his life in Prague where he wrote many works, most of which have been lost.

Encouraged by the RAMA, Rav David published the historical work for which he is most famous: *Tzemach David.* The book is in two parts: one part deals with Jewish history; the other with general history.

This work has become a standard reference work for later chroniclers.

Gishmei Brachah:

see *Epstein, Rav Baruch haLevi.*

halkriti:

see *Rav Shemariah ben Eliyahu halkriti.*

Heilprin, Rav Yechiel b. Shlomo:

(1660-1746).

Lithuanian Rav, Kabbalist and historian.

He was a descendant of RASHAL (Rav Shlomo Luria), and traced his ancestry back through Rashi to the Tanna, Rav Yochanan haSandlar.

He was Rav and Rosh Yeshivah at Minsk, where he studied Kabbalah and published several works.

He is most known for his *Seder haDoros,* a history from Creation down to his own time.

He based his work on *Sefer haYuchsin* of Rav Avraham Zacuto; *Shalsheles haKaballah* of Rav Gedaliah ibn Yachya; and *Tzemach David* of Rav David Gans, as well as on an abundance of Talmudic and Midrashic references.

Hirsch, Rav Shamshon Raphael:

(1808-1888).

The father of modern German Orthodoxy. He was a fiery leader, brilliant writer, and profound educator. His greatness as a Talmudic scholar was obsured by his other monumental accomplishments. After becoming chief Rabbi and member of Parliament in Bohemia and Moravia, he left to revitalize Torah Judaism in Frankfort-am-Main which he transformed into a Torah bastion.

His best known works are the classic six-volume *Commentary on Chumash* noted for its profound and brilliant philosophical approach to Biblical commentary; and *Horeb,* a philosophical analysis of the mitzvos.

Ibn Ezra, Rav Avraham:

(Born 1089 in Toledo; died 1164).

Famous poet, philosopher, grammarian, astronomer — and above all — Biblical commentator. He also wrote a *Commentary on the Megillos* — including Ruth.

In all his Bible commentaries he strived for the plain, literal meaning of the verse. His aim was to explain the etymology of difficult words within their grammatical context. Next to Rashi, his commentary on the Torah is most widely studied, and appears in almost all large editions of the Bible.

In France, he met Rav Yaakov Tam ['Rabbeinu Tam'] — grandson of Rashi], and a deep friendship between the two followed.

According to some, he married the daughter of Rav Yehudah haLevi, and had five sons.

Legend has it that he once met the Rambam and dedicated a poem to him on the day of his death.

Ibn Shushan, Rav Yehudah

Rav in Magnesia, about 1500.

Member of illustrious Ibn Shushan Spanish family of Toledo, which can be traced back to the 12th century.

Little is known about Rav Yehudah. He is the author of a **Commentary on Ruth,** and is quoted extensively in many halachic works, and by Iggeres Shmuel.

Ibn Yachya, Rav Yosef.

Bible commentator; member of the famous Ibn Yachya family of which many scholars were descendants.

He was born in Florence, Italy in 1494, his parents having fled to that country from Portugal.

He relates in his preface to his Torah Or that in her first month of pregnancy with him, his mother, under threat of being ravaged, had thrown herself off a roof in Pisa, in order to preserve her modesty, and she was miraculously saved.

She then fled to Florence where he was born.

He published his **Commentary to the Five Megillos.** Two of his other works: Derech Chaim and Ner Mitzvah were consigned to flames at the burning of the Talmud in Padua in 1554.

Rav Yosef had three sons, one of whom was Gedaliah, the author of Shalsheles haKabbalah.

Rav Yosef died in 1534. Ten years after his death his remains were brought to Eretz Yisrael. Rav Yosef Caro arranged for his burial in Safed.

Iggeres Shmuel:

See Uzeda, Rav Shmuel de.

Ima Shel Malchus:

see Bachrach, Rav Yehoshua.

Josephus, Flavius

[Hebrew: Yosef ben Gorion haKohen].

Jewish, Roman general and historian (born in 37 or 38; died after 100).

He boasted of belonging to the Hasmonim dynasty on his mother's side. As a boy he was distinguished by his profound memory.

During the great Jewish war in 66, he was entrusted by the Sanhedrin with the defense of the Galilee.

Captured in the war and led before Vespasian, he prophecised that Vespasian would become Emperor (just as Rav Yochanan ben Zakkai had also done) — and Vespasian released him, rewarding him with a command in the Roman army.

He spent the rest of his life writing a history and 'apology' of the Jews — which is a classic, eye-witness account of the period. The accuracy, however, of the religious sections is questionable. He was generally despised as a traitor and turncoat by the Jews.

It is said that a statue of him was erected in Rome after his death.

Kimchi, Rav David:

French grammarian; known by his acronym 'RADAK'.

Born in Narbonne, 1160; died there in 1235.

His father, Rav Yosef, also a grammarian died when Rav David was a child, and he studied under his brother, Rav Moshe, who had also published several volumes on grammar.

Radak's commentary on Bible is profound, and is included in most large editions of the Bible.

Many have applied to him the saying from Pirkei Avos: 'Without kemach ['flour' i.e. 'Kimchi'] no Torah; such was his great influence.

His main work was the **Michlol,** the second edition of which came to be known independantly as the Sefer ha-Sharashim.

In his commentary, he stressed the derech ha'peshat, the plain sense, wherever possible, striving for clarity and readibility, rather than the compression and obscurity of some of his contemporary commentators.

His **Commentary to Ruth** was published in Paris, 1563.

Kitov, Rav Eliyahu.

Israeli scholar and author; died, 1976.

Famous for his *Ish uBeiso* ('The Jew and His Home'); **Sefer haTodaah** ('The Book of our Heritage'), both of which have been translated into English by Rav Nathan Bulman; and his series of *Sefer haParshios* on the Five Books of the Bible.

Kol Yaakov:

See *Kranz, Rav Yaakov.*

Kol Yehuda:

Kabbalistic and philosophical commentary to **Ruth,** *Lamentations,* and *Esther,* by Rav Yehudah Leib ben Eliezer published in 1727.

Rav Yaakov Kranz:

(1741-1804).

Known as the 'Dubna Maggid.'

Born near Vilna; Rav Yaakov demonstrated his skill as a preacher at an early age, and was barely 20 years old when he became *darshan* in his city. He later became *darshan* in several cities, but he achieved his fame as preacher in Dubna where he served for 18 years.

He came into frequent contact with the Vilna Gaon, who, it is said, enjoyed his homiletical interpretations, stories, and parables.

The Dubna Maggid's works were printed posthumously by his son Yitzchak, and his pupil Baer Flahm. Among these works were: *Ohel Yaakov* on *Chumash;* **Kol Yaakov** on the *Five Megillos;* Commentary on the Passover *Haggadah;* and *Mishlei Yaakov,* a collection of his parables.

Rav Levi ben Gershom:

(Acronym: RALBAG).

Born in Bangols, France in 12⁸8; died 1344.

One of the most important Bible commentators of his time, he was also a mathematician, astonomer, philosopher, and physician.

He wrote commentaries to *Job, Song of Songs, Ecclesiastes;* **Ruth**; *Esther;* the Five Books of the Torah; Former Prophets; *Proverbs; Daniel; Nechemiah;* and *Proverbs.*

His commentary to *Job* was one of the first books printed in Hebrew (Ferrara, 1477).

Lipowitz, Rav Yosef:

Noted Israeli Bible scholar and lecturer of the last generation.

Rav Lipowitz was one of the outstanding pupils of Rav Nosson Finkel *(der Alter)* of Slobodka.

He published several works on Bible, among them the very philosophical **Nachalas Yosef**, his commentary on *Ruth.* Written in poetic Hebrew, the author appears to be lecturing, as it were, weaving the various Midrashim and philosophical *hashkafos* [perspective] into a flowing, lucid commentary.

Luria, Rav David:

(1798-1855; Known as RADAL).

Lithuanian Rav and *posek.* Student of Rav Shaul Katzenellenbogen of Vilna.

After the death of his mentor, the Vilna Gaon, Radal was considered one of the Torah leaders of is generations. His scholarly writings embrace almost all of Torah literature. Among his works is his commentary to the Midrash, **Chidushei Radal**, printed in the Romm edition of the *Midrash Rabba.*

Luzatto, Rav Moshe Chaim

(1707-1746)

Kabbalist; author of Mussar ethical works; and poet.

Born in Padua, Italy, Rav Moshe Chaim was regarded as a genius from childhood, having mastered *T'nach*, *Midrash* and *Talmud* at an early age. He later went on to delve into Kabbalistic and ethical studies.

He is most famous for his profound ethical treatise, *Mesilas Yesharim* ('The Path of the Upright') which has, alongside the *Chovos haLevavos* of Rav Bachya ibn Paquda, became the standard ethical-Mussar work.

Among his Kabbalistic works were: Razin Genizin, **Megillas Sesarim;** *Maamar haGeulah;* **Derech Hashem.**

In 1743, he emigrated to Eretz Yisrael. He lived a short time in Acre, and died there, with his family, in a plague.

Maharal:

see *Rav Yehudah Loewe ben Bezalel.*

Maharsha:

see *Eidels, Rav Shmuel Eliezer ben Yehudah haLevi.*

Malbim, Rav Meir Leibush:

(1809-1879).

Rav, preacher and Biblical commentator.

The name Malbim is an acronym of 'Meir Leibush ben Yechiel Michel.'

The Malbim was also known as the 'ilui [prodigy] from Volhynia.' He was Rav in several cities, but he suffered much persecution on account of his uncompromising stand against Reform, leading to his short-term imprisonment on a false accusation. He wandered much of his life, serving as Rav in various cities for several years at a time.

His fame and immense popularity rests upon his commentary to the Bible which was widely esteemed. His first published commentary was on *Megillas Esther* (1845). His commentary to the remaining books of the Bible were published between then and 1876. His commentary to *Ruth* is entitled **Geza Yishai.**

Margolios, Rav Chaim Mordechai.

Polish Rav and *Posek*; died in 1818.

Rav Chaim was Rav in Great Dubna, where he operated a printing office.

Together with his brother Rav Ephraim [author of *Bais Ephraim* and *Mattei Ephraim*], he published **Shaarei Teshuvah**, a digest of the Responsa literature dealing with the laws of the *Shulchan Aruch Orach Chaim*, from the time of Rav Yosef Karo until his day.

This work was continued on the three remaining sections of *Shulchan Aruch* by Rav Tzvi Hirsch Eisenstadt and published under the name *Pis'chei Teshuvah.*

Mashal Umelitzah

Collection of homiletic interpretations on the Torah by Rav Avraham Naftali Galanti. Published in New York City during the last generation.

Matanos Kehunah:

see *Rav Yissachar Berman haKohen.*

Megilas Sesarim:

see *Luzatto, Rav Moshe Chaim.*

Michtav me-Eliyahu:

see *Dessler, Rav Eliyahu Eliezer.*

Michlol:

see *Kimchi, Rav David.*

Meishiv Nefesh:

see *Sirkes, Rav Yoel.*

Midrash:

see *Midrash Rabbah.*

Midrash haNe'elam:

see *Zohar Chadash.*

Midrash Lekach Tov:

Early Midrash on various Books of the Bible. This *Midrash* has been published at separate times on the various books of the Bible as the manuscripts have been discovered. **Ruth** was published in 1867.

Midrash Rabbah:

[Lit. 'The Great Midrash'].

The oldest Amoraic classical *Midrash* on the *Five Books of the Bible and the Megillos.*

[Note: Throughout the commentary of this Book, whenever 'Midrash' alone is shown as the source, the reference is to Midrash Ruth Rabba.]

Midrash Tanchuma:

The ancient *Midrash* on the Torah which has come down to us in two versions.

One of the versions is the oldest collections of *Midrashim* known.

Midrash Zuta.

Also called *Ruth Zuta* ('Minor Ruth'). This *Midrash* was probably compiled before the 10th century. It is quoted by the author of *Midrash Lekach Tov* which was written in the 11th century.

It was published by Buber from a Parma manuscript in 1894.

*Miller, Rav Avigdor:

Contemporary Rav, noted lecturer and author. A major force on the American Orthodox scene. Rav in Brooklyn, New York. Author of *Rejoice O Youth!; Sing You Righteous; Torah Nation; Behold A People.*

Minchas Shay:

see *Rav Yedidiah Shlomo of Norzi.*

M'lo haOmer:

see *Zeunz, Rav Aryeh Leib.*

Rav Moshe ben Maimon:

Known by his acronym: RAMBAM; Maimonides.

(1135-1204).

One of the most illustrious figures in Judaism in the post-Talmudic era, and among the greatest of all time. He was a rabbinic authority, codifier, philosopher, and royal physician. According to some, he was a descendant of Rav Yehudah haNasi.

Born in Cordoba; Moved to Eretz Yisrael and then to Fostat, the old city of Cairo, Egypt.

At the age of 23 he began his commentary on the *Mishnah,* which he authored all through his wanderings. His main work was *Mishneh-Torah Yad-haChazakah,* his codification of the spectrum of *Halachah* until his day. This was the only book he wrote in Hebrew, all his other works having been written in Arabic, a fact he regretted later in life.

He is also known for his *Moreh Nevuchim* ('Guide for the Perplexed'), and for his many works in the field of medicine, hygiene, astronomy, etc.

Truly it may be said 'from Moshe to Moshe there arose none like Moshe.'

Rav Moshe ben Nachman:

Known by his acronym: RAMBAN; Nachmanides.

(1194-1270)

One of the leading Torah scholars and authors of Talmudic literature during the generation following Rambam; also a renowned philosopher, biblical commentator, poet and physician .

Born in Gerona, to a famous rabbinic family. He is sometimes referred to, after his native town, as Rabbenu Moshe Gerondi, where he spent most of his life, supporting himself as a physician. He exercised extensive influence over Jewish life. Even King James I consulted him on occasion.

Already at the age of 16 he had published works on Talmud and Halachah.

Among his works were: *Milchemes Hashem,* in defense of the Rif against the 'hasagos' of Rav Zerachiah haLevi in his Sefer haMaor; *Sefer haZechus,* in response to the 'hasagos' of the Ravad on the Rif; *Sefer haMitzvos; Iggeres* haRamban; Iggeres haKodesh; and his profound and encyclopedic **Commentary on the Torah,** which is printed in all large editions of the Bible.

in 1263 he was coerced by King Jame I into holding a public disputation with the apostate Pablo Christiani which led to a victory for the Ramban, but which aroused the anger of the of the church and resulted in his barely secceeding to escape from Spain. He then emigrated to Eretz Yisrael. In 1268 he became Rav in Acco, successor to Rav Yechiel of Paris.

He died in 1276; his burial site has not been definitely ascertained.

Nachalas Yosef:

see *Lipowitz, Rav Yosef.*

Nachal Eshkol:

see *Azulai, Rav Chaim Yosef David.*

Niddah:

Talmudic tractate in *Seder Nashim.*

Ohr Yohel:

See *Chasman, Rav Yehudah Leib.*

Pirkei Avos:

"Chapters" or "Ethics" of the Fathers. A Talmudic tractate in *Seder Nezikin.* Read in the Synagogue on Shabbos afternoons from Passover to Rosh Hashanah.

Pirkei d'Rabbi Eliezer:

Ancient aggadic work attributed to the first century *Tanna,* Rabbi Eliezer ben Hyrcanos.

Pri Chaim:

Commentary to the *Five Megillos* by Rav Chaim Knoller, published in Premyshla, Poland c 1903.

The **Commentary on Ruth** is based on the approach of the *Malbim* whom the author quotes extensively and upon whom he elaborates in a most original manner.

Also by the same author is *Kavod Chachamim* in which he explains what may seem to be discrepencies between the *aggados* of the Talmud and quoted verses in the Bible, as well as Masoretic differences.

Pri Tzaddik:

See next entry.

Rabinowitz, Rav Tzadok haKohen:

(1823-1900)

Born in Kreisburg, Latvia, young Tzadok attracted attention as a phenomenal genius. Orphaned at the age of six, he was raised by his uncle near Bialystock. Such was the child's reputation, that Rav Yitzchak Elchanan Spektor of Kovno made a point of testing him when he happened to be near by.He prophesied that 'the boy will light a great torch of knowledge in Israel.

In later years, Rav Tzadok lived in Lublin where he became acquainted with Rav Leibele Eiger, a disciple of Rav Mordechai Yosef of Izbica. Rav Tzadok became their disciple, and, with their passing, became Rebbe of the Chassidim of Izbica. He became known far and wide as the 'Kohen of Lublin'. The breadth and depth of his thought were astonishing. Many considered him the greatest Torah scholar in all of Poland.

Pri Tzaddik, is a collection of his discourses on the weekly portion, and festivals. He was a very prolific writer. Although much of his works have been published, he left many unpublished manuscripts that were destroyed during World War II.

Among his other works are Responsa *Tiferes Zvi; Meishiv Tzaddik;* and *Resisei Layla.*

Radak:

see *Kimchi, Rav David.*

Ralbag:

see *Rav Levi ben Gershom.*

Rambam:

see *Rav Moshe ben Maimon.*

Ramban:

See *Rav Moshe ben Nachman.*

Rashba haLevi:

see *Alkabetz, Rav Shlomo haLevi.*

Rashi:

see *Rav Shlomo ben Yitzchak.*

Saba, Rav Avraham ben Yaakov.

15-16th Century Kabbalist, Bible commentator and Darshan.

Rav Avraham was among those expelled from Spain in 1492. He moved to Portugal where he wrote his commentary **Eshkol haKofer** to the *Chumash,* the *Five Megillos,* and *Pirkei Avos.*

In his youth, many of his works were lost, and he was forced to rewrite them later in life from memory.

His commentary to the *Chumash* was entitled *Tzror haMor.*

According to the *Shem haGedolim,* he died on board a ship on Erev Yom Kippur 1508.

Sanhedrin:

Talmudic tractate in *Seder Nezikin.*

Seder haDoros:

see *Heilprin, Rav Yechiel b. Shlomo.*

Seder Olam:

Early Midrashic-chronological work. *Seder Olam* is mentioned in the Talmud *(Shab. 88a; Yev. 82b et al.)* and is ascribed to the *Tanna* Rav Yose ben Chalafta.

Sefas Emes:

See *Alter, Rav Yehudah Aryeh Leib.*

Shaar Bas Rabim:

Scholarly and erudite anthology of commentaries on the Torah and *Megil-*

los by Rav Chaim Aryeh Leib Yedvavnah; late 19th century.

Sefer haTodaah:

see *Kitov, Rav Eliyahu.*

Shaarei Binah:

see *Rav Eleazar ben Yehudah of Worms.*

Shaarei Teshuvah:

see *Margolios, Rav Chaim Mordechai.*

Rav Shaul ben Aryeh Leib of Amsterdam:

Born 1717 in Risha; died in Amsterdam, 1790.

Member of famous rabbinical family.

Served as Rav in many important cities, and upon the death of his father he replaced him as Rav of the prestigious Ashkenazi community of Amsterdam, where he served until his death.

He published many works on Bible, Talmud and Halachah, most famous of which was **Binyan Ariel.**

When the Chidah visited Amsterdam, he stayed at the home of Rav Shaul and was so awed by his erudition and righteousness, that he praised him most flourishingly in his *Shem haGedolim.*

Rav Shemariah ben Eliyahu haIkriti:

(1275-1355).

Italian Bible commentator and philosopher. When he was a child, his family moved to Crete where his father was appointed Rabbi; hence his surname 'haIkriti' ['the Cretan'] or, as he is also known, 'haYevani', ['the Greek'].

Until the age of thirty he studied Bible almost exclusively; then he immersed himself in Talmud and philosophy. His reputation as a Bible scholar was so great that he was invited to the court of King Robert of Naples, a patron of Jewish learning, where he devoted himself to his studies, and published *Philosophical Commentaries* on the Bible, of which his commentary to *Song of Songs* is still extant.

He is quoted extensively by the early commentators, among them: *Rav Alkabetz; Alshich;* and *Iggeres Shmuel.*

Among his other works were *Elef haMagen,* a commentary on the Aggadah in tractate *Megillah;* and *Piyyutim.*

He tried to reconcile the Rabbanites and Karaites, and because of this certain zealots leveled accusations against him, and he died in prison.

Shem haGedolim:

see *Azulai, Rav Chaim Yosef David.*

Rav Shlomo ben Yitzchok:

(RASHI)

Leading commentator on the Bible and Talmud.

He was born in Troyes, France in 1040 — the year in which Rabbeinu Gershom M'or haGolah died. According to tradition, Rashi's ancestry goes back to Rav Yochanan haSandlar and to King David.

The summit of Rashi's commentaries was his commentary on the Talmud — an encyclopaedic and brillian undertaking. Nothing can be compared to the impact this commentary has had upon all who study the Talmud. Rashi's commentary has opened to all what otherwise would have been a sealed book. Without his commentary, no one would dare navigate the 'Sea of Talmud.' Every word is precise and laden with inner meaning. Rashi's corrections of the Talmud text were, for the most part, introduced into the standard editions and became the accepted text.

Rashi's **Commentary to the Bible,** too, made a similar impact — and virtually every printed Bible contains his commentary which is distinguished by its conciseness and clarity.

Many Halachic works from the 'School of Rashi' have come down to us: *Sefer haOrah; Sefer haPardes; Machzor Vitry; Siddur Rashi;* and responsa.

Rashi died on Tammuz 29, 1105. His burial place is not known.

Shabbos:

Talmudic tractate in *Seder Moed.*

Shoresh Yishai:

See *Alkabetz, Rav Shlomo haLevi.*

Sirkes, Rav Yoel:

(known as 'BACH' from his work 'Bayis Chashash')

Polish *Rav, Posek* and Commentator. Born in Lublin in 1561.

Student of Rav Shlomo, Rav of the City, he then studied in the Yeshiva of Brisk under Rav Meshullam Feivish (later Rav of Cracow), and Rav Zvi Hirsh Shur, a student of the RAMA.

Rav Sirkes was Rabbi in many cities, among them Lublin, Brisk and Cracow.

His most famous works are *Bayis Chadash* [BACH] on the *Tur, Hagahos HaBach* on the *Talmud,* and his Responsa.

He published an analytical commentary of *Ruth* entitled **Meishiv Nefesh** along with his super-commentary on *Rashi, Be'er Mayim.*

In his old age he wanted to emigrate to Eretz Yisrael, but he never did. He died in Cracow at the age of 79 in 1640.

Soloveichik, Rav Yitzchak Zev haLevi

(1889-1960)

Known as Rav Velvele Brisker.

Son of Rav Chaim Brisker, Rav Velvele was regarded by many to be the supreme *Talmudic* authority of his day.

Born in Volozhin, he was the student of his father Rav Chaim, who was his only teacher.

His erudition and acumen were evident in his early youth, and upon the death of his father, he succeeded him as Rav in Brisk where he became a central figure in the Torah world. During World War II his wife and four children were murdered in Brisk; he fled to Vilna with his surviving five sons and two daughters, and managed to flee from there to Eretz Yisrael.

He settled in Jerusalem, where he founded a kollel for a group of select young men. Later a yeshiva was founded which was administered by his Rav Yosef Dov.

He confined himself to his studies, and was considered the spiritual heir of the Chazon Ish (Rav Yeshaya Karelitz).

He exercised a great influence over extensive circles in the Torah world.

Sotah

Talmudic tractate in *Seder Nashim.*

Tanchuma

See *Midrash Tanchuma.*

Targum

The ancient, authoritative translation of the Bible into Aramaic.

Toldos Am Olam:

See *Rottenberg, Rav Shlomo.*

Torah Nation

See *Miller, Rav Avigdor.*

Torah T'mimah

See Epstein, *Rav Baruch haLevi.*

Tzemach David

See Gans, *Rav David.*

Uzeda, Rav Shmuel de

Born in Safed c. 1540.

He studied Kabbalah with Rav Yitzchak Luria [ARI zal] and Rav Chaim Vital.

In 1557 he traveled to Constantinople where he published his commentary, an encyclopedic super-commentary on Ruth, *Iggeres Shmuel,* which has been reprinted many times and appears in large editions of the Bible.

His most famous work is *Midrash Shmuel,* a detailed commentary on *Pirkei Avos* with reference to many connecting sources such as Rabbenu Yona of Gerondi, Meiri, Rav Yosef Ibn Shushan, and Rashbam, which were at that time in manuscript, but have since been printed.

Rav Velvele Brisker

See *Soloveichik, Rav Yitzchak Zev haLevi.*

Vilna Gaon

See *Rav Eliyahu ben Shlomo Zalma of Vilna.*

Rav Yaakov ben Asher

(1270-1340)

Posek and codifier.

Son of Rav Asher ben Yechiel (the 'ROSH') under whom he studied. He was born in Germany, and in 1303 he accompanied his father to Toledo, where he lived in great poverty, and devoted his life to Torah.

Rav Yaakov's enduring fame rests on his encyclopaedic Halachic codification *Arbaah Turim,* which is the forerunner of our Shulchan Aruch today, and as a result of which he is referred to as the "Baal haTurim."

The arrangement and wealth of content made it a basic work in halachah and it was disseminated greatly through the Jewish world. It became so widely accepted, that when Rav Yosef Caro wrote his major work, *Bais Yosef,* , he decided to "base it upon the *Turim* "because it contains most of its views of the *Poskim."*

Rav Yaakov also wrote a comprehensive commentary on the Chumash anthologizing the literal explanations (*p'shat)* by earlier Bible commentators. To the beginning of each section he added "as a little appetizer, *gemmatrios* and explanations of the *Masorah,* in order to attract the mind." Ironically the whole work was printed only twice. It was just these "appetizers" that were popularly published alongside most editions of the Bible under the title *Ba'al HaTurim.*

Among Rav Yaakov's students was Rav David Abudarham.

According to *Shem haGedolim* Rav
Yaakov died en route to Eretz Yisrael.

Yalkut Shimoni

The best known and most
comprehensive Midrashic anthology
covering the entire Bible.

It is attributed to Rav Shimon ha-
Darshan of Frankfort who lived in the
13th century.

The author collected *Midrashim* from
more than 50 works, arranging them
into more than 10,000 statements of *Aggadah Halachah* according to the verses
of the Bible.

Yavetz, Rav Yitzchak ben Shlomo

Turkish Bible commentator in the
second half of the sixteenth century.

He published commentaries on *Pirkei
Avos* and most of the Bible.

His commentary on *Ruth* is called
Tzemach Tzaddik. He is quoted extensively by *Iggeres Shmuel*.

Rav Yedidiah Shlomo of Norzi

Rav and Commentator.

Born in Mantua 1560; died in 1626.
Became Rav in Mantua in 1585.

Rav Yedidiah consecrated the greater
part of his life to studying the *Masorah*
of the Bible — and by studying every
previously printed *Masorah* text, com-
paring the various readings scattered
through *Talmudic* and *Midrashic*
literature, as well as in published and
unpublished manuscripts.

The resulting work was entitled *Poretz
Geder* but was published under the
name *Minchas Shai*.

This work, which was as perfect as
thorough learning and conscientious
industry could make it, has become the
most accepted work in establishing the
Masorah. The *Minchas Shai* is printed in
the back of all large Bibles.

Rav Yehudah Loewe ben Bezalel.

Known as the MAHARAL of Prague.

One of the seminal figures in the last
500 years of Jewish thought, Rav
Yehudah was born c. 1512 and died in
Prague in 1609. His genealogy can be
traced to King David.

Although he was universally acknowledged as one of the rabbinic greats
of the era, while his life was not an easy
one. He delayed his marriage for 20
years due to financial difficulties. He
was Chief Rabbi of Moravia, residing in
Nikolsburg, for 20 years.Then, in 1573,
he transferred his yeshiva to Prague, the
Torah metropolis of Europe. Upon two
different occasions, he accepted the
rabbinate of Posen in order to settle
communal strife.

He was elected Chief Rabbi of Prague in
1597 as a very old man. It appears that
the position had been denied him up to
then because of his outspokenness in
attacking social evils and religious laxity.

Though commonly known as a folk
hero and miracle worker, his greatest
contribution was his formulation of a
self-contained system of Jewish
thought. His many books and lengthy
sermons formed the basis for much of
the significant writing of succeeding
centuries.

Among his many erudite works were:
Novellae on *Shulchan Aruch Yoreh
Deah; Gur Aryeh* on the Torah; *Be'er
haGolah* on the *Passover Hagaddah;
Derech Chaim; Netzach Yisrael;
Nesivos Olam,* etc. Many of his works
are extant and were recently
republished in an 18-volume set: *Sifrei
Maharal.*

Yefe Anaf

See *Ashkenazi, Rav Shmuel Jaffe.*

Yerushalmi, Peah

Tractate *Peah* in the Jerusalem Talmud.

Yevamos

Talmudic tractate in *Seder Nashim.*

Rav Yissachar Berman haKohen

Known as Berman Ashkenazi.

16-17th Century commentator on the Midrash.

Very little is known about him except that he was born in Sczebrzesyn, Poland, and that he was a student of the Rama (Rav Moshe Isserles).

He is the author of the famous commentary to the Midrash Rabba, *Matanos Kehuna,* first published in 1584, and appearing subsequently in nearly every edition of the Midrash.

Rav Yissachar makes it very clear in his introduction that he was very concerned with establishing the correct text for the *Midrashim,* basing his text upon all the various printed editions up to his time and on various manuscripts.

Zohar Chadash

A part of the *Zohar* which was printed slightly later than the main body of the text. Incorporated within the *Zohar Chadash* is the **Midrash haNe'elam** on the Torah and **Midrash Ruth haNe'elam. Midrash Ruth haNe'elam** as also appeared as a separate work called *Tapuchei Zahav.*

Zos Nechemasi

Commentary on *Ruth* by Rav Shlomo ben Chaim Chaykl Yanovsky of Warsaw; early 19th Century.

Zuenz, Rav Aryeh Leib

(1773-1833)

Polish Rav and Kabbalist. At a young age his genius was recognized and he became known as Leib Charif ('sharp-witted').

For a time he was Rav of Prague, then Warsaw, then he became Rosh Yeshiva in Praga, a suburb of Warsaw.

He was the author of many works, and on his deathbed he promised to intercede in Heaven on behalf of anyone who published his works, with the result that many Jews came forward to publish them.

He is known for his *Get Mekushar* and *Geresh Yerachim.* His commentary on Ruth is called **M'lo ha'Omer.**